Object Worlds in
Ancient Egypt

MATERIALIZING CULTURE
. . . .

Series Editors: Paul Gilroy, Michael Herzfeld and Danny Miller

Barbara Bender, *Stonehenge: Making Space*

Gen Doy, *Materializing Art History*

Laura Rival (ed.), *The Social Life of Trees: Anthropological Perspectives on Tree Symbolism*

Victor Buchli, *An Archaeology of Socialism*

Marius Kwint, Christopher Breward and Jeremy Aynsley (eds), *Material Memories: Design and Evocation*

Penny Van Esterik, *Materializing Thailand*

Michael Bull, *Sounding Out the City: Personal Stereos and the Management of Everyday Life*

Anne Massey, *Hollywood Beyond the Screen: Design and Material Culture*

Wendy Joy Darby, *Landscape and Identity: Geographies of Nation and Class in England*

Joy Hendry, *The Orient Strikes Back: A Global View of Cultural Display*

Judy Attfield, *Wild Things: The Material Culture of Everyday Life*

Daniel Miller (ed.), *Car Cultures*

Elizabeth Edwards, *Raw Histories: Photographs, Anthropology and Museums*

David E. Sutton, *Remembrance of Repasts: An Anthropology of Food and Memory*

Eleana Yalouri, *The Acropolis: Global Fame, Local Claim*

Elizabeth Hallam and Jenny Hockey, *Death, Memory and Material Culture*

Sharon Macdonald, *Behind the Scenes at the Science Museum*

Elaine Lally, *At Home With Computers*

Susanne Küchler, *Malanggan: Art, Memory and Sacrifice*

Nicky Gregson and Louise Crewe, *Second-Hand Cultures*

Merl Storr, *Latex and Lingerie*

Object Worlds in Ancient Egypt

Material Biographies Past and Present

Lynn Meskell

Oxford • New York

First published in 2004 by
Berg
Editorial offices:
1st Floor, Angel Court, 81 St Clements Street, Oxford, OX4 1AW, UK
175 Fifth Avenue, New York, NY 10010, USA

Berg is the imprint of Oxford International Publishers Ltd.

Library of Congress Cataloging-in-Publication Data

A catalogue record for this book is available from the Library of Congress.

British Library Cataloguing-in-Publication Data

A catalogue record for this book is available from the British Library.

ISBN 1 85973 862 1 (Cloth)
     1 85973 867 2 (Paper)

Typeset by JS Typesetting Ltd, Wellingborough, Northants.
Printed in the United Kingdom by Biddles Ltd, King's Lynn.

www.bergpublishers.com

For Emma, Dorothy and Peggy

Socrates: Let us suppose the existence of two objects: one of them shall be Cratylus and the other the image of Cratylus, and we will suppose, further, that some god makes not only a representation such as a painter would make of your outward form and colour, but also creates an inward organization like yours, having the same warmth and softness; and into this infuses motion and soul and mind, such as you have, and in a word copies all your qualities, and places them by you in another form. Would you say that this was Cratylus and the image of Cratylus, or that there were two Cratyluses?

Cratylus: I should say that there were two Cratyluses.

Plato, *The Dialogues of Plato*

The production of ideas, of conceptions, of consciousness, is at first directly interwoven with the material activity and the material intercourse of men, the language of real life.

Karl Marx, *The German Ideology*

The possibility of desire is the possibility of the objects of desire.

Georg Simmel, *The Philosophy of Money*

Contents

List of Figures

Acknowledgements

The book was written on sabbatical at the School of American Research in Santa Fe, possibly the most wonderful place one could think and write. In many ways New Mexico seemed to be the perfect place to write a book on material biography. In my first few days in Santa Fe I attended a festival at the Santa Domingo pueblo; it was a mass of stalls with exquisite pottery, jewelry and things in general. I stopped by a table where a group of women were selling story-teller dolls, their clay bodies covered with the bodies of numerous children and their mouths open, ready for the telling. One of the women casually asked as I looked intently at the figures, "which one speaks to you?" I remember feeling awkward in her attribution of agency to the piece; perhaps she was teasing me, but I felt altogether inadequate to make any sort of coherent answer. It is common here to experience out of placeness. I could study such a phenomenon in the past, but I certainly was reticent to confront it in the present. Since then I have learnt more about fetishes, *milagros*, *katsinas*, the concomitant politics of looking, and the cultural difference embodied within systems of belief and experience. Though one could be here and witness the vitality of Native American culture, someone like me is always removed and can only use that distance and difference to reflect upon other places and times and other ways of being in the world.

Both SAR and NEH fellowships provided financial support for the project. Richard Leventhal was the best boss one could imagine and everyone at the school has been incredibly helpful and generous. My colleagues for the year, Jennifer Denetdale, Natasha Schull, Gelya Frank, Stephen Houston and Michael Dietler have been great company and I am especially grateful to Jennifer and Natasha for their warm friendship and inspiration. Rebecca Allahyari and James Brooks were also generous with their ideas and their time. SAR librarians, Sandy White and Len Leschander, were tireless in their assistance, adeptly moving between obscure Egyptological publications and exposés on Las Vegas. A special thank you to the Friday night group, Norm Yoffee, Barbara Weber and Kathy Schreiber, who provided an alternative environment of support, camaraderie and intellectual stimulation. They really made New Mexico a wonderful experience for me because they love the southwest as much as I have come to.

Many friends and colleagues have kindly provided references, sent offprints, and read sections of the book at various stages: Lila Abu Lughod, Janaki Bakhle, John Baines, Victor Buchli, Denis Byrne, Rick Elia, Doris Francis, Liz Frood, Elizabeth Gray, Ian Hodder, Rosemary Joyce, Danny Miller, Barbara Mills, Peter Pels, Bob Preucel, Stephen Quirke, Richard Parkinson, Tom Patterson, Ted Robinson, Chris Rojek, Kathy Whitaker, and Alison Wylie. Others were brave enough to read the entire manuscript and were my most rigorous interlocutors. I am indebted to Emma Blake, Ian Hodder, Nan Rothschild, Natasha Schull, and Norm Yoffee. Nan particularly has been an incredible support in this year away, enduring daily emails and calls about all manner of things. Danny Miller and an anonymous referee provided rigorous and enlightening peer review of the book. I am eternally grateful that Danny spent so much time on the project, making it altogether a better book. Our conversations over the phone and by email ranged from Egyptian cats to Jean Baudrillard and I am much in his debt. As always, my students were generous with their enthusiasm and assistance with references: Erin Hasinoff, Marisa Lazzari, Carrie Nakamura, Matt Palus, and Lindsay Weiss. Anna Boozer helped gather many of the source materials in New York.

Photographic assistance was kindly provided by Henry Glassie, Katrina Lasko at SAR, Tania Watkins and Richard Parkinson at the British Museum, Helen Nicholl at National Museums of Scotland, Olivia Zorn at the Ägyptisches Museum und Papyrussammlung in Berlin, Jaromir Malek at the Griffith Institute, and Ove Kaneberg at the Medelhavsmuseet, Stockholm. Geof Thompson, Rebecca Denning, and Carolyn Jones at the British Museum Company and British Museum Publishing were incredibly helpful and I could not have managed Chapter 7 without them. Kathryn Earle and Ian Critchley at Berg deserve special mention for their patience and support, for seeing this book through to fruition, and for all their help along the way.

This book is dedicated to Emma, Dorothy and Peggy who have been like a second family to me during my last few years in the United States. Their kindness, generosity and good humor have kept me sane through all the dramas of life, especially academic life. Emma particularly has been a great friend and constant inspiration ever since our days at Cambridge, and this dedication is just a small expression of my gratitude.

LMM
Santa Fe

Introduction

We constantly drift between the object and its demystification, powerless to render its wholeness. For if we penetrate the object, we liberate it but we destroy it; and if we acknowledge its full weight, we respect it, but we restore it to a state which is still mystified.

Roland Barthes, *Mythologies*

In this book I engage with issues of materiality in a well-documented ancient context and demonstrate that archaeology can provide a sophisticated disciplinary medium for that worldly engagement. It is not a dialogue with the usual objects archaeologists have previously described to make their analogies, including favorite coffee mugs, madeleines, wedding rings or art works by Duchamp (e.g. Knappett 2002). These forms of cathexis, or the libidinal energy we invest in objects, are extremely personalized and subjective meditations that ultimately reflect little upon ancient experience. Potentially they collapse cultural difference and may even instantiate unhelpful distinctions around ancient and modern sophistication. Clearly, what we have lacked are substantive archaeological accounts of materiality in ancient contexts. There is a growing body of scholarship on materiality, produced in fields including anthropology, sociology, communication, and media studies (Schiffer 1999: 4–5), much of which has yet to be translated productively into archaeology. Archaeologists have yet to deal with the implications of materiality, with the constitution of the material world in antiquity, although they have delved into contextual studies of material culture (Chilton 1999; Hodder 1989; Schiffer 1999). Semiotic approaches have also been popular as a strategy for reading archaeology as a textual enterprise (Bauer 2002; Hodder 1991; Preucel and Bauer 2001; Tilley 1990). Following a relatively independent French intellectual tradition Leroi-Gourhan (1993), Lemonnier (1992, 1993) and Latour (1991) pursued the material aspects of technology, interrogating the cultural

1

logics that underlie choice and ultimately transform society. This strand forms a related yet different tangent to our engagement with material culture. However, the study of material culture is not necessarily tanta-mount to materiality which takes as its remit the exploration of the situated experiences of material life, the constitution of the object world and, concomitantly, its shaping of human experience. Studies of material culture can be read as oscillating between empirical studies and more theoretical evocations of cultural analysis. The empirical trend is devoted to precise object analyses of form, materials and manufacture, but is not automatically concerned with social relations. It can be associated with deterministic models deriving from economic processes (e.g. DeMarrais, Castillo, and Earle 1996) or notions of cultural progress, and is not always attendant to subtle changes in meaning or reception. Theoretical trends focus more directly on broader interpretive connotations around and beyond the object (Attfield 2000: 40–1), on the unstable terrain of interrelationships between sociality and materiality and the neglected area of the cultural constitution of objects. Studies of materiality cannot simply focus upon the characteristics of objects but must engage in the dialectic of people and things. Archaeologists, because of our dependence upon the interpretation of the material world as our ontological bedrock, ideally should lead the way in terms of theorizing and evocation.

Perhaps it is not surprising that archaeologists have left the investiga-tion of materiality to ethnographers who have at their disposal materially rich contemporary settings from which to explore questions of con-sumption, variability, classification, meaning and, my favorite question, when is an object not an object? These questions largely form the basis of the following chapters. Arguably much the same materials are available to many archaeologists and we simply have to ask a similar suite of questions, to reconfigure our old materials in new ways. Since materiality is not readable as a given set of conditions or practices common to all cultures and all times, it is surely necessary to study specific cultural moments to understand contextual notions of the material world and its propensity to forge, shape, interpolate, and possibly even challenge and undermine social relations and experiences. Materiality is thus a set of cultural relationships (Pels 2002). Imbued matter and embodied objects exist in relationship to specific cultural moments and contexts. Like all ethnographic writing, this gives us pause to reconsider our own under-standings of materiality, its qualities and limitations, but also to eschew essentialism and naturalism. Considerations of materiality today, the conditions of material life and our relationships to the object world, cannot stand in isomorphic relation to the deep past or to other cultural configurations, as ethnographers have amply demonstrated. In Chapter 2 it will be argued that to challenge those essentialisms entails an interrogation of the very limits of taxonomy and classification.

This challenge entails deconstructing our own notions that objects and subjects are discrete and essential entities that inhabit particular, impermeable worlds. Recent writing on the specific contours of agentic objects or fetishes, as interlocutors between persons, things and worlds, undermines the fixity of our imposed boundaries. Yet we should acknowledge that humans create their object worlds, no matter how many different trajectories are possible or how subject-like objects become. Materiality represents a presence of power in realizing the world, crafting thing from non-thing, subject from non-subject. This affecting presence is shaped through enactment with the physical world, projecting or imprinting ourselves into the world (Armstrong 1981: 19). Such originary crafting acknowledges that there are no a priori objects; they require human interventions to bring objects into existence. The being of objects can never be inferred logically, it is apprehended through our perception, which can be sensed, experienced and believed (Simmel 1979: 61). Those qualities are both human and subjective. Alternatively, persons exist and are constituted by their material world: subjects and objects could be said to be mutually fashioning and dependent. This inherent tension is very much part of the current project. New literatures in archaeology suggest that many have been seduced by the potentials that objects are actors in the same ways as individual persons, thus collapsing the subject:object dichotomy. Such a slippage elides important cultural and temporal specificities. A single theory of materiality that proposed to stand for modernity and antiquity, and all the myriad cultural valences assumed therein, will never suffice. Here I am following Miller and Tilley's (1996: 6) call to investigate object–subject relations through developing theoretical perspectives and empirical studies, drawing on different evidential bases and contexts. While archaeologists desire to apprehend the theory, we have been rather less successful at deploying it convincingly. Ancient Egypt provides an altogether different context from the bulk of material culture studies: it is neither contemporary nor familiar, yet is data rich and the subject of endless fetishization.

The subject:object divide is very much our concern and we should not get too preoccupied with trying to resolve this epistemic tension, probably irresolvable, that may not have impinged so pervasively upon other cultures at other times. Cartesian bifurcations such as mind:body, reason:emotion, subject:object, may be a central projection and source of concern within Euro-American culture but, as I have argued extensively

(Meskell 1996, 1999, 2002; Meskell and Joyce 2003), were not a fundamental way of structuring Egyptian relations. By definition artefacts are
made by humans, but the distinction between these and natural places
can also be unstable and permeable when certain groups, whether
Egyptians, Aborigines or Native Americans, incorporate places, natural
features, stones, animals, plants, and so on. It may be more accurate to
"think of ancient objects and places being constantly recycled through
new systems of meaning, constantly recontextualised and 'updated' with
new roles, new significance" (Byrne 2003). This is a book about things,
but equally about practices of transformation, since objects are merely
things without the world of practice to embed, mobilize and metamorphose them. We have to be careful not to privilege the moment of
an object's creation, or simply its divine birth as a sacred being (see
Chapter 4), as some art historians might, but to trace the many afterlives
of images. All subsequent reinterpretations are equally of biographic
interest, as reinforced by the structure and focus of this book.

   Dualisms are categorical structures that haunt our particular experience
of the world. In many fields they have been considered as inherently
negative, primarily because of the privileging of one half over the other,
most graphically seen in the mind:body dualism which has necessarily
occupied a primary position in feminist theory for political reasons. Of
course it is necessary to note that taxonomies such as subject:object are
political products, not universals, and are not salient to all cultures at all
times. But given contemporary writing on materiality in anthropology
some of the tensions between domains require addressing. Daniel Miller
(in press) succinctly argues that while "an artifact does not exist prior to
history and socialization which gives it its cultural form as material
culture ... equally people do not exist outside of being born into a
material environment which they absorb as habitus and which socializes
them into particular social beings." This recursive thinking has led to
much writing in terms of mutual constitution: we make objects and they
in turn make us. This simple equation can be taken as read, but a problem
ensues when objects are *de facto* considered as agentic, as having lives of
their own outside of human constitution. While the theory of object
agency is appealing, especially for archaeologists who feel that material
culture has traditionally been sidelined in social disciplines, it cannot
be applied uniformly, at all places and all times. One major proponent
of object agency, Alfred Gell (1998: 23), conceded that manufactured
objects assumed a patient position with their maker (or primary agent),
and without whose agency they would not exist. Another proponent,
Bruno Latour (1991, 1996, 2000), has gone further by imputing that

agency is intrinsic to objects and that they are, in fact, society's co-producers. In this book I want to contain the limits of agency, to contextualize the agency of objects, rather than subscribe unthinkingly to a simple, unidirectional thesis. A critical engagement with these issues, namely the historical and theoretical underpinnings of object knowledge, is explored in the first two chapters. While I do want to place more emphasis on the material, this is not deployed at the expense of the social or the processes of materialization or objectification; it is very much a hybrid project.

The aim of Chapters 3–6 is to uncover and examine the past lives of artefacts, sometimes as objects and other times as active entities, things that we have become accustomed to viewing as unproblematic or residing in intransigent taxonomies. It is crucial to interrogate the specific moments of crafting, forging, exchanging, installing, using and discarding objects, their histories in a variety of contexts. One can do this coherently with Egyptian materials, documenting the various stages of an object's life cycle and even taking it into the contemporary period where Egyptian things are desired and commodified. Not all objects have such rich and illustrious histories, but the materials investigated largely have magical, ritual, religious or commemorative inflections rather than mundane utilities. Things that have the status of "work" are defined by virtue of their lack, since they are not accorded the deference or assigned the rights and personae reserved for powerful things, people or divinities (Armstrong 1981: 7). Looking at the quotidian in the material record, it is unsurprising that few posit the agency of domestic ceramics, lithics, basketry, and so on. This is a clear instance where the simple equation that objects have agency cannot hold, although it is rarely explicated. However, in specific settings the mundane can be considered efficacious. Early ethnographers such as Lévy-Bruhl (1966: 28) avidly reported the beneficent or terrifying qualities of ordinary Zuñi objects. It is one thing to say that the material world produces effects and another to say it has agency; to impute agency and intentionality to things can be rhetorically provocative, yet difficult logically to sustain. Nick Thomas critiques the "curious idea that artefacts are subjects rather than objects," but more specifically, he challenges that we cannot predict the kinds of engagements between people and things and "it is perhaps this instability, historicity and lack of historical containment that epitomizes the entanglement we all have with objects" (1991: 208). To be effective, theories of object agency are more cogent when they enhance our understandings of people's intentions and practices, rather than diminish their participation in favor of simply objects themselves. The objects examined in the following chapters are bridges between abstraction and concretization, and I would assert that they are bound by human intention. They represent radical forms of materiality that require thinking through in concert with the deep stratigraphies of social and cultural understandings.

Cultural context remains the most salient determinant, and we can expect no rules of materiality external to situated practice. A stark example of this would be an Egyptian statue; it can be considered an embodied being in its original context, a non-object at its point of installation and cult worship, then reductively considered an art object in contemporary museum display. As Ingold (2000: 64) cautions, "the more that objects are removed from the contexts of life-activity in which they are produced and used – the more they appear as static objects of disinterested contemplation." Context is everything no matter how momentary or fleeting those relationships of connection may prove. One could ask, when did the materials and the making eventuate or culminate in the deity? At what point was it no longer the work of human hands, no longer wood or stone? It is not simply a then and now structure, but a series of culturally steeped moments, actions and experiences. Ultimately these moments of transformation are mutually forging: we make our object world and it recursively shapes us. What I am concerned with here are the situations and processes that transform materials into more than their constituent parts, specifically when they assume new taxonomic roles as beings, deities, oracles, agents, mediators, and so on. It is one thing to say that objects can operate as agents and another to document those classificatory shifts in antiquity. Makers and users imbue specific objects with agency, which recognizes the active role of things in constitutive rather than simply reflective terms. Those things can take on their own life histories, and they may be perceived as acting independently, which is subsequently read by cultural participants as significant. Many manufactured objects in particular cultures are considered of divine origin or to have mysteriously made themselves. And lastly, depending upon the groups involved, this may result in the attribution of agency to objects or a realization that this is largely a projection. In all instances we need to redefine those specific contexts and moments in time and contour the suspensions of disbelief that may be required. Although these are imaginative and sometimes magical geographies, in Egypt they were equally part of the quotidian world. I want to document the instabilities, the swerving moments between events and objects, between intentions and forgings, the circumstances that blur classificatory boundedness. I also want to introduce the disruptions and resistances to culturally embedded taxonomies, when individuals challenge authority and the status quo, where fixity is called into question.

Egyptian culture placed enormous emphasis upon material rendering and representation as an instantiation of individual permanence, cultural longevity and the endurance of powerful socio-religious concepts. For a society obsessed and to some degree constituted by cultural institutions of doubling and pairing (Upper and Lower Egypt, paired gods and goddesses, red land and black land, order and chaos, etc.), the act of doubling and mimesis was the perfect expression of Egypt's organizing core. The processes of fabrication and copying, imbuing doubles with the potency of the original, are central to the examples that follow. Egyptian culture had its own understanding of materiality and its significations, its sense of ontology and religion, that may in turn impinge upon our own contemporary and profound debates about subjects and objects. Statues, figurines, carved and painted images of the individual were all doubles for the self that could extend the biography and trajectory of the individual. The images were the bearers of the owner's identity, personality and visual likeness, and could be called upon as referents in the afterlife. These material renderings also had the power to improve upon reality, such as portraying a person as youthful, beautiful and without imperfections. The physical reality of the depiction was thought to have such efficacy as to bestow that desired corporeality upon the person at death as they entered a new domain of existence. If any harm were to befall the deceased's body, those doubles would also physically substitute for his person and guarantee a successful embodied afterlife. The mummified body as a material instantiation for, and carapace of, the person; personalized coffins and cartonnage representations; numerous substitutes in statue and figurine form; wall paintings depicting the deceased, and so on, were each physical doubles considered to have long-term vitality and power. At a meta-level one could see the construction of the tomb, and tomb culture in general, as the most salient evocation of the specific configuration of Egyptian materiality and its potency. In the New Kingdom (1539–1070 BC), a man could devote much of his adult life and his wages to constructing a tomb for himself, and in many cases for his family. One could think of the tomb as a time machine that housed all the materials necessary for eternal life: bodies, coffins, statues, paintings of the deceased and his family, ritual paraphernalia, furniture, clothing and jewelry, household goods, food, wine, and so on – *every good thing* as the Egyptians would proclaim. It was clearly not enough simply to aspire to having it all next time around; it was necessary to provide that material world in the context of the tomb so as to secure it for the future. This buried object geography provided the mimetic basis for this next life. Investing significant sums having tombs carved into the bedrock as we see in ancient Thebes, having the walls of this complex subterranean architecture painted, and provisioning the tomb with both the quotidian and highly ritualized objects was, for many, a lifetime project.

Materiality could also work against the individual in Egypt: iconoclasm was the most extreme example. Since the physical representation substituted for the individual and their afterworld trajectory, it could be effectively enhanced or harmed through human agency in the present. Throughout much of Pharaonic history, defacement and physical damage were common ways of perpetuating extreme forms of injury upon the person. What was enacted in this world would extend far into future scenarios. Like the sensational toppling of political statues in present times, the Egyptians mobilized campaigns to destroy and desecrate the images of Pharaohs such as Akhenaten, who attempted to instigate new forms of religious worship in the New Kingdom. This was not only a damning of his memory, of past actions, but, more pointedly, the damnation for all potential futures. Acts of *damnatio memoriae* that effaced and erased were also extended to ordinary individuals. Many of these persons were criminals or wrongdoers, whose punishment thus persisted beyond this life. Physical punishment in Pharaonic times, such as the cutting of the nose, was mimetically transferred to the nose and face of images of the perpetrator whose breathing was thus terminated in the hereafter. Altering the historical record, attacking personal enemies, censoring a religious event, are all motives for the "mark of the second hand," erasure, which presupposes a certain level of knowledge by the perpetrator (Der Manuelian 1999: 286). Bodily mutilation easily destroyed earthly wholeness and perfection and similarly removed any chance of surviving into the hereafter, let alone achieving the physical perfection that Egyptian culture required. Corporeal mutilation extended beyond representational spheres since we know that ordinary criminals had their feet beaten, their noses cut, ears removed and, for heinous crimes, they could be burned alive or impaled on sticks. Effigies of enemies, in this case Nubians, have been found in their hundreds near the Egyptian fort at Mirgissa. Clay figurines depicting bound prisoners were burnt in a kiln, then buried or nailed to the walls of the fort. A similar fate awaited traitors or foreign enemies (Pinch 1994: 93). This torturous treatment effectively erased all bodily trace and subsequently any chance at attaining an afterlife. Such practices were not only horrific as a torture but ensured long-term humiliation since the crime was perpetually signified through materiality. At a less dramatic level, the erasure of a name on a monument meant obliteration. Even the bodies of birds such as ducks or owls, which were common in the hieroglyph script, were also mutilated since they might easily fly away, leaving the inscription and the tomb bereft (Goldwasser 1995: 79). It was believed that the iconic image could also be reanimated and brought back to life through magical prowess. Thus the erasure or mutilation of persons, animals or things alternatively diminished their agency, reducing them to ineffectual non-beings in all worlds. Just as statues were considered beings in their own right, images of people, animals and others could have real-time efficacy.

We can also look toward the micro-practices of more mundane orientation to uncover the specificities of materiality within the Egyptian lifeworld. Examining the ritual sphere, which was in itself pervasive throughout domains that contemporary audiences might designate domestic or sexual (Meskell 2000), it is clear that the process of rendering the immaterial material was a potent and necessary practice. Egyptian magic operated in the interstices, requiring materialization of immaterial spells and invocations to be truly efficacious. Magic was thought to coalesce in the body of the magician, but it required conscious manipulation through spells and rituals. Effigies of people, their embodied doubles, were made and manipulated for ritual purposes. Numerous spells were written on papyrus or linen and transformed into amulets that were worn on the person's body. Other practices relied on the materiality of the body and particularly its bodily substances including saliva, blood, and excrement. Magic was thought to be "on the mouth," and this oral dimension involved the physicality of spitting, licking and swallowing. Medico-magical spells were written on the flesh then licked off; other texts were written on papyri then burnt, ground up, dissolved in water and drunk so that the power of the spell was ingested corporeality. Specific deities like Maat, the goddess and personification of cosmic order, could also be painted on the tongue. The power of representing and giving form to the individuals and entities invoked or entreated was key. Power was transmitted through these animated and empowered substances, and became efficacious around bodily boundaries, orifices and surfaces. For pregnant women who feared miscarriage, spells were recited over pieces of knotted material that were then placed inside the vagina. The materiality of the knot and the process of tying it was a powerful symbol that literally bound together positive forces and blocked out malevolent ones. This concept was materialized in many jewelry forms, including knotted bangles and amulets that acted as both decoration and protection for sexually mature women. They wore them in life and were subsequently buried with them, offering material protection in the journey to the next life. The Egyptian project of materiality was so complex and central within the lifeworld that its potency could promise to secure the future, and similarly threaten to manifest eternal annihilation. It was an ever-present reminder of the tensions between the two potentialities of empowering and divesting. Ancient as well as ethnographic accounts challenge our presumed normativities and offer alternative modes of being in the world. Alternatively they show the constructedness of our own experience and undermine any notions of naturalism or essentialism. In this regard Egypt is evocative, yet such studies could clearly be undertaken for many cultural locations, past and present.

Finally, this book is ultimately tied to the projects of phenomenology and existentialism which captivate our attention through the exploration of practice, embodiment, experience, agency, biography, memory, reflexivity and narrative that have become central to our field. While phenomenology has been central to landscape approaches in archaeology (Bender 1998; Edmonds 1999; Tilley 1994) it has been less influential in theorizing the material constitutions of our world and has similarly been subject to critiques of poor self-reflexivity and false familiarity in constructions of place (Bender 2001). Phenomenology is both wed to empirical rigor and to the jettisoning of our own cultural privilege as the substrate for examining world-views and the complicated nature of the human condition (Jackson 1996: 1; Merleau-Ponty 1962, 1963). It is an attempt to ground human consciousness in its lived experience and to resist the entrenched concepts and systemic explanations that seek to flatten out, even efface, the qualities of life one desperately seeks to apprehend. That entails challenging the taxonomies we have happily projected across other cultural domains and concentrating on the contextual understandings of other cultures, past and present. Egyptian constructions of the subjects and objects as porous, overlapping, sometimes indistinguishable entities provide a salient example. Ancient and moderns share complex but different theories and embodied understandings of materiality, and, from that standpoint, contemporary culture is not especially modern. In Egypt, the materialization of selfhood and the extension of material biography were significant concerns (Meskell 2002; Meskell and Joyce 2003) that have resulted in the now-famous cultural materiality of pyramids, tombs, monuments, statues and images of individuals and divinities that have both encapsulated ancient understandings of this world and the next, but also serve as materials for our own fascination and existential questions about permanence, value, religiosity, and the world to come. It is this flipside of ancient materiality, the physical and residual force of specific Egyptian things, which leads me to my last chapter. These evocative and concrete images, whether pyramids, temples or statues, instantiate a potent presence from the deep past for contemporary culture. In turn they implicate a particular theory of materiality as held by their creators. Perhaps it is not possible to situate any contemporary study of Egyptian materiality without an acknowledgement and analysis of our own theorized experience of Egypt, its vast legacy on the one hand and its tantalizing reinvention on the other. Materiality is our physical engagement with the world, our medium for inserting ourselves into the fabric of that world, and our way of constituting and shaping culture in an embodied and external sense. From that perspective it is very much the domain of archaeology.

Objects In The Mirror May Appear Closer Than They Are

[C]ommodities are in love with money, but the course of true love never did run smooth.

Karl Marx, *Capital: A Critique of Political Economy*

In our time there has come to the front a special study of human life through such object-lessons.

E.B Tylor, in F. Ratzel, *The History of Mankind*

In all cultures things exist which may assume the status of ordinary objects in our contemporary eyes, but are in fact treated very differently and are accorded an altogether other status for their creators; many of these were deemed to be enlivened. We confer enormous respect upon fabricated things; we are known by them and they in turn bestow prestige upon us. They materialize our engagement with the world, our understandings, and our desires to shape its physicality. Materiality subsumes the object world, its tacit *thingness* and virtuosity, which is difficult to define or contain. Even in a world of increasing virtuality and immateriality, the material realm remains just as germane to our worldly engagement. And yet we cannot privilege the material alone since materiality is ultimately bound up in creative cultural contexts and transformative acts that constitute in-between spaces. And in our current academic climate that celebrates postmodernism, postcolonialism, postnationalism and revels in hybrid positionalities and fluid categories, it seems imperative that we give contrasting and adequate weight to the intransigence of physical evidence and the material conditions constitutive of

13

social life (Desmond 1999: 251). I have found in writing this book that materiality necessarily bleeds into the related domains of exchange, consumption, waste and excess. It links both to the radical ideas of mimesis, simulacra and agency and to the more mundane notions of goods, services and economic structures. While each deserves a monograph-length treatment, I have tried to understand, tease apart, and subsequently enmesh these topics in my understandings of materiality as it pertains to the object world of ancient Egypt and the concomitant objectification and fetishization of things Egyptian under modernity. Some objects have the *presence* of identity, others have the *presence* of excellence (Armstrong 1981), and this duality is what defines my comparative analysis of the reification of Egyptian things in their original settings as opposed to their voracious decontextualized consumption in the present.

"Material culture" has long served as a gloss or umbrella term synonymous to "artefacts"; it simply accounts for what archaeologists deal with in the archaeological record, yet it can signify much more. Artefacts have not been traditionally treated for their *thingness* or their sociality, but rather as a mediating window onto ancient life. *Thingness* lends objects an elusive inflection that impels us to think through the specificity and salience of the object world within the larger constitutive social frame (Attfield 2000: 15). Material culture is the physical marker of humanity's intrusion into the natural world and our way of demarcating the natural and cultural with the knowledge that they inhabit permeable categories. We can also refashion nature to our desire, shaping, reshaping, and arranging things during life. We live within material culture, enmeshed and dependent upon it, take it for granted and, through our most sublime aspirations, seek to attain it (Glassie 1999: 1). Anthropology, from its inception, had concerned itself with material culture and from the 1800s this was largely inseparable from the ethnographic project. Tylor used the word "object-lessons" in the foreword to Ratzel's (1896) magisterial three-volume work on ethnographic artefacts, modestly titled *The History of Mankind* (Buchli 2002b: 2). Yet with the historical particularism of Boas and the ethnographic tradition of Malinowski, anthropology began broadly to devalue materiality as a study of cultural phenomena in preference for more abstracted systems of belief and meaning (Ellen 1988: 232). But given the burgeoning corpus of writing in an array of disciplines, material culture can no longer be treated as external or epiphenomenal to culture. A disciplinary chauvinism has long been in effect where sociologists, archaeologists and anthropologists have tended to read within their intellectual domains, irrespective of the benefits of cross-over scholarship (Miller and Tilley 1996). The *Journal of Material Culture* has been one vehicle designed to escape the enforced ghettoization and has effectively brought interdisciplinary work devoted to materiality to the fore. Despite this new surge of interest many valuable anthropological or ethnographic accounts focus more directly on exchange or social relations rather than on the specificities of material life (Appadurai 1986b; Hoskins 1998). More successful are a new generation of material culture specialists whose focus is firmly on contemporary Euro-American life (Buchli and Lucas 2001; Dant 1999; Graves-Brown 2000; Hallam and Hockey 2001).

Archaeology is usually glossed by those external to the discipline as a technical purveyor of data or ancient technology (ceramics, lithic, metalworking, art), whereas it should occupy a central place in developing sophisticated notions of materiality. Alternatively, archaeologists have become so enamored of description and classification that they have yet to pursue convincingly the implications of materiality as a defining relationship in social life. Others have desperately entered the fray with theoretical contributions yet lack the ancient data to evince a compelling connection. For the most part, my own work attempts to address this lacuna by uncovering the constitution of object worlds and assuming that material life is inflected with social relations and thus can be read as a window onto larger cultural structures. The objects under investigation have elusive properties and were infused with a power that demands our attention (Armstrong 1981: 6). My account of materiality stems from the objects and the social relationships that imbue and transform them, from the position that the material is constitutive and active, and that the taxonomies of people, things, deities, and so on, sometimes overlap or are at least complicated by porous cultural beliefs and practices. Unsurprisingly, none of this is entirely new despite the outpouring of recent scholarship that signifies it as *de rigueur*. As this chapter makes clear, we owe an enormous intellectual debt and, at the same time, we must acknowledge the centrality of materiality as a philosophical concern, repositioning archaeology as a discipline with something tangible to contribute.

Man Makes Himself

The project of understanding materiality and its central constitutive force in the phenomenal world was set very early on in the work of philosophers like Vico, and later by Marx and Mauss – so much so that it is quite striking to find how much recent work is simply a refining and reshaping of their original projects. Quite simply there is nothing new about our fascination with materiality. Before the influential work of Gell, there was Marx, Mauss, Weiner, Armstrong, Godelier and a host of other anthropological thinkers who struggled with the relationship between humans and their object world, with objects that transcended Western categories, and the circulation of things that retained bio-graphical residues. I argue that these conceptual arguments have a long history in anthropology, and it is simply archaeology's reticence to engage that posits this is a new endeavour. While Gell has been a pervasive and, for the most part, positive force, much of his theorizing was deeply enmeshed in the seminal ethnographies and debates many decades before. He also retained the problematics surrounding attributing agency and intentionality to objects that was construed more excessively than asserting the human-like qualities of particular things, or that objects affect our lives (see Chapter 2).

Back in the early 1700s Giambattista Vico was already propounding the idea that man makes himself, or, to put it less succinctly, that human knowledge developed from the ground of fabrication, from the processes of creating, crafting and making and their concomitant materialities: "for when man understands he extends his mind and takes in the things, but when he does not understand he makes the things out of himself and becomes them by transforming himself into them" (Vico 1984: 130). In his understanding God crafted nature, while man was the God of artefacts. Termed *syndesis* by Armstrong (1981: 13), this captures the basic process of apprehending and constructing the world while enacting the self in tandem. For philosophers like Vico, the most sublime work of poetry is that of giving sense and emotion to insentient things. He suggested that "the first poets attributed to bodies the being of animate substances, with capacities measured by their own, namely sense and passion, and in this way made fables of them" (Vico 1984: 129). In his view real poems are made not of words, but of things. One might ask how different is this to the position espoused by Tim Ingold (2003) writing on the sensuous practice of crafting, proposing that the material forms we encounter emerge out of practical activity, crystallizations of activities within fields of relationships? Imagining and dreaming are all forms of creative production that have their material substrate. He goes as far as suggesting that doing anthropology could be equally a project of acquiring a craft and making objects rather than simply writing one's work. While the individual specificities of these works are notable, my point is simply that materiality has historically occupied a central place in a philosophy of being and the constitution of society, and that, secondly, scholars have been refining and re-tracing the steps of earlier theorists.

Hegel, for one, viewed society's self-creation through objectification and sublation (Miller 1987: 214). In *Phenomenology of Spirit* he spoke specifically of *thinghood* and the particular manifold properties of objects, realized by individual viewers in particular contexts. These multiple properties of things interpenetrate, each characteristic is everywhere and co-existent, but it was the very medium of *thinghood* that bound them together. The medium was crucial for Hegel, the constituent elements or matters that existed together in sensual form, albeit perceived subjectively: "since the object is the true and universal, the self-same, while consciousness is the variable and non-essential, it may happen that consciousness apprehends the object wrongly and deceives itself" (Hegel 1977: 70). He acknowledged the diverse moments of sensual apprehending and the subjective perceptions of individuals, what archaeologists would later describe as being *multiply constituted*. Hegel was also interested in the relationship between spirit and matter, especially as embodied in artistic manifestation in the sphere of divinity. Spirit takes form through instinctive actions and objectifications embedded in cultural practice. Using the examples of pyramids and obelisks, he outlined the differences between manufacture as human activity, producing material effects, and the reception or suffusing of spirit that entered into these works imbuing them with real significance. This results in a collapsing of the body:soul dichotomy, bringing both into concert and blurring the distinctions, the aim being to endow the spirit with embodied shape. In his discussion of divine being, the indwelling god (see Chapter 4) is a unity that must transcend both the elements of nature and self-conscious actuality, despite individuals realizing that the thing in itself is not an animated thing; instead the creator or onlooker must dispense with reality, forget themselves and dispense with certain moments of consciousness (Hegel 1977: 427–30). There are two sides to this abstraction, recognizing the characteristics of *doing* and of *being a thing*, resulting in a return to ultimate unity. In retracing Hegel's writing on material being it is clear that his initial theorizations reappear in the work of Egyptologists and anthropologists alike.

Objects and persons take on new hues with Marx's writing of *Capital*. To gloss superficially, things become personified and individuals are reified under capitalism. The fetishization of things also looms as a specter that haunts capitalist society, and Marx's writings on the subject have become set pieces in later work on person/object relations. Individuals are perceived as embodying capitalist society, further blurring the taxonomic boundaries: they are considered the members of the body of Capital (Pietz 1993: 149). The three key terms reappear throughout Marx and are similarly those that have informed contemporary treatment of materiality, whether based in antiquity or modernity: *alienation*, *fetishization* and *reification*. It is for these, and many other reasons, that we should look again at Marx's writing on the constitution of the object world and its mutually constitutive effects on the forging of society. This connection was certainly picked up by V. G. Childe who proposed that people transform natural materials into objects that satisfy their culturally embedded needs and in the process transform themselves as they create new desires and acquire new knowledge of their lifeworlds (Patterson 2003). While Marx's work has impacted significantly on archaeological theorizing for some seventy years (see Patterson 2003), it has yet to be fully appreciated within the new turn toward archaeologies of materiality (but see Miller 1987).

For Marx, the commodity is an object outside us, a thing that satisfies human desires. It is a way of doing things with things. The utility of a thing is its use value, and that is only determined by use or consumption. Exchange value, a quantitative relation, is the proportion in which value of one sort is exchanged for another sort and is shaped by contextual and temporal factors. The use values of commodities must afford expression in different qualities whereas the exchange value of commodities should be expressed in different quantities (Marx 1992: 45). When goods are transformed they can no longer be regarded simply in terms of their use value, rather they are the product of many forms of labor that coalesce into something relative to a system of exchange. Human labor is both embodied in the object and also abstracted. The object then assumes "value" by accruing crystals of social substance to itself: "as values, all commodities are only definite masses of congealed labor-time" (Marx 1992: 47). Thus every object, whether iron, paper or Marx's famous coat (Stallybrass 1998), has to be considered from this dual perspective. Productiveness is determined by circumstances, including skill, scientific knowledge, practical application, means of production, physical conditions, and so on. Productiveness also depends on time; good seasons or poor will obviously affect notions of value and so on. And so the value of a commodity is in direct relationship to its quantity. As Simmel and others have made clear, we have come to value objects because of their rarity and devalue those that are abundant and easy to extract.

Objects or goods always form embodied or sensual constructions for Marx, so that one cannot separate out the physicality that lies at the root of an object's making, as Hegel before him outlined. Goods are a

synthesis of matter and labor and as such assume a bodily form encompassing their utility and residual value that might manifest as a
physical form or as a value form. In a capitalist society money is a crystal
formed of necessity, according to Marx – an external expression to the
contrast between use value and value, which can be an independent
category. Money is a vehicle of circulation that provides value with
an independent reality. For Habermas, "Money is a special exchange
mechanism that transforms use values into exchange values, the natural
economic exchange of goods into commerce in commodities." Money
has structure-forming effects only when it becomes an intersystemic
medium of interchange (Habermas 1987). This is very different to ancient
societies where pre-monetary barter systems were in effect, leading to
different manifestations of complexity as we will see with Egypt. Simmel
underscored that money is reified, abstract and relational and transforms
social interaction into anonymous action on many accounts. This
accords well with Marx's own concept of the detaching of products from
their producers. Money comes to stand as a medium for all other
relationships (Miller 1987: 71). For Godelier (1999: 137) the insertion of
money as an independent apparatus characterizes our double existence;
the inversion of relations between subject and object, between producers
and products, is materialized in economic and political spheres. The
processes whereby humanity and the world is split and duplicated are
ultimately materialized in objects involving a mix of tangible and
intangible realities, albeit embodied in matter.

But for Marx the commodity, or object, was "a very queer thing,
abounding in metaphysical subtleties and theological niceties" (Marx
1992: 76). Some of his observations are directly relevant for the crafting
of the Egyptian object world, he too marveled at the object, the everyday
thing derived from natural materials, wood or stone for example, that
was transformed through labor into something transcendent. It stands
with its feet on the ground, but also in a sphere of relations with other
commodities and individuals. Thus the mystical nature of goods does
not originate with their use value because the social character of labor
appears as an objective character, premised upon relations between the
producers and their labor being presented to them as a social relationship
existing primarily between the products of their labor. We desire things
irrespective of the exploitative relations of labor in which they are
embedded. From another perspective, the human agency of the maker
is effectively erased in specific contexts of making. This was especially
necessary for the production of ritual objects in the Egyptian context.
From a Marxist perspective, one could posit that ritual operated as the

overarching symbolic field that erased labor from the production of value within the political sphere. Thus a certain degree of opacity is deemed necessary, both in ancient and capitalist societies. How else would one reconcile the fabricating of the divine by the hands of mortals (see Chapters 4 and 5)? Egyptian goods were not authored in modern ways; they were not signed, for example, and the attribution to discernible individuals was irrelevant. For Marx these ancient trading societies existed in the interstices and, compared to bourgeois society, he claimed that they were simple and transparent. He found them to be immature in their development, or hopelessly collective in their connections to community or upon the direct relations of subjection (Marx 1992: 84). As I hope to demonstrate, this was an over-simplification.

Following on from his thesis of alienated goods Marx developed the concept of commodity fetishism that derived from the peculiar social character of the labor that produced them (Marx 1992: 77). It is the disjunct and ultimate displacement between human activity and the object that instantiates the notion of the fetish (see Chapter 2). Human labor sets up a material relationship between persons and social relations between things. Goods become the receptacles of human labor and assume the role of supra objects. Using a semiotic metaphor, Marx claimed that it is value that converts every product into a social hieroglyphic (Marx 1992: 79). With respect to consumerism and capitalism Marx imputed that the devaluation of the human world grows in direct proportion to the increase in value of the *world of things*. For Marx, the product of labor is labor embodied and made material in the object: it is the *objectification* of labor. In commodity fetishism goods are worshiped by consumers and thought to bestow happiness and fulfillment, inferring that happiness is only a purchase away. Here again the object world is believed to confer a magical transformation upon the consumer (Belk 2000: 84). Following Marx, Hannah Arendt considered that human world-building was based on the reification of permanence as underscored by our relationship to the object world. Objects possess the durability Locke needed for the establishment of property, the value Smith needed for the exchange market, and the productivity Marx considered to be the test of human nature (Arendt 1958: 136). Through their inherent durability things assume their relative independence, their "objectivity" for which they can endure the voracious desires of their living makers and users (see Chapter 7). Things operate as stabilizing devices; objects anchor familiarity to constructions of identity that are constitutive for human subjectivity.

Given his enormous contribution to the world of things, it is clear that many social theorists have simply refined Marx in their discussions of objectification, value, and object relations. In using the self-aware object as a frame, Marx argued that if they could only speak objects would inform us that while their use value is what captivates the consumer, it does not constitute them as subjects. What is particular to them as objects is their value – specifically their exchange value. Thus objects are always embedded and contextualized in networks of social action and social knowledge. Human agency interpolates them into fields of exchange and the will of persons inheres in those objects. Commodities must be acknowledged as values before they can be realized as use values. Yet concomitantly they also have to demonstrate their use value before other value can be accorded. Objects are thus engaged in recursive, mutually constitutive notions of value. Exchange is the mechanism through which value is assessed and calculated, despite the subjective and situational nature of the process, as we will see in the next section.

Traveling Things

Since objects are external to individuals, as Marx wrote, they are rendered alienable. And what enables exchange in the first place is the willingness of owners or producers to alienate their objects, and through that iteration exchange becomes socialized. A distinction then arises within the object world between those goods created for consumption and those for the purpose of exchange (Marx 1992: 91). Drawing on Mauss (1990), the difference between commodities and gifts can be summarized as follows: commodities are generally entirely alienable, independent and object-like, and tend to be characterized by quantity, whereas gifts are inalienable, dependent and subject-like and are strongly demarcated by quality (Myers 2001: 4; Thomas 1991: 15). In useful shorthand the designation primarily hinges upon what is socially consequential and hence what *may* or *may not* be circulated. Provocatively, Miller (2001a: 95) suggests that today the vanguard of inalienability rests with reproductive technologies and organ transplants which underscore how the property of personhood itself is now under threat. To this I would add the controversial procedures of cloning where individual genetic materials and signatures of individuality are poised to enter the fields of circulation and commodification.

Commodities metamorphose within various circuits into a mode of circulation that is different to barter in both form and substance. Today we find ourselves in a society where commodities produce commodities by means of commodities. "Whether the sacred things that are not given or the valuables that are given appear to have an in-dwelling spirit which drives them, or the commodities have an exchange-value, a price which fluctuates independently of conscious awareness and the control of those who produce or consume them, we are in either case in the presence of man-made worlds, but ones which become detached from man and are peopled by phantasmatic doubles, duplicates" (Godelier 1999: 71). Godelier imputes that the phantasmatic beings that dominate humans, for whom people offered their labor and goods willingly, are no different from the opaque impersonal relations prevailing in the market-based and state-bureaucratic societies. Only the intercessors are different, such as priests, spirits, and ancestors to whom offerings must be made. Indeed he argues that no social identity can survive over time or provide a material foundation for society if there are no fixed points, these being material realities that are exempted (provisionally but lastingly) from the exchange of gifts or from trade. But what are these realities? Godelier (1999: 8) asks whether they were merely the sacred objects found in every religion? From an external viewpoint one could take such a stance with ancient Egypt, arguing that the durable materiality of Pharaonic religion and the edifices of culture are what enabled the civilization's longevity, that the detachable and inalienable objects of culture were a form of Egyptian world building. It is almost as if he had Egypt squarely in mind. However, Godelier's is a purely materialist reading that fails to account fully for the more invisible, but no less influential, social and cultural phenomena.

The community that forms the focus of several chapters, Deir el Medina, preserved some of the most detailed economic documents of the ancient world. This was a workmen's community charged with the responsibility of constructing and decorating the royal tombs in the Valley of the Kings, on the Theban West Bank. This New Kingdom village (1539–1070 BC) was called the "Place of Truth" in antiquity, referring to the location where the reigning Pharaoh, upholder of truth and order or Maat, was buried. Other sites throughout Egypt were, at various times, also known by this toponym. The first settlement was probably constructed at the outset of the 18th Dynasty. It was expanded during the 19th and 20th Dynasties when the team of workmen increased, as the scale of the royal tombs grew more and more ambitious. The official role of the village came to an end during the reign of Rameses XI, when civil unrest made the occupants gradually leave the site. More information has been gleaned from this community than from any other in Pharaonic history. The site is remarkably well preserved and today it includes some sixty-eight houses within an enclosure wall and approximately 400 tombs surrounding the village. The tombs were largely constructed in the New Kingdom but contained material from many centuries afterwards, since the site was continually reused for mortuary purposes (Montserrat and Meskell 1997). In fact, it was the impressive materiality of the site, replete with decorated houses and pyramid-topped tombs, that suggested Deir el Medina was a numinous place to later Ptolemaic and Roman visitors. Many individuals physically recorded that they fell to their knees and offered up prayers to the spirits of this place. Rock graffiti suggests that travelers passed through Deir el Medina on their way to visit the popular tourist destination of the Valley of the Kings, and some at least were moved to record their experience of the place by making an obeisance (or *proskynemata*) to the local deities. *Proskynemata* may be seen as expressions of awe and piety, a way of propitiating the dangerous aspects of local deities to obtain a sort of safe conduct through their domain. At Deir el Medina and its environs, Roman travelers made obeisance *in the presence of the great gods in the holy mountain* or to *the holy place in the presence of all the gods* (Montserrat and Meskell 1997: 183). This was a material investment in the landscape: individuals took the time to inscribe a permanent record of their feelings in the correct ritual wording. Despite the cultural cadences and possible misreadings of Deir el Medina as a sacred site, rather than settlement site (Meskell 2003), it was the potent materiality and symbolic landscape that much-later visitors revered and re-crafted to their own understandings.

At New Kingdom Deir el Medina, its highly literate occupants left a wealth of documentary data. Due to their educated scribal social position and the very nature of the *raison d'être* on the Theban West Bank, the workmen kept detailed records of exchange. The community existed on rations supplied by the state from a variety of institutions such as the Granary, Treasury, various temples, and so on. Unsurprisingly, these goods did not entirely satisfy the villagers' needs or tastes, resulting in a widespread network of trading within and outside the community for both goods and services. It is well attested that the workmen took private commissions to make furniture, statuary and funerary goods, as well as accepting paid contracts to paint the tombs of their neighbors. One such artist was a man called Meryskhmet who painted the vault of Aanakhte's tomb for the following sum of goods: loincloths, sandals, baskets, wood, pigment and vegetables (McDowell 1999: 69). The barter economy was in full force and every item had a notional price that was measured in weights of grain, copper or silver. Most transactions were estimated in *deben*, a weight of copper around 91 grams that could be used to determine equivalence. Raw materials such as copper were simply a medium of exchange for assessing the value of the goods. In this sense the Egyptian economy represented a money-barter system rather than a pure-barter one, where no value of commodities exchanged is outlined (Janssen 1975: 495). And it is likely that exchange was recorded primarily when significant sums were involved, as opposed to exchange of inexpensive commodities, since ostraca (inscribed flakes of limestone or potsherds) had a quasi-legal status. Inscribed ostraca were more than *aides-mémoire*. On occasion it was pertinent to have witnesses present and oaths were sworn publicly (Haring 2003): *This day of giving goods to Pendua by Rehotep: two beams, and again one. Month 2 of akhet, day 26. What is given to him: 50 bricks, 3 khar and 3 oipe of water, in the presence of Haremwia and Penbuy.* Swearing of oaths conferred an almost magical inflection to the exchange.

Terms such as buying and selling are probably inappropriate here since it was more that both parties received what they wanted rather than guaranteeing the correct price as such. A person desiring a specific object or service had to find another party who was in a position to make, provide or hand over such things in exchange and would concomitantly be interested in what was being offered in return. As a result of all these contingencies prices were rather vague. Exact prices in our sense were secondary; it was the nature of the commodity that determined the transaction (McDowell 1999: 74–5). A man called Hay purchased an ox from the chief policeman Nebsemen, a wealthy individual within the community. However, while the ox was valued at 120 *deben*, Hay ended up handing over 130 *deben* in goods, including jars of fat, clothing and an animal hide. In the end the extra 10 *deben* did not seem to matter as much as acquiring the desired commodity. Other situations seemed rather difficult and often urgent, as in the case of the correspondence between two women: *Please pay attention and seek out for me one tunic in exchange for the ring; I will allow you ten days.* This can been described as true target trading, and when one could not find the exact payment suitable to the seller a system of open credit could be established. People could hold off settling until they had the appropriate payment, or debts incurred by various kin could also be paid out by helping to pay off someone else's purchases. This ensured complicated social relationships for individuals connected and enmeshed in a web of exchange networks. Transactions both reflect and constitute social relationships between individuals and groups: affines, strangers, enemies and lovers (Thomas 1991: 7). Gifting was also a well-established social practice and evidence from Deir el Medina suggests that prestation occurred around special events such as childbirth, *founding a house* (glossed as marriage [Meskell 2002]), festivals, and so on. Festival preparations involved many individuals bringing food, drink, and various goods: *I sent you by the hand*

of the policeman Pasaro two cakes baked at the ratio of ten per oipe-measure
of grain, five deben of incense, and again five deben of incense on the day of
offering which you made for Amun during the Feast of the Valley (Wente 1990:
139). Material arrangements were correlates for new social formations,
as evidenced in the terms we interpret for marriage including *founding*
a house, bringing a bundle, and so on. Since the villagers of Deir el Medina
recorded these socialized transactions this would suggest a supra-
economic value to gifting in particular contexts. Following Derrida
(1992), these gifts are non-gifts or impossible gifts because they establish
a suite of obligatory relationships of reciprocity with an expected return,
whether between mortals or between mortals and divinities. The very
condition of gifts, such as the *ex votos* we see in Chapters 3 and 5, is a
material evocation of social contracts within a political economy of
goods, services, credit, and capital.

It was Mauss who cogently demonstrated that things create bonds
between people through exchange, for the thing itself has an inalienable
and originary spirit. This was a theme taken up for many later ethnographers such as Lévy-Bruhl (1966: 61) in his discussion of the "primitive
mentality" and its propensity for imbuing objects and things with mystic
qualities. He framed this collective representation as "participation"
between persons and objects, and thus the researcher might view these
new taxonomies as *things in themselves* or something other than themselves. Thinking beyond traditional categories, this entailed "an unstable
ensemble of mystic actions and reactions, of which persons, things,
phenomena, are but vehicles and manifestations, an ensemble which
depends on the group, as the group depends on it" (1966: 82). However,
with Mauss we have the first iteration of the idea that in giving an object
part of the person was imbricated in the materiality of exchange. Giving
creates obligations between the living and between the living and other
entities. Things and persons take each other's place. The same processes
are at work through ritual practices associated with statue cults, the
dedication of votives, veneration of ancestors, and in festive contexts
that instantiated memory in Egypt. This is a form of sacrifice (Bataille
1988), an exchange with the gods where a material and immaterial future
is forged, and where desires for the future are solidified. "In all societies
– whether or not they are divided into ranks, castes or classes – humans
make gifts to beings they regard as their superiors: divinities, nature
spirits, spirits of the dead. People pray to them, make offerings, and
sometimes even 'sacrifice' possessions, or a life. This is the famous 'fourth
obligation' that constitutes gift exchange" (Godelier 1999: 13). It is a
personal, inherently biographical act, set within specific moments and

mobilized by individual needs within a life trajectory. People have always felt indebted in other words, and it is not by accident that Godelier repeatedly draws on ancient Egypt as his archaeological correlate: "The Egyptians believed they owed their life, fertility, and abundance to the gods, and the Pharaoh in particular" (1999: 31). A social contract is set in place whereby goods and services were offered in the desire for a hoped for return.

For Mauss and all that have followed his lead, the exchange of goods belies a deeper concern with social relations and social cohesion. From this perspective objects are really transparent vehicles that forge alliances and dependencies. Mauss described this as society paying itself in the false coin of its dream. He was fundamentally interested in the notion of archaic jurisprudence and early forms of contract, another notable domain of object entanglement (Thomas 1991: 16). Yet no system of exchange can fully account for society's functioning or can hope to explain the totality of the social. Following Mauss, Godelier (1999: 105) provocatively suggests, "things" no longer exist, there are only persons, sometimes in the guise of humans and other times in the guise of objects. Objects and symbols are polysemic since they have symbolic logic and multiple interpretants, yet they cannot be simply reduced to the status of symbol. Before becoming signs and symbols, objects are material things that possess a spirit and thus power. "Man finds himself a prisoner of the world of his representations and his desires, of his volition. And in the course of this process, his social relationships become constructed in such a way that the opacity necessary for them to exist and to reproduce is produced at the same time" (Godelier 1999: 136). The individual is linked to one's entire universe and, conversely, an entire universe comes to dwell in the embodied person. Recursively, the sacred comes to inhabit the object world, leading to a state of enchantment.

Finally, in his famous discussion of Haida and Kwakiutl potlatches, Mauss outlined that objects such as coppers had a power of attraction and that other objects felt their efficacy. Each copper was unique, had its own name and design and had the capacity to accumulate its own history (Graeber 2001: 207). Objects were described as alive and autonomous, inspiring other objects to follow, and they could also be killed. "Things possess a personality and the personalities are in some ways the permanent things of the clan. Tiles, talismans, copper objects and the spirits of the chiefs are both homonyms and synonyms of the same nature and performing the same function . . . Yet it is giving oneself, and if one gives oneself, it is because one 'owes' oneself – one's person and one's goods – to others" (Mauss 1990: 46). This could be seen as an early articulation of the agency of objects thesis. However, as Sahlins has shown through more recent translation of Mauss's informants, sometimes Mauss tended to omit details that would provide important situational information that colored the gifting. Mauss's idea that things keep their identities over time took hold of the ethnographic imagination: identities crystallize in the object and concomitantly reaffirm the existence of hierarchical differences between individuals and groups. Later studies have positioned these material objects as "metamessages about eschatology, power, and rank, as well as success in subsistence activities, trade, warfare and key cultural values and structural principles" (Kan 1989: 209). Potlatches were also vehicles for expressing social and power relations and expressing feelings and attitudes. Tlingit objects were often perceived as extensions of the body or person and were often rubbed on the faces of hosts before being dispatched. This links back nicely to Mauss's thesis that the gift was a component of the giver's person. Yet as Kan argues (1989: 212), for the Tlingit Mauss's notion that the efficacy of the person is perpetually imbued in the object and retains a magical force over the recipient does not hold, thus reinforcing the contextual specificity and variability of exchange practices.

Working in the Pacific and echoing this social dimension, Weiner argued that the primary value of inalienability was expressed through the valence certain objects have to define historicity, identity and their ability to fuse past and present (Weiner 1985: 210; 1992). She was referring to heirlooms that possessed an identity and a biography and embody a transcendent value. Weiner demonstrated that material culture may enhance rather than detract from the capacity to objectify social values. Here we see the formative shift from classic exchange theory towards an object-oriented notion of material culture (Myers 2001: 13). There are goods that are clearly alienable and in Egypt this can even extend to sacred objects such as coffins, stelae, and ritual goods that need to be manufactured by craftsmen and circulated. Then, theoretically, there are inalienable things, such a statues of gods and Pharaohs destined for the temples, that were not for barter. In Egypt, as in all cultures, there were radical disjuncts that challenge any hard and fast categorical division. For instance, a man called Amenemope exchanged goods in order to acquire a statue of the deity Seth, but then willingly gave it to another man for a month so that he could take advantage of the divine power of the piece (McDowell 1999: 84–5). This sharing of both an object and its particular service suggests that ritual objects, incarnations of gods in fact, could in specific circumstances be alienable property. For *things to work* they must be beyond the object-as-taxonomy approach that we are comfortable with in Western societies. There must be a pervasive presence, constant influence and agency traveling between spheres. Those objects that travel are substitutes for people and for more sacred entities.

Cool Exchange

The focus of the book is materiality and the constitution of ourselves through the object world, therefore it is impossible not to enter the terrain of exchange and consumption. As Thomas critiques, ethnographic analyses of such transactions tend to leave the nature of things exchanged as an absent space, a matter of no particular import. Many assume objects are uniform, so that all that counts is the social relationship irrespective of whether the exchange involves axes, food or sex (1991: 204). Briefly I want to chart the major issues within ethnography that impinge on the concept of materiality, specifically the permeable categories of persons and objects, or when objects themselves are imbued with life.

In his discussion of the kula, Mauss famously remarked that objects *have a gender*, rather than as archaeologists might say *were gendered*. Objects were similarly endowed with a soul, encompassed in the concept of *vaygu'a*. These objects were human substitutes, and in some ways equivalents to the person's life history. More specifically, these objects encapsulated the history of exchanges and the concomitant relationships they have made manifest. *Vaygu'a* have a name, personality, a past, even a legend attached to them, and people are often named after them. With kula, the object can be both kept and given, it is neither sold nor bought. Objects move with reason and with agency and with them detach parts or essences of individuals. Nancy Munn (1986) famously demonstrated how objectification and sublation could exist outside of alienation and how these processes were firmly enmeshed within social relations. Inspired by Polanyi, she sought to examine the time–space–person system in Gawa and its inter-island worlds of understanding, moving from mere facticity of exchange to the internal relations and their contextual significance and meanings implicated in practice. Kula is an arena of lived experience, construed by human actions and imbued with cultural meanings. Within that system material goods have supra-economic value, they are redolent of potential and their value is relational and socially situated in spacetime (Munn 1986: 9). Material and non-material can be exchanged within the system as the products of agents and the bodies of agents themselves. The locus of self, or fame, of Gawa is extended and dispersed overseas through acts of hospitality, through gifting.

Certain objects of variant status can also be withdrawn from circulation in specific contexts such as kula or in particular structured deposits found in prehistoric Europe. In the Balkan chalcolithic hoards have ranged from two to over 10,000 objects with remarkable variability, combining complete and fragmentary objects in a ritual economy of sacrifice. Copper or gold objects comprise some deposits, while others were replete with bodily ornaments, lithics or shell. Chapman (2000: 117) situates material objects within hoards as having individual biographic elements; each tells a narrative to be recounted and is thus socially linked within kin and power relations. People exchange themselves as they do objects and the concomitant chain of personal relations forged leads to enchainment. Accumulation is the obverse process and forms a tension with enchainment, linking people and things to the experiential domain of place. This is reminiscent of Bradley's influential long-standing work on structured deposits in Western Europe and his ethnographic interest in Saami practice. Depositions of metalwork by the Saami have been read as sacrifice and reflect long-distance exchange networks: one suggestion is social leveling, another is a mechanism through which to secure wealth in the afterlife (Bradley 2000: 50). In Bronze Age Europe, however, depositional practice was very much tied to place, with the recognition of both spatial and temporal variability. Going back to the neolithic Bradley traces the trade and ritual deposition of stone axes across Britain and further into Europe. Hundreds of stone axes were uncovered in river beds and bogs, perhaps as a return offering to the earth where the stone was originally extracted as a form of exchange reciprocity. Withdrawing, hoarding, caching, disposing, and secluding are all ways of excluding materials from circulation while similarly bestowing reverence upon their materiality. Bataille argues that these are all gifts of rivalry within sacrificial economies. Objects are withdrawn from profane circulation, yet these liberated things are ostensibly useless from the start (Bataille 1988: 76). Turning to the ethnographic present, Küchler (1997) imputes that part of the reason for such large collections of Oceanic material abroad is this peculiar willingness to offer objects into the realm of the invisible (see also O'Hanlon and Welsch 2000). Her discussion of museum acquisition, and the Melanesian exchange of ritual objects that facilitated these collections, is an eloquent reconfiguration of alienable circulation – a modern spin on a traditional practice. Absence is thus marked as a ritually constituted practice and space.

Egypt also utilized the sacred deposit, a withdrawing of objects from the world for symbolic reasons. Often termed caches, these were official deposits usually associated with temple activities, specifically the excess of statues and ritual paraphernalia that accumulated over successive dynasties. Some time around 300 BC when major restoration on Karnak temple was underway, a large pit over 10 meters deep was dug in the temple courtyard and in it were placed some 1,700 objects, including 750 stone statues mostly from the New Kingdom or later (Russmann and Finn 1989: 82–3). The deposition of these works within the sacred precinct of the temple shows a level of respect for the spiritual presence of past Pharaohs who were both long dead and, in many cases, long forgotten. There were remarkable statues of Tuthmosis III, Amenhotep III, and Rameses II, as well as many images of the gods. Given the longevity of the Egyptian pantheon it is likely that the images of the gods, their statue embodiments, were plausibly more potent than those of past Pharaohs for successive generations. As Mauss originally noted, objects forge ties between people, between souls, because the thing itself has a soul (1990: 12). And deposition serves as a series of obligations between persons and objects that are culturally coded, a buried geography (Pollard 2001: 318) that retains its implications and reciprocities for the living. Souls are meshed with things just as lives are mingled together, and that is why persons and things become so entangled in the sphere of contract and exchange (Mauss 1990: 20). Those responsible for assembling the Luxor cache were simply fulfilling their end of the contract – to unite and bury Pharaohs and gods within the divine sphere of the temple, constituting a buried cosmos. As archaeologists we need to construct the total social phenomenon, where economics is only part of the complete social exchange, with the acknowledgement that in some societies (such as ancient Egypt) these spheres were inseparable.

Impossible Exchange

In taking an interdisciplinary stance upon objects, objectification and exchange one must tackle to some degree the prodigious work of Jean Baudrillard. For Baudrillard, contemporary society is acquisitive and material culture is oriented to a system of meanings. Late modernity is thus distinctive since humans are not so much surrounded by other humans as they are by objects (Baudrillard 1998: 25). The age of production that demarcated the nineteenth century has been replaced by the twentieth as the age of consumption (Dant 1999: 27). Baudrillard constructs a landscape of proliferation with a myriad of natural species running wild in a system where the fundamental balance has been lost. Pullulation of objects – their multiplication, mutation and variability – requires an adequate classification system. Yet there are as many criteria for classification as objects themselves and the whole process is both speculative and contingent, as set out in the next chapter. What I aim for here is a kind of natural history of the object, grounded within a specific historical trajectory. People and objects are bound together in collusion and take on a dense layering of memories, emotional and historical valences (Baudrillard 1996: 16). Our objects bear silent witness to our unresolved ambivalence in making sense of, and controlling, the world around us. Some objects serve as mediation with the present, others as mediation with the past, the value of the latter being that they address a lack (1996: 83; see Chapter 7).

In Baudrillard's view, consumption is a system of signs to be read, distinct from symbolic meanings and lived experience. In *The System of Objects* (1996: 200), what is consumed is not the object itself but the system of objects, their sign values. He argues that *"to become an object of consumption, an object must first become a sign*. That is to say: it must become external, in a sense to a relationship that it now merely signifies. It is thus *arbitrary* – and not inconsistent with the concrete relationship: it derives its consistency and hence its meaning from an abstract and systematic relationship to all other sign-objects" (emphasis in original). And further, this "conversion of the object to the systematic status of a sign implies the simultaneous transformation of the human relationship into a relationship of consumption – of consuming and being consumed. In and through objects this relationship is at once consummated and abolished; the object becomes its inescapable mediation – and before long the sign that replaces it altogether." Baudrillard is not interested in the objects themselves as embodied matter; he would see them today as potentially divorced from webs of meaning. But objects are never merely signs or symbols functioning as proxies, they *are* whatever they are (Armstrong 1981: 5). His obsession with function and sign value impedes a more nuanced understanding of contextually activated objects resulting in the erasure of meaning. However, he has argued that objects have double lives, they have function and they express meaning and value. "Plural identities, double lives, objective chance or variable-geometry destinies – all this seems very much like the invention of artificial, substitute facts. Sex, genes, networks, desires and partners – everything now falls within the ambit of change and exchange" (2001: 77). Embedded within this narrative however, Baudrillard does acknowledge that certain sorts of objects lie beyond his specific system of signs – namely, exotic, antique, folkloric and generally unique objects. These run counter to functional demands and operate within the spheres of memory, nostalgia and escapism, perhaps as remnants or survivals from a "traditional" system. The application of this reasoning, the idea of double meaning of the ancient under modernity, is more fully explored in Chapter 7 on the reification of ancient Egypt in contemporary theaters of collection and desire.

Central to Baudrillard's (2001: 3) later work is the premise that everything starts from impossible exchange, the uncertainty of the world being reflected in the fact that it has no equivalent anywhere; it cannot be exchanged for anything. This is a provocative thesis that meshes well with both archaeological and ethnographic studies of exchange. He imputes that all our systems are converging in a desperate effort to ward off this radical uncertainty, "to conjure away the inevitable, fateful fact of impossible exchange. Commercial exchange, exchange of meaning, sexual exchange – everything has to be exchangeable. With all things we have to find their ultimate equivalence, have to find a meaning and an end for them" (2001: 14). And further:

> Commodity exchange, the abstraction of commodity, of the general equivalent, and everything which describes the movement of value and the historic form of capital is one thing. The current situation, in which money is the object of a universal passion reaching far beyond value and commodity exchange, is quite another. This fetishism of money, before which all activities are equivalent, expresses the fact that none of these activities any longer has any distinct end-goal. Money then becomes the universal transcription of a world bereft of meaning. (Baudrillard 2001: 127)

Thus he sees a three-tiered structure of development: natural stage (use value); a commodity stage (exchange value); and a structural stage (sign value) (1997: 157).

For Baudrillard every "good" is rendered a service under modernity, every object comes with a suite of features that mimic services (machines say thank you after dispensing, a product such as soap looks after your very well-being). He sees a conspiracy lurking under the mantra of devotion and good will (Baudrillard 1998: 159). Yet he elides the culturally grounded properties of objects that are spatially and temporally marked. Consider the difference in a culture where work and life are not separated, where different spheres of activity overlap or are indistinguishable. How different ancient Egypt is, where products were more than objects, since they also provided a service that might stretch from one world of existence into the next. In consumer culture, however, we are faced with the phenomenon of object profusion, like an uncontrollable vegetation. We live by object time and at the pace of objects and their ceaseless succession. Contrasting modernity with antiquity, Baudrillard quips that now we watch objects as they are born, mature and die, whereas in the past the monuments and timeless objects outlived mortal beings (1998: 25). Baudrillard has a bleak, rather uninformed view of premodern societies: here there is no concept of time, behavior is collective and every-thing ritualized. This, of course, raises issues for archaeologists and ethno-graphers similar to the assertions of Mauss or Giddens, modernity is forged in relation to a fictional and unknown past that seemingly requires no investigation (Meskell 1999: 26). There are, however, other more serious problems with Baudrillard's analysis of social relations and objects. As Miller (1987: 194) underscores, Baudrillard's critique of Marx unfolded into a wider critique "in which objects not only did not signify use value but were found not to signify anything outside of themselves." In the modern context objects were considered so totally interchangeable that there was no value that was not be reducible to the cycle of exchange. Objects are presented as signs whether of function or ostentation: it is a surface rendering of gloss minus depth. Meaning and personal connection are erased in his tacitly post-structuralist account. According to Miller, Baudrillard presents people simply as vehicles for expressing the differences between objects. The source of sign value is progressively disconnected from social practice and thus becomes overdetermined. Baudrillard's oeuvre is stimulating for discussion of consumption under modernity, but rather more heuristic and less instructive for musing upon networks of exchange and sociality in antiquity.

Miller and the New Material Culture

Writing in the late 1980s, Roy Ellen had accused anthropologists of effectively eliding material culture for some fifty years. While nineteenth-century anthropologists like Tylor and Haddon forged an incipient study of material culture, the project had largely stalled. Yet the new material culture studies, stemming largely from British (and more specifically Cambridge) archaeology, offered a new challenge and direction to the study, fusing archaeological approaches to materials with ethnographic savvy and real world complexities. Daniel Miller's prodigious writing heralded, and continues to confront, the disciplinary confines of anthropology and archaeology. His original, early work on material culture recognized that archaeology has been somewhat limited in its engagement with material culture and that such a project would be necessarily interdisciplinary. Later he was to impute that "there is at present no academic discipline which sees as its specific project to examine the nature of artefacts as cultural forms" (1987: 100). This position lies at the core of his construction of material culture studies, a particularly British configuration of scholars and subjects that has forged new ground in anthropology abroad.

The central premise of his early work is that "artefacts, as objects created and interpreted by people, embody the organisational principles of human categorisation processes" (Miller 1985: 1), following the work of Mary Douglas and other structuralists. Miller was adept in documenting the variability of material forms, something that is reflected in his later work, and the idea that human creativity and expression in material forms are inflected with social relations and social life. Miller was one of the first to recognize the fetish aspect of artefacts; that archaeologists have tended to substitute material relations for social relations. In his own words, Miller conducts an archaeology of the minutiae of the mundane. He is interested in the biographical constitution of the material – in this case specific ceramic forms, their every contextual movement and pursuant meaning, and their embodied, performative potentials. Yet the ceramics are also constitutive objects; they are enmeshed in social relations, neither strictly determining them nor being determined by them. This would be to attenuate the capacities of material culture. Biographical moments also inhere in the Indian ceramics under investigation: they were "created by individuals of one generation and become the given environment through which individuals of the succeeding generation are themselves constructed as subjects" (Miller 1985: 204). In this dialectic, mundane objects such as pottery aid in the contextual understanding of the lifeworld but also simultaneously constitute that world. His micro-analysis contributes to our understandings of the ways society and culture reproduce and transform, much as I argue in Chapter 6 for Egyptian lifeworlds.

Adeptly Miller situates archaeology's problematic tendency to interpolate objects as signifiers for culture itself and the reductive readings that ensue from that conflation. This might be seen as an inherently functional interpretation and handling of materiality, effectively erasing the *thingness* of things. In *Artefacts as Categories* he engages in a close reading of categorization – its scientific and anthropological underpinnings and tacitly subjective indeterminacy. His account is still certainly relevant for archaeology's historical engagement with taxonomy and, to some degree, still speaks for what archaeologists do in terms of category and classification. I will not attempt to revisit it in the present work, suffice to say "there is no 'true' typology or taxonomy, but equally, the producers cannot be disestablished as the creators of order under study"

(Miller 1985: 11). Here the material world is used to objectify conceptualization, to naturalize social relations and to mark social categories.
To date only a sparse literature exists, mainly directed at consumption,
and these studies are firmly lodged in disciplines outside archaeology.

In *Material Culture and Mass Consumption* (1987), Miller's central
premise stems from the Hegelian recognition that subject and object
are tacitly framed within a mutually constitutive relationship. Objectification is an inevitable process by which all expression, conscious or
unconscious, social or individual, takes form. Cultural objects are the
externalization of value and meaning embedded in social processes and
further transferable and negotiable by individuals (Myers 2001: 20).
Objectification, which for Hegel is a process of alienation and its return,
are therefore seen as positive, providing a non-reductionist and dynamic
subject–object context from which to pursue the topic of material culture.
For Hegel, property and other things were an externalization, an embodiment of the will. It is not surprising then that Hegel significantly influenced
Marx, although he lacked Marx's historicity and political positioning.
Both suggest a material constitution of society, that objectification and
culture can be defined with respect to one another (Miller 1987: 33).
Subjects and objects are thus unthinkable without each other. And as
Marx made clear, the separation and estrangement of producers and their
products, coupled with the alienation of their labor, formed the central
problem of capitalism. Much of his book is focused upon the question
of contemporary consumption in Britain, an area that Miller subsequently grounded in a series of ethnographic studies. Miller draws from
a wide range of scholarship, including psychology, psychoanalysis, and
philosophy, as well as the classic ethnographies of Mauss, Weiner, Munn
and Bourdieu. Significantly, archaeology does not play a central role in
his formulation of a new materiality and consumption. Yet the way he
repackages materiality has obvious benefits for an archaeological
endeavor. In his view "an object may always signify its own material
possibilities and constraints and thereby the more general world of
material practices. What is of importance is certainly not the idea of
physicality as some 'ultimate constraint' or final determining factor, but
rather the manner in which everyday objects continually assert their
presence as simultaneously material force and symbol" (1987: 105). This
goes some way to his original Hegelian position of the mutually
constitutive play of subject and object and, moreover, that materiality
is always present in cultural configuration and transformation.

Miller's later work has taken materiality and consumption to new
levels, effectively crafting the new discipline of material culture studies

that developed within the interstices of archaeology and anthropology and appears to have surpassed both its parent disciplines. In later work he argues that the ways in which people interact with objects are largely shaped by discourse, a circulation of signs and values, albeit in a more nuanced vein than Baudrillard. Possessions are key in the project of self-construction. Valued material possessions act as signs of the self on the micro scale and are key in the maintenance of culture on the macro. Thus the world of meaning that we create, and through which we too are constituted, extends in the object world and into our objective surroundings (Belk 2000: 78). For Miller, a theory of consumption focuses upon recovering objects from the alienated process of production, consumption thus being a strategy of self-creation in the face of alienation (Dant 1999: 32). Miller also positions consumption as the "vanguard of history" in shaping global and social order:

> The authenticity of artefacts as culture derives, not from their relationship to some historical style or manufacturing process – in other words, there is no truth or falsity immanent in them – but rather from their active participation in a process of social self creation in which they are directly constitutive of ourselves and others. The key for judging the utility of contemporary objects is the degree to which they may or may not be appropriated from the forces which created them, which are mainly, of necessity, alienating. This appropriation consists of the transmutation of goods, through consumption activities, into potentially inalienable culture. (Miller 1997: 215)

Kopytoff (1986) and Miller (1987) have both demonstrated that the degree of inalienability is an index of the object's personification through the act of consumption. If persons and relationships become the primary medium through which we achieve a sense of the transcendent or inalienable, then in turn any objects that express persons or relationships become the vehicle for expressing these higher values (Miller 1998b: 146). As Miller perceptively points out, when reading *The Gift*, "we often ignore the fact that his first example is not the much quoted case of the *hau*, in which objects in non-commodified societies are found to have person-like qualities, but rather the *taonga*, in which persons are found to have object-like qualities" (1995: 157). Greater emphasis must be applied to the dialectical relationship; namely, the ways in which objectification changes and develops the subject. Bourdieu, through habitus, was similarly interested in the ways social beings are constructed through the geographies of the material world, interpolating that human agency is always to a degree an act which reproduces the agency of the things that socialize those persons (Miller in press). Bourdieu claimed to be drawn to mimesis and the ineffable nature of the art object, how it speaks and conveys through matter. Yet he was trapped by the linguistic model in terms of generative practice and social reproduction that placed undue emphasis upon the replication of enduring structures. He too returned to Mauss and gifting (Bourdieu 1977), yet ultimately focused more upon the structural setting than the meanings that inhere in material exchange.

Consumption has certainly provided one avenue to understanding materiality. For Marx the material world was a reflection of congealed labor, but also one in which subjects and objects are mutually constitutive, much like Simmel (1979). For Bourdieu consumption signified status and identity, whereas Baudrillard views materiality as a bearer of aesthetic value. Douglas and Isherwood (1996) see it as the arena in which culture is shaped, Weiner and Munn see it as potentially inalienable and reflective of individual and societal constitution. Finally, Miller posits that consumption occurs at precisely the moment at which the alienable becomes inalienable and where both relationships and persons are forged. This approach is perhaps closest to the kinds of ancient Egyptian engagements with materiality and exchange that I outline in the following chapters. Archaeologically the traces for such interleaved processes and beliefs are more scant and ambiguous yet still worth pursuing. Influenced by the work of Mauss, Munn and Miller we can begin to see that separating out objects and experiences into the familiar spheres of religion or economics will never suffice to explain indigenous understandings, so we must try to reconfigure these spheres into contextually significant arenas of knowledge. This can be achieved to some degree in antiquity as well if we are willing to problematize taxonomies and to look for local understandings of the phenomenal world.

Materialization of the physical world is a human project, predominantly though not exclusively involving a project of creation or objectification. The material culture of everyday life acknowledges the physical object in all its materiality and examines its fabrication, distribution, consumption, use, discard, and so on. Like many ethnographers I am interested in specific historical moments, whether celebrations or crises, where the material transactions undertaken by Egyptian individuals were ritually charged and saturated with meaning. One could perceive the Egyptians as highly acquisitive since they accumulated material goods during life and much of it was taken with them to the grave. Things such as tombs, houses, statuary, furniture, clothing, and personal adornment signified wealth and status, but many things were inseparably redolent of ritual potency. Many objects were not simply goods in the modern commodity market sense, and this is why we need to re-examine our categorizations, as outlined in the next chapter. However, this is not to say that they viewed all objects as animistic, that a spirit resided in each thing, natural or manufactured. Such a generalization would also erase the significance of context. However, in magic and ritual domains the acts of inscribing, speaking, and fabricating, and the very materials that concretized those actions, were regarded as efficacious. More specifically, the following chapters explore how the biographies of objects progress through various stages of the mediation process between people, divine beings and the physical world (Attfield 2000: 3). And there is a world of difference between the *conceptualization* and *materialization* of experiential reality. Many Egyptian things can be posited as intermediaries between individuals and their phenomenal worlds, anchoring a dynamic complex and non-dualistic interplay of subjects, objects, beings, things, people, animals, landscapes, and so on. We require a language, a contextually appropriate discourse that calls into question or destabilizes those taxa with which we feel most comfortable.

Taxonomy, Agency, Biography

Could we classify the luxuriant growth of objects as we do flora and fauna, complete with tropical and glacial species, sudden mutations, and varieties threatened with extinction?

Jean Baudrillard, *The Sytem of Objects*

Inspired by a passage from Borges describing the wild profusion of things and the desperate attempt to classify and collapse the distinction of same and other, Michel Foucault wrote *The Order of Things*. The Chinese encyclopedia Borges described suggested that "animals are divided into: (a) belonging to the Emperor, (b) embalmed, (c) tame, (d) sucking pigs, (e) sirens, (f) fabulous, (g) stray dogs, (h) included in the present classification, (i) frenzied, (j) innumerable, (k) drawn with a very fine camelhair brush, (l) et cetera, (m) having just broken the water pitcher, (n) that from a long way off look like flies" (Foucault 1973: xv). This fabulous taxonomy proffers a direct challenge to the naturalism of categories, that they constitute objective knowledge. The impossibility of the Chinese taxa transgresses the fixity of our own categories, ironically deconstructed (or excavated) by Foucault in his own form of archae-ological practice. Archaeology, as a methodological trope, is particularly adequate to the task since it provides general spatial and temporal knowledge, investigates cultural configurations, and offers a kind of natural history of culture. More evocative still is the real example from Australian Aboriginal culture, specifically the taxonomic distinctions inherent in traditional Dyirbal language. In their object universe the word *Bayi* can encompass men, kangaroos, possums, bats, most snakes and fish, the moon, storms, rainbows, and boomerangs, among other things. While the term *Bala* refers to parts of the body, meat, bees, wind, yamsticks, some spears, grass, mud, stones, noises and language, to name a few (Lakoff 1987: 92–7). Understanding the internal logic that saturates these classifications is difficult from a Western perspective, yet the Dyirbal system reflects Aboriginal domains of contextual experience and learned understandings of the world. Archaeology, as an inherently taxonomic discipline, is also well placed to interrogate the tacit pervasiveness of Western classificatory systems that elide or impede culturally contextual understandings of the phenomenal world.

Following Foucault, what is taxonomy if not a classificatory convenience based on resemblance, on visual observation, a sense that became privileged in Western thought some time during the seventeenth century? As a graduated scale of proximity, taxonomy pertains less to the world of things than to the world in which they exist, a world structured and fashioned in particular ways by distinct groups. We witness a radical change in the episteme from the sixteenth century when the determining configurations were based upon kinships, resemblances, and affinities, and where words and things were deeply enmeshed. The next century heralded in the age of scientific order – what we know as rationalism (Foucault 1973: 54) – characterized by the search for a general grammar, a fixed grid that might overlay the known world. Finitude seems to be the ultimate goal, the act of knowing the concrete forms of finite existence, reconciling similarities and differences, difference being rendered the same as identity (Foucault 1973: 315). But what about the intermediate productions, as Foucault cites them, the blurred organisms between animal and vegetable, the flying squirrel and the bird, monkey and man? One need only think of the recent realizations that birds are dinosaurs and that birds (avian dinosaurs to be exact) are more closely related to dinosaurs, in current classificatory thought, than say lizards. This new approach to classification is known as cladistics or phylogenetic systematics. The story goes that Thomas Huxley, while eating quail one night, made the connection between his dinner and the tibia of a dinosaur that he was currently studying. His theory failed to find support, and only in the 1960s did the dino-bird theory assume scientific credence. Even this theory has been challenged by scientists who deconstructed one set of supposed resemblances and examined other variations: taxonomy is like that, it forms a subjective ontology where some similarities are privileged and some differences are elided. In some senses our construct of natural history is far from natural. The division of mineral, vegetable and animal was originally formulated around the concept of movement: which entities can grow, which are susceptible to sensation and which are capable of independent mobility. For Darwin all classification was genealogical, although one could not base a classification upon a single unit of resemblance. He sought to critique naturalists for their subjective renderings of uniformity and connectivity, the separating and uniting of species more or less alike.

Questioning taxonomy is no different to challenging any body of what are claimed to be incontrovertible facts. Mary Poovey provocatively asks, what are facts?

> Are they incontrovertible data that simply demonstrate what is true? Or are they bits of evidence marshaled to persuade others of the theory one sets out with? Do facts somehow exist in the world like pebbles, waiting to be picked up? Or are they manufactured and thus informed by all the social and personal factors that go into every act of human creation? Are facts beyond interpretation? Or are they the very stuff of interpretation, its symptomatic incarnation instead of the place where it begins? (Poovey 1998: 1)

Playing with these provocative questions, one may substitute the word "classification" or "taxa" for Poovey's "facts" to good effect here, exposing the same level of constructedness and interpretation and the inherent subjectivity that permeates throughout.

The Problem of Taxonomy

At the heart of this argument lies the originary problem of taxonomy that extends beyond the heuristic frame. It is not simply a matter of the classificatory schemes that scholars employ, but rather the fundamental understandings and interpretation of other cultural times and spaces; ultimately, cultural difference. All categories are artefacts (Goodman 1992). I am advocating a recognition and adjustment to take account of the underlying cultural complexity of the world. In the early seventeenth century Francis Bacon remarked that it was human nature to enforce order and regularity upon the world around us despite our recognition that so much in nature is singular and unmatched. Irrespectively we devise parallels and conjugates that do not, in reality, exist. Following this work, philosopher John Dupré takes as his project the issue of unity or diversity of the world's ultimate contents. He asks the question: what underlies and shapes the intent to classify the object? In essence a contextual investigation, Dupré argues that any move toward taxonomy entails understanding the goals underlying the motivations for categorization. The notion that things belong unambiguously to discoverable natural kinds is intimately connected to essentialism, the idea that things possess inherent properties or qualities that make them one kind of thing or another (1993: 6–7). Many resounding critiques have been launched at the concept of essentialism from feminists and philosophers alike;

however, fewer realize that essentialism as a model also fails in biology. In its place Dupré advocates pluralism, a doctrine that recognizes many equally legitimate ways of dividing the world into kinds – what he terms a "promiscuous realism." Within pluralism one can avert the pitfalls of reductionism, insisting rather on the equal reality and causal efficacy of objects, large and small.

Dupré proposes that science is best viewed, in Wittgenstein's sense, as a family resemblance concept (1993: 10). While distinctions may be easy to draw, making meaningful decisions on the basis of culturally relevant criteria may be another matter. Biology is Dupré's main test case, where taxonomy really came to the fore in classificatory and intellectual terms. Organisms are organized into a hierarchical series of taxa with species being the narrowest. Classification tends to be treated as an outcome of an ordering process or an end in itself. Teleologically, this ordering process itself is couched in prior social action that shapes and directs every stage (Douglas and Hull 1992: 2). This leads to the age-old question: are there natural kinds? As Douglas and Hall suggest, if biological species evolve according to the mechanisms proposed by evolutionary biologists then species are not *kinds*, much less *natural kinds*. What we have is a typical case of induction. And as Douglas makes clear (1992: 243), anthropologists need to revisit their own constructed notions of similarity and taxonomy since inductive practice forms the basis for canons of similarity. Anthropologists are, she imputes, very interested in implicit understandings, highlighting some meanings, eliding others, weighting specific elements, and together this too recalls the process of world-making.

Taxonomic practice may change, and some examples clearly demonstrate a divergence between scientific terms and ordinary language. The gross morphology of a plant is of little import to taxonomic theory, so that the term "tree" has no place in scientific taxonomy, although it is clearly relevant to a discipline like ecology. And this is how I suggest we consider taxonomy within the archaeological workings of material culture and its analysis. While I do not deny that certain categorizations are useful in the archaeological organization of objects, it is perhaps more productive to also be able to complicate our heuristic strategies and try and restore some emic or contextual meaning to the frame. Some categories are clearly meaningful for us: figurines, wall paintings, ceramics, lithics, worked bone, and so on. In some archaeological excavation these categories are being collapsed and reorganized to attempt a closer fit with ancient systems of meaning. What if the sorts of things one makes from clay all belong to one coherent category? This sort of thinking has recently been pursued at Çatalhöyük (Hodder 2000).

Suppose magical items, whether clay, wax or wood, were more meaning-fully grouped from the outset, as would be the case in Egypt. These strategies can be pursued later in more synthetic works but often are not followed up on, leaving a static and unrepresentative picture of material life in place. Archaeologists tend towards morphological, followed by evolutionary, classification whereas it is conceptual taxonomies that allow insight into past meaning.

Today it is commonplace for ecologists to write broadly of the powers of humans, gods, and nonhumans and to include discussions on religion, power, ancestors, cosmology, plants and animals (Latour 1991: 14). For some scientists the poles of object and subject are more difficult to maintain and in their place new positions, or hybrid situations, are emerging: we should be talking about morphisms rather than anthro-pomorphism. Social context is also crucial here (see also Haraway 1991, 1997). From a Latourian perspective (1991: 130) moderns have often failed to realize the entwining of objects and societies, the nonseparability of cosmologies and sociologies. Past societies recognized this conver-gence, but the onslaught of terrifying revolutions has to some degree severed the link – that mixture of rational constraints and the needs of their societies. We continue to identify with Enlightenment thinking, the separability of the human and nonhuman, when in fact we need to reconfigure modernity in new ways, perhaps even a little like that of the distant past. This is akin to Latour's hybrid systems of thought and hence his argument that we have never been modern. To take an ethnographic example, Tambiah, in his famous study of Thai amulets (1984: 208) redescribes amulets as "sedimentations of power," with the acknow-ledgement that the Thai do not have a single system of categories that exhaustively label and classify amulets. Each individual amulet is named and some named amulets fall in larger classes. This goes back to the concept of Dupré's argument for pluralism – specifically methodological pluralism. Scholars may design classifications that facilitate certain aspects of their research, but this does not entail getting any closer to one's subject or understanding the embedded cultural meanings.

Relics and fetishes are perhaps the most evocative examples of cross-classification. With the recognition that categories can be mobilized to different degrees of inclusion and exclusion, sometimes equivalent to species, or genera, or families, Ellen (1988: 223) argues for strong cultural variability, as well as differences between domains, contextual specificity, and so on. He too focuses on the natural kind argument. However, I would like to push the analysis to the object world itself, collapsing those categories of meaning and experience. Metonymic fetishes such as saintly body parts that circulated in the Middle Ages are compelling examples of the cross over and collapsing between persons and things. Sacred objects and texts realize the synthesis of the real and the imaginary which make up humanity's social being (Godelier 1999: 138). They are loaded with symbolic value for this reason and belong to already existing social codes and can never inhere in reductive categories whether as pure symbols or pure objects. Examining the production, exchange, sale and even theft of sacred relics, Geary reveals that this category was very much culturally grounded and included clothing, objects, dust, oil and actual body parts. Objects, persons and parts of person could all be subsumed within the category of the relic, although the body was the most potent agent of god, viewed as a security deposit that guaranteed their perpetual interest in the earthly community (Geary 1986: 176). There were two periods of high demand, between 750–850 AD, and in the eleventh century AD, where efficacy and value were at a premium. Some holy men were even in danger of being murdered to thus transform their bodies into relics, while others stole their bodily remains once dead. Like those of St Mark, the remains of many pious individuals were periodically lost or rediscovered, and quite simply if the human remains/objects "worked," they were authenticated. Apart from their thaumaturgic power relics could also operate, and substitute, for public authority to protect, secure, and determine the status of individuals and churches and their economic prosperity. But what is insightful in this well-documented context is the juxtaposition of belief and skepticism. On the one hand, person-objects (relics) were almost universally accepted in their efficacy, while on the other the recognition of fraud, the ubiquity of similar items, and intense competition that undermined specific relics, were widespread detractors. Both positions were simultaneously embraced and accommodated. This case provides a valuable insight into those cultural moments where emic rationality around taxonomic difference is challenged, negotiated and ultimately reconciled.

These are incisive examples from Western culture where the Cartesian duality obviously breaks down, with concomitant moral and ethical dilemmas. One salient example is the circulation of body parts that subsequently become objects, objectified, and certainly commodified. They are objects in that they do not assume subject status, but they also are intimately connected to the very fabric of corporeal being. Objects in this context become embodied and, for some, enlivened. This begs the much-debated question of when does personhood begin? This undermines one of our fundamental moral dilemmas in regard to abortion and human reproduction, although not one that is universally shared (Kopytoff 1986: 84). This is reminiscent of a rather more ancient set of contexts. First in ancient Egypt, body parts became objectified and the living body turned into another sort of product (Meskell and Joyce 2003). The dead body was transmuted into almost object status, a body that was rendered permanent and artificial through the elaborate processes of evisceration and mummification. For most Egyptians the mummy was a sacred self, an embodied subject with a future trajectory, yet numerous individuals who robbed the tombs with mummies *in situ* perceived them very differently. Many Egyptians feared that the rituals and processes would fail them and there would be no return from death (Parkinson 1997). Such examples complicate the notions of bounded-ness, classificatory schemes, agency and trajectory, and each could be said to be extending the biography of the entities involved.

There remains the unavoidable question: to what extent do individuals recognize themselves in their replicas? Do they see themselves as authors of their own sacred objects? To what extent do they believe their beliefs; are they convinced that someone else is the force behind society and do they simply turn a blind eye? To what extent do people have to repress, sublimate, or metamorphose the facts for the good of social cohesion (Godelier 1999: 178)?

> The sacred is a certain relationship with the origin of things in which imaginary replicas step in and take the place of real humans. In other words, the sacred is a certain type of relationship that humans entertain with the origin of things, such that, in their relationship, the real humans disappear and in their stead appear duplicates of themselves, imaginary humans. (Godelier 1999: 171)

In this relationship human beings need to disappear, specifically in their role as authors – authors of one's social being. Baines amply demonstrates this with regard to the creators of Egyptian art, including the statues or illustrated ostraca discussed later, who have left little trace of their own intentions. What mattered most was maintaining social order as conceived by a small elite group who commissioned, designed and perhaps executed such works, practices that recursively constituted a self-legitimating program (Baines 1994: 88). In explanatory frameworks, humans become not simply actors but those acted upon. This results in an occultation of reality and an inversion of the cause and effect dynamic. This too leads to a situation of alienation and a fictional account of origins that effaces the agency of humanity. We can see this clearly in the origin myths of ancient Egypt, the repressing of human achievement and action, a necessary forgetting in order to produce and reproduce society. The sacred conceals something from society collectively and individually; it produces alternative accounts, the opacity of which is essential to conceal the social from itself and ultimately legitimate this sacred character. Sacred objects mystify, they embody and signify with over-elaborated meaning, but they also come to obfuscate, expressing the inexpressible and representing the unrepresentable, that which cannot truly be known (Godelier 1999: 174).

Fetishism and its Objects of Desire

"Fetish," as a term, derives from the Latin *facticius*, meaning "to do" or "a thing made by art." Already by the late fifteenth century it was applied widely to objects such as charms, and later to religious relics. Another interpretation cites "fetish" as a Portuguese derivation, from *feitico*, which also means "charm" and stemmed from sixteenth and seventeenth century colonial expansion into West Africa. The term itself was, and continues to be, one of contestation. It reaches scholarly dogma, according to Ellen (1988: 214), in the second half of the eighteenth century when it was used in the French parliament by De Brosses to describe the worship of stone figures and other material objects, and was used to repudiate the "savage mind" that could only grasp the tangible object rather than abstract concept. He also devoted his writing to his own mis/understandings of ancient Egypt in his book *Du culte des dieux fétiches, ou Parallèle de l'ancienne religion de l'Egypte avec la religion actuelle de Nigritie*. And it was De Brosses' writing that also influenced Marx, fusing materialism and fetishism together. Many have since argued that religion originated with fetishism: Comte espoused this position in his three-stage development of religion: fetishism, polytheism, and monotheism. Tylor modified this narrow usage, arguing that fetishism could be understood as the "attribution of human mental qualities to inanimate animism, while restricting fetishism to the doctrine of the spirits embodied in, attached to or conveying influence through certain material objects" (Ellen 1988: 214). Through its history, the fetish has come to be strongly associated with African tribalism and witchcraft, where the fetish and poison were regarded as isomorphs (Lévy-Bruhl 1966: 53). Yet the concept itself is widespread and could easily apply to many cultures and practices, both ancient and modern. What underscores the African connection is an overt and racist substrate of *primitivism*, a legacy that gives a negative inflection to modern uses of the word. These Western connotations were constructed initially due to a combination of Christian suspicion of idolatry and the accounts of beliefs and practices. By the eighteenth century, the meaning had become so confused that African religion was inextricably linked with European ideas of witchcraft. In many ways it has come to stand for the entirely European failure to understand Africa (Shelton 1995). This pervasive negativity shrouds many studies of fetishism, as if moral, religious or socio-sexual risk is always a spectral possibility.

Most recently definitions of the fetish underwrite its inherently material qualities, its thingness. Much is made of its magical, ritual, and ultimately sexual characteristics: the examples used are typically African. Similar to many of the examples, the Egyptian context can also be read as a technology, the desire for a predictive or divinatory mechanics of practice through material means: the active deployment of an agentic materiality. This is not to undermine the concept of cultural historically situated difference with understandings of fetishism. As Taussig (1980: 37) notes, within pre-capitalist societies fetishism arises from an organic unity between people and things, as opposed to the strongly contoured divide between persons and the things they produce to exchange in capitalist societies. The latter results in the subordination of persons to the things they produce under capitalism and the fetishization of commodities where objects of private property stand in for real human relations.

The shift towards fetishization entails a move from the balanced simultaneity of signifier and signified towards the "thing in itself" (Ellen 1988: 213). Baudrillard achieves this with his re-reading of Marx, imputing that the "formal analysis of the commodity grounds a first-level fetishism, connected with exchange-value. But when the passion for value becomes embodied, beyond value, in the doubly abstract passion for money, this becomes the object of fetishism, connected now not with exchange-value, but with the unexchangeable" (Baudrillard 2001: 129). It is also a flattening of the distinction between subjects and objects. One can read the fetish as "a displacement of meaning through synecdoche, the displacement of the object of desire onto something else through the process of disavowal" (Gamman and Makinen 1994: 45). That desire may be provoked by religious, economic, or erotic value that accrues to the object. Anthropology has studied the religious fetish, Marxism has pursued the economically inflected object, and Psychology has examined the sexualization of the object. Few studies have attempted to blur those domains. The fetish as an entity crystallized into an object beyond value that possesses an unexchangeable singularity. From these various perspectives one might argue that many Egyptian objects would fall into the religious category, the traditional focus of ethnographic investigation. Through veneration or devotion the object is attributed power or effectiveness, and may appear to act independently of its manifestation. As Ellen casts it:

> Animation, through analogy (ultimately with the sentient human body), provides a means for representing, comprehending and evoking; the inevitable consequence of which is the socialization of the natural, material, world. But the socialization of nature releases ambiguities, most notably in terms of the semiotic status of the objects or categories (their simultaneity as both signified and signifier) and in the perceived power relations between object and person. (Ellen 1988: 230)

Given the axiomatic nature of the fetish's physicality, Pels is correct in challenging the elision of materiality in recent discussions. Specifically he attacks Appadurai's notion of methodological fetishism, largely because it leads away from the salience of materiality and historicity. Things talk back, Pels (1998: 94) imputes, and can undertake this action in two ways. One way is via animation by another entity, another is though their own "voice." Appadurai refers to the former in his discussion of human traffic enlivening the object, thus their agency is derivative. More controversially, some might say that things act on their own, affect change and insert themselves into life trajectories. Thus we have traditional notions of animism on the one hand, and fetishism on the other; namely, the capacity for objects to communicate their own messages. Parts of the book are devoted to exploring the ramifications of this second premise, the cultural moments whereby power is accorded or bestowed upon things that are then perceived as transcending their manufacture – oracular statues and statues of the gods for example. As Tambiah (1984) declares, probably all cultures have their versions of object fetishism, it is only the manner in which persons and objects are intertwined that varies according to contextual understandings of the cultural grid.

Writing this book in the American Southwest it is impossible to overlook the visual and material power of Native American fetishes, specifically objects created by Zuñi carvers, past and present (Figure 2.1). Zuñi fetishes are carved stone objects of either animals or revered gods (Fane, Jacknis, and Breen 1991). Legend has it that when the children of the sun touched the animals they encountered they were rendered into stone. Animals are closer to the gods than humans, they have corporeal and sensory attributes that demarcate them as special, and thus they can act as messengers or intercessors between divine and earthly orbits.

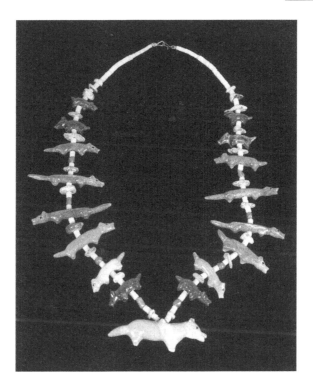

Figure 2.1 Zuñi fetish necklace, carved by Leekya Deyuse in the 1940s, comprised of turquoise, coral, shell and rycolite. Courtesy of the School of American Research.

Embellishments such as arrowheads, shells and feathers increase the power, and fetishes bring these as offerings, sometimes known as power packs and medicine bundles, to the gods. Since they are animate agents they are traditionally fed, well treated, and called upon to help treat diseases, gambling, fertility, bring rain, and to protect from witchcraft. Large animal fetishes that represent animal gods were kept in fetish jars and ceremonially fed on a daily basis, some with ground and powdered turquoise. In sum, the power resides within the spirit within the fetish, not the fetish itself. Zuñi fetishes operate as indexes of cumulative agency and can be perceived as a material knot entwining the invisible threads of spatio-temporal relations (Gell 1998: 61). Unconsecrated fetishes can be sold to tourists, like myself, interested parties who are outside ritual tribal practice. These are disengaged objects or empty vessels, yet still operate as objects of another sort of veneration and fetishization. As Taussig (1993a: 233–5) would have it, the fetish is where thought and object interpenetrate. Through praxis, there is a peeling off of the signifier from the signified and the representation acquires more than the *power of* the represented, but subsequently *power over* it.

Finally Benjamin (1968), and Simmel (1979) before him, anticipated the contemporary sexualization of things: objects provocatively draw persons into desiring and acquisitive states. And in contemporary modernity objects are impregnated or saturated with the recognition of absent value (Apter 1993: 2). This has real repercussions for the practices of collecting, particularly the ancient artefacts of glittering cultures such as Egypt. Fetishization always requires historical and cultural grounding, objects require territorialization, an evocative locality and personalization that both intensifies and undercuts the connectivity. I am struck by the very phrase, "objects of desire," and how commonly we employ it, even in describing the mundane rather than those things that undergo a transference through our emotional needs. Unsurprisingly, Baudrillard conveys a negative spin on the fetishization of such objects of desire. For him, the destiny of all these desired objects is an artificial survival, to be resurrected as reservation fetish, like endangered animal species that are rehabilitated, like the musealized ghettos and all the things that survive in intensive care or on a drip-feed (Baudrillard 2001: 43). A more sustained engagement with modern reification, consumption and collection of objects is undertaken in Chapter 7.

Subject and Object Problems in Archaeology

The fixity of our taxonomies is cogently demonstrated in the terms "objectivity" and "subjectivity" and their distinct frames of reference: "objectivity" is employed to represent knowledge imbued with unquestioned and universal validity whereas "subjectivity" is used to convey attitudes or judgments that are changeable, relative and unstable (Riggins 1994: 1). As Latour (2000: 115) cautions, "objectivity" does not imply a special quality of mind, but rather to the presence of *objects* that have been rendered able to *object* to narratives and explanations imputed to them. Given the context of analysis we might do well to deconstruct if not jettison these predetermined categories. Following Lévi-Strauss, we are all *bricoleur* who speak with things but also through the medium of things (Mark 1994: 90). The instability of definitions of materiality, of objects and subjects, might not be a source of epistemic anguish, but rather allow for a spectrum of contextual understandings. As Miller cautions, it is unlikely that a single theory of materiality is either possible or even desirable. Approaching the study of material culture in terms of its shifting states of materiality and immateriality might also offer some possibility towards gaining insights into the agent-like qualities of material culture itself. Yet any simple strategy to make things more human or animating objects, with a simple attribution of agency, still resorts to the same dichotomies (Gosden 2001: 164) and fails to reconfigure our essential thinking. Following Buchli, the imputation of agency, notably in the work of Gell and Latour, has eroded the totalizing effects of discourse-based analysis and social constructivism that view materiality as determined by discourse and language at the expense of corporeal and phenomenological accounts. Yet in archaeology this is often achieved through blanketing, while the cultural specificity and con-textual understandings of categorical shifts are usually left unexplored. Moreover, there is still the danger of slippage within the attribution of agent-like qualities to material culture, if this assertion is understood as more than a proxy (Buchli 2002a).

For many, materiality implies that we attribute agency both to subjects and objects, working back from a particular effect to an original cause. One need only think of the recent spate of Gell-inspired case studies in archaeology. From one perspective, persons and things are encountered in some mutually constitutive sense of a shared material environment; alternatively, this taxonomic collapse references the ways in which agency and intentionality are imputed. In either or both these guises, the agency of subjects and objects appear as *things* because they are encountered as ready-formed images (Rowlands 2002). A materialist approach, following Rowlands, should instead emphasize the real sense of how people are shaped through the production of their material life, with the recognition that objects do not exist a priori. It should also treat the sensuous, grounded nature of things as having serious experi-ential and ontological weight. The mutually constitutive model has provided an appealing shorthand, albeit rather lazily, in understanding the processes of shaping: we envision and shape things as they recursively impact upon us. It is superficially descriptive rather than explanatory, but has served to interpolate the social constitution of the object world, as a palliative to traditional, reductive economic or technological accounts. As Rowlands (2002) makes clear, even some phenomenological and semiotic approaches lack the insights of an earlier materialism that took for granted that not only do we make ourselves, but that this is in itself a political act (see Chapter 6).

The work of Alfred Gell, largely his *Art and Agency* volume, has contributed much to the refining of discussions concerning agency. He posited that agency is attributed both to persons and things that are seen to initiate causal sequences by acts of mind, will or intention: agents cause things to happen in their vicinity. Action is always social, as are the indexes of agency attributed to art objects. These objects are not self-sufficient agents, but secondary ones that operate in conjunction with particular human subjects. Gell conceded, axiomatically, that things cannot have intentions and what they cause to happen should be positioned as *happenings* not *actions* referable to the agency exuded by the thing. This entails a paradox from which he tries desperately to disentangle himself. He acknowledges that a "'sociology of action' premised on the intentional nature of agency, undermines itself fatally by introducing the possibility that 'things' could be agents, because the whole interpretative exercise is founded on the strict separation between 'agency' – exercised by sentient, enculturated, human beings – and the kind of physical causation which explains the behaviour of mere things" (Gell 1998: 19). To escape the trap Gell elaborates upon the notion that human agency is exercised within the material world and that primary (intentional beings) and secondary agents (things) are involved. "We recognize agency, *ex post facto* . . . but we cannot detect it in advance, that is, we cannot tell that someone is an agent before they act as an agent, before they disturb the causal milieu" (1998: 20). This allows objects to act, since we cannot detect them in advance as one would a primary agent. Pol Pot's landmines are the salient example of secondary agents, tools of destruction that were deployed through primary agency, but no less effective on the ground as "embodiments of the power or capacity to will their use." Landmines are a valent signifier of the proliferation of fragments of primary intentional agents in their secondary objectified form. Pol Pot's soldiers themselves were similarly efficacious agents of their leader's distributed personhood.

Agency itself is a problematic taxonomy and has been the subject of much debate in archaeology (Blake 1999; Dobres 2000; Dobres and Robb 2000; Johnson 1989; Meskell 1999; Saitta 1994). Avoiding the pitfalls of extreme methodological individualism, one can posit that people have degrees of agency or intentionality while acknowledging that this exists within a specific cultural location; their actions are embedded in contexts of grounding and webs of dependency. Persons do not come to their understandings of the world or act upon them in a vacuum, but this does not mean that they are incapable of choice or self-reflexivity in those practices. For Gell, the act of *doing* was tantamount to an evocation of agency, and delineating a shift from an analysis of meaning to an analysis of effect was a direct challenge to restricted, Western notions of art and the role/s it performs (Gosden 2001: 164). To propose that objects, as an index of an individual's agency, act as a secondary agent is to propose a different sort of agency: agent by proxy, rather than as an agent of primary intent. For Gell social agents and art objects are indistinguishable in specific interactive settings, prompting us to interrogate the qualities of specific objects at particular times and places: one of the central themes of this book. However, as Gosden argues, the secondary agents theory does not ring true: since objects cannot act independently as persons do, and thus their "agency" must always be circumscribed and context-driven, there can be no universal claim to intentionality. Indeed many have argued that Gell's contentions have been overstated (see papers in Pinney and Thomas 2001). Objects, of course, can shape human action and potentialities, as famously outlined by Mauss and legibly incorporated by Gell. The *abduction of agency* as a cognitive operation has to be tempered and contextualized. Using the language of semiotics, the relevant indexes are those that permit the abduction of agency, thus the index is perceived as the outcome or instruments of social agency. Following his structuralist assumptions Gell presumes that agency is similarly constituted in all cultures and he further instantiates the dualisms intentional/mental and causal/material, that are clearly not universal (Keen 2001: 32, 33). He also developed a notion of *captivation*, defined as a special kind of agency affected through performance that embodies a certain level of indecipherability (Bolton 2001: 101). While not exclusive to aesthetically powerful objects, Gell applied the concept to the imputed agency to Trobriand canoe prows and decorative art, both of which have continuity and discontinuity, synchrony and succession, that make these intricate designs challenging to comprehend. These were seen as attempts to communicate the incommunicable. Indirectly Gell was accumulating contexts; concentrating on specific social settings of significance, relations between artist, object and audience as agent, index and recipient, analyzing various intentions and permutations, and unraveling the threads of functions, interpretation, evaluation and meaning (Campbell 2001: 134).

Gell's main contribution was to assess more rigorously the qualities and effects of objects, specifically those created for effect (e.g. Jones 2001). From Gosden's perspective, the term "aesthetics" and its attendant sensory meanings would have been more appropriate, given the notorious baggage that accompanies the term "art." In fact Gell did attempt to jettison "art" in favor of a theory of efficacy. Yet despite his assertion that both anthropological and semiotic approaches had failed to theorize visual art successfully, Gell was influenced by writings in the anthropology of art such as Cole's framing of *art as a verb* and Layton's (1991) suggestion that art objects were agents of ideology directly impacting upon social relations. Layton employs Saussurean semiotics to analyze the ways in which the ideas, values and emotions given expression in artistic form are both a mediation and reflection of sociality. Moreover, Armstrong (1981) had already developed a sophisticated theory of the affective presence of art objects, with human and agentic qualities, and had similarly vigorously critiqued the baggage accompanying aesthetics; however, he is never cited. Art historical theory was similarly significant and Gell capitalized upon Freedberg's *powers of art* argument and Mitchell's formulation of *what pictures really want*. However, he pointedly stated that the "innumerable shades of social/emotional responses to artefacts (of terror, desire, awe, fascination etc) in the unfolding patterns of social life cannot be encompassed or reduced to aesthetic feelings"; nor was he "happy with the idea that the work of art is recognizable, generically, in that it participates in a 'visual' code for the communication of meaning" (Gell 1998: 6). His own perspective is more akin to art sociology, examining the ways in which objects mediate social agency within a social–relational matrix. *Art and Agency* is not simply a study of material culture for its own sake, but an insistence of the agency of things (Thomas 2001: 2). Marilyn Strathern has charged that objects are merely illustrative in his work and not a focus of study in themselves, although this view is highly debatable. Others have imputed that Gell's theory is not specific to art objects but to all things, and that very few objects do not mediate social agency in some ways – whether a chipped stone or a landmine, as previously illustrated. Despite these obvious criticisms, Gell successfully directed our attention toward the ways in which objects mediate sociality: the charge now will be to document contextually the specific and complex relations that mobilize objects. That mandate is taken up within this book, and a critical engagement with Gell's ideas concerning object agency and mediation resides as a recurrent backdrop in the discussions of Egyptian materialities.

Anthropology, as evinced by Tylor in *Primitive Culture*, has always been primarily concerned with the peculiar relations between persons and things that appear as, or perform as, persons (Gell 1998: 9). This position has recently influenced Strathern (1999: 15), yet ironically is similarly derivative of her partible or networked selves thesis. Strathern has previously argued that social agents can be identified with objects and that their identities can circulate through things. Materiality is thus external to sociality, yet both person and things are forms by which we have knowledge of agency and relationships. In a sense we read them teleologically to impute what must have happened for them to exist.

She has more recently underscored the interpretative force of relational effects that makes things and persons co-presences in the field of effectual actors. She then questions the status of the art object, implying that such reifications form objects of attention and that objects of objectification tend to be social relations. In Mount Hagen objects are not always seen as made by individuals, but rather are the outcome of relationships (Graeber 2001: 39). Semantics, she admits in this case, can be misleading. Reification can operate as a form of abstraction, whereas personification seems absurdly mystical. Thomas remains critical of her position, nonetheless, arguing that she deliberately excludes considerations of individual subjectivity and biographic experience in her accounts of people and things (1991: 10–13). Interestingly her lack of individual or biographic specificity remains why she has been so popular for prehistoric archaeologists, since there has been a problematic elision between the deep past and the ethnographic present.

Material objects operate as vehicles to explore the object/subject relationship, a condition that hovers between physicality and visuality, between the reality of physical presence and fantasy, the empirical reality and representation. The object is both the point of origin and return (Attfield 2000: 11). Material culture theorists such as Miller (1987) have drawn upon psychoanalytic scholars such as Winnicott and Klein who have formulated theories of object relations and the role of trans-itional objects in negotiations between subjects and objects. Following Winnicott, the object is depicted as facilitating separation (in early child development), to both join and separate the subject from the object simultaneously. One might also think of Freud's famous *fort da* case study or Latour's framing of the *faitich* (see Chapter 4). Rather than splitting, objects perform a transition from subjectivity to objectivity (Attfield 2000: 127–8). The distinctive and unstable quality of things makes them particularly potent in these dynamic human relations and development. While these are provocative theories, the several strands of cathexis out-lined here derived from psychoanalysis or psychology are not the focus of the current work.

Categories of Biography

The genre of biography, however loosely applied, and the notion of object lives, has been a pervasive modality in archaeology, influenced primarily by two papers by prominent anthropologists (Appadurai 1986a; Kopytoff 1986). Their work has been framed as a form of cultural biography, yet both scholars have very specific notions of commodities as a particular sort of thing, rather than objects or artefacts more broadly construed. Following Marx, Appadurai positions commodities as things with precise forms of social potential; thus they are distinguishable from products, objects, goods and artefacts. Specifically, he is concerned with the classic issue of exchange, circulation and value as culturally embedded, and traverses the familiar ground of *kula* and *keda*, cargo cults and commodity fetishism. His famous sound bite, "tournaments of value," refers to specific, complex and periodic events that are removed from quotidian economic life. While this might conjoin with notions of caching, feasting or excess in the archaeological record, its referential sphere is well circumscribed. Another phrase, "regimes of value," has proven more elusive. Since Appadurai follows Simmel's notion that value is regulated on the basis of exchange value, it is difficult to interpolate sentimental or emotive value into the equation, and thus Appadurai's notion of objects passing back and forth between regimes of value is difficult to assess (Graeber 2001: 32). Following Maquet, he divides commodities into four useful types: *commodities by destination* (objects made and intended for exchange); *commodities by metamorphosis* (things intended for other uses that are turned into commodities); *commodities by diversion* (objects commodified but originally protected from it); *ex-commodities* (things removed from the commodity sphere and re-contextualized). For archaeologists these distinctions are most clearly evinced in the latter types when objects move contexts and take on new meanings; one need only think of the musealization of objects (see Chapter 7). However, Appadurai's concerns are very much tailored to economic exchange, the processual mode of "commoditization" (1986a: 17). Of course, one might modify this stance and interpolate objects for commodities, but this also entails a rather different schema with variant meanings and outcomes.

Appadurai cogently argues that exchanging value through the exchange of commodities is political, even if buyer and seller do not share the same system of values. He suggests commodities have social lives and that their resonant values may change over time. His work has been incredibly influential for archaeologists, yet he still does not offer an embodied account; rather, it employs the object to reflect upon cultural and historical processes. It is not its thingness *per se* that is entirely worthy of investigation for Appadurai. Types of objects have a cultural history and individual pieces have their own biographies with value residing in provenance, like religious relics or perhaps some forms of memorabilia. But again the focus has always been on exchange. For Appadurai it is the social history of things and how that reflects back upon complicated shifts in the organization of knowledge and modes of production that characterize our relationship to object worlds. These economic valences have cultural implications and are not merely refractions of technology or economics. Importantly, he underscores the dualistic techniques of anthropologists: us versus them; materialist versus religious; objectification of persons versus the personification of things, and so on. This, he argues, leads to a flattening out of cultural difference and also produces self-fulfilling taxonomies. Kopytoff is similarly keen in deconstructing taxonomies of people and things, beginning with a discussion of slavery, that insidious transformation of people into objects and potential commodities. His interpretive contribution can be encapsulated by the proposition that commodities have life history, a biography, albeit a culturally regulated formulation. He aims to convey the life narrative of the object, since objects cannot narrate their own biographies, and thus we have to fabricate them. Telling object stories has subsequently become a popular genre common to many domains (Baudrillard 1996; Hoskins 1998; Miller 1998a), yet many ethnographic accounts have been tightly focused on the concept of exchange, as has Kopytoff himself. The experiential and sensuous dimension of materiality has often been elided.

Objects might be framed as having mutual or overlapping biographies, shared biographies or even conferred and cumulative biographies. No object is isolated, unconnected from other objects or a dense network of relationships, and Kopytoff's biographical details reveal an entwined suite of aesthetic, historical, and political judgments alongside convictions and values. Yet Kopytoff refers to inherently alienable commodities and networks of exchange. Perhaps his most evocative statement is that society constrains the world of people and the world of things, and in constructing objects society also constructs people (Dant 1999: 90). Archaeologists influenced by Kopytoff have tended to focus upon the afterlife of archaeological artefacts, the shifting contexts of things in and out of their original embeddings (Hamilakis 1999; Seip 1999). Often these reflect the politics of museum display or colonial collection and disembedding, the renegotiation of meaning through the life history of the object (Gosden and Marshall 1999: 170). Using objects as focal points to reflect upon social setting and institutions has also impacted on ethnographic projects. These studies, often conducted around Pacific materials, are most evocatively retold through the lens of colonialism (Gosden and Marshall 1999; Thomas 1991, 1994, 1999). Another direction is one that employs the trope of biography, yet is somewhat indistinguishable from previous studies of site histories, reuse of places and monuments, recontextualization and memory: a rather business-as-usual approach (Gillings and Pollard 1999; Moreland 1999; Rainbird 1999). Both are interesting approaches, implementing the structural framework of biography in varying degrees of applicability and success. Other studies have attempted to cover both aspects of biography: artefacts as understood in their original context and then projected into other times and places, complemented by thickly described networks and resonances (Eckardt and Williams 2003; Saunders 1999, 2001). This is more the approach I aim to pursue here as well, to anthropologize the embedded object, understanding the thing in itself (*Ding an Sich*) and then trace the capricious terrain of meaning and significance.

The task for archaeology, then, is to think critically about our imposed categories inflected with Western monadic thinking, our constructions of the object world, and to think contextually about local understandings of the world and its constituents. This is certainly not a new endeavor: at a heuristic level archaeologists have been debating the epistemic implications of imposed taxonomies for decades. As Wylie (2002: 42–3) has demonstrated, from the "1930s and 1940s and continuing through the 1950s, questions about the efficacy and status of typologies – specifically, questions about whether they capture fundamental and inherent empirical structure or whether these are heuristic, problem-specific constructs – became the primary locus of debate about the goals and epistemological underpinnings of archaeology." All classification, and the subsequent taxonomies we create, whether in archaeology or the world at large, are constructs that serve context-specific purposes. For archaeologists, the constituents of the past we find worthy of investigation necessitate distinct bodies of data and classificatory schemes that we designate appropriate at particular times and places. They form perhaps part of our own biographical projects in our relationships with the object world. Yet this recent reconfiguration of taxonomy goes even further at challenging the nature of subjects and objects as essential and given types of things in the world. Several strands of ethnographic thought are potentially instructive here, the art and agency thesis and the trope of biography or life histories, though each needs to be tempered beyond rhetoric to encompass the grounded meanings and embodied practices accorded to the tasks of fabrication, installation, transformation, and enlivening, as well as the afterlives of things, as we see in the chapter to follow.

Material Memories:
Objects as Ancestors[1]

[W]e have to conceive that the mnemonic presentation within us is something which by itself is merely an object of contemplation, while, in-relation to something else, it is also a presentation of that other thing. In so far as it is regarded in itself, it is only an object of contemplation, or a presentation; but when considered as relative to something else, e.g. as its likeness, it is also a mnemonic token.

Aristotle, *On Memory and Reminiscence*

[E]very portrait that is painted with feeling is a portrait of the artist, not of the sitter. The sitter is merely the accident, the occasion.

Oscar Wilde, *The Picture of Dorian Gray*

Perhaps the most evocative modern account of an agentic portrait or enlivened image is that of Oscar Wilde's masterpiece *The Picture of Dorian Gray*. We continue to identify with Enlightenment thinking, the separability of the human and nonhuman, when in fact we need to reconfigure modernity in new ways, perhaps even more from the distant past. Doubling is key throughout the tale, as is a strongly contoured bio-graphic connectivity. The double is an imaginary figure that, like one's soul or shadow, haunts the subject with a faint death that has to be constantly warded off. If it materializes, death is imminent (Baudrillard 1990: 168), just as it was for our anti-hero. Following Benjamin's seminal thesis on the progression of art in the industrial age, the artwork first assumes the status of a ritual object with a singular history and an

1. An earlier version of this chapter appears as 'Memory's materiality: ancestral presence, commemorative practice and disjunctive locales,' in R. van Dyke and S. E. Alcock (eds), *Archaeologies of Memory*. pp. 34–55. Oxford: Blackwell.

individuated spatio-temporal presence. Progressively, the authority and authenticity of image are diminished through the process of technical reproduction, and so finally the aesthetic form submits to political form, and this form outweighs content (Baudrillard 1990: 180; Coombe 1998: 102). While this progression is central for the move from original context to artefact and then collectible, as we will see in Chapter 7, this template equally speaks to the auratic quality of the painting and specific histories in which it is enmeshed. The timeless, static quality underpinning Western notions of the image is inverted in this case with disastrous effects. Dorian Gray realizes a horrible sympathy exists between him and the portrait, a relationship that lies at the heart of a Maussian construction of magic, discussed below. The painting is itself a possessed technology, facilitating and dictating change in the life of its subject, albeit as a result of Wilde's projected desire. The very image comes to control and direct his actions during life, including the taking of a life, acting as a portal for the pervasive evil that comes to inhabit his being.

Wilde's creation is a perfect account of the context whereby an image supersedes the category of art, and where its agency appears to extend beyond the confines of representation and materiality. In this account the fictional, supernatural nature of the genre allows for a power beyond the scope of its material constituents. It represents a collapsing of object and subject, much as Foucault has argued in his famous study of Velázquez's *Las Meninas* (Foucault 1973: 308). This is clearly a recurrent fantasy or desire that has captivated people at various times and places throughout history. How different is this construction from the now popular claims espoused by Gell who provocatively suggested that the Western taxonomy of "art objects" might in some cases be productively reconfigured as persons, deities, and so on? It is not dissimilar from an older idea that a novel, poem, or picture could all be perceived as individuals; that is, beings in which the expression is indistinguishable from the thing expressed, their meaning, and accessible only through direct contact (Merleau-Ponty 1962: 115).

As archaeologists our contribution will be to assess and redefine the transitional moments, the taxonomic shifts pertinent to specific cultures, the technologies and practices that facilitate those transformations or mark cultural categories as different in the first instance. This chapter examines how we might then apprehend the material presence of ancestral beings in ancient Egypt and understand the importance of imbuing spirit with form. The making and venerating of an ancestral image was very much a local affair, residing in the domain of the domestic and the realm of the magical. Using the Deir el Medina community as a primary locus of study I interweave the varied hues of archaeological, textual, iconographic and cross-cultural materials to embody the magical and material practices that coalesced around ancestral stelae and busts. These objects existed outside our traditional taxonomies, yet we cannot be sure whether they were considered animated beings themselves or simply that they provided physical connections between living and dead. The nuances here are significant. Did Egyptian participants see these objects as ancestors or as intercessors? Following Baines (1984) we must adopt a strategy of interpretative pluralism where a variety of practices, personal beliefs and aspirations, possibilities for devotion and reflexivity are all embraced within the sphere of religious practice. This incorporated aspects we might term symbolic, intellectual, cognitive, social and psychological yet was not reducible to any or all of these factors.

Egyptian religion was both traditional and a locus for innovation, as we see with the rising popularity of ancestor busts and stelae in the Ramesside period. Religious practice infused other cultural phenomena as a pervasive mode of discourse and was so diverse and encompassing that no one interpretative strategy can adequately suffice. There was no single word for religion or cult in ancient Egypt (Baines 1984: 36): religion imbued the world with meaning and assembled a world of meaning for individuals through its enactment. Mauss famously considered magic rather differently to religion in its lack of institutionalization. Magical rites as a whole are traditional facts that should be separated out from legal actions, techniques and religious ritual (Mauss 2001: 23). But magic is not opposite to knowledge since both attempt to deal with life's uncertainties. Ritner (1993: 13; 1995) has pointed out that magic in Egypt was quite legal, unless sorcery was directed against the Pharaoh himself (see Chapter 5), and the spheres of magic and religion were quite permeable. Interestingly, Mauss states that there is "not a single activity which artists and craftsmen perform which is not believed to be within the capacity of the magician," which accords well with the Deir el Medina community. It is "because their ends are similar that they are found in natural association and constantly join forces" (Mauss 2001: 24). Effectiveness of these rites should not be distinguished from that of the techniques: they are one and the same. Object worlds furnished the medium for mediation between realms, direct communication between individuals, and desired outcomes for living and dead in specific situations. One need only think of the ever-popular role of the tarot reader in our own times, with his/her symbolic armory of cards or personal objects, who makes predictive statements about the future and creates links with the deceased. In New Kingdom Egypt ancestral images were prefigured as congealed memory and also operated as contextual technology, a pre-science, or technics of communication and effective change, and offered strategies to induce change. The technology of enchantment is thus political with individuals manipulating and entrapping other agents by intentional use of material culture (Thomas 2001: 9). Drawing on the classic insights of Mauss it is possible to reinstate some of the sensual, embodied practices of memory, magic and mediated materiality in an ancient Egyptian setting.

Past Lives: Remembering and Forgetting

Philosophers have long given meaning to the particular qualities of materiality in the mobilizing and mediating of memory. Foucault (1972) argued that the reality of the past resides in the artefacts of its representation. From that perspective our very grounding in the present, by virtue of our recognition of temporal passing, is anchored in material residues. For Merleau-Ponty, in a Proustian reflexive sense intellectual memory limits itself to a description of the past, a past as idea, from which it extracts characteristics or communicable meaning rather than discovering a structure. Yet this would not constitute memory if the object that it constructs were not still held by a "few intentional threads to the horizon of the lived-through past" (1962: 85–6). Those threads are experientially woven, forming a rich, diverse and subjective tapestry of memories. Given archaeology's disciplinary concern for materiality and the tangible residues of the past, this ideally should be our sphere of expertise. Yet as stated above, only recently have we become ensconced in the relationship of memory to the material in highly elucidated, discursive contexts.

Focusing on the lived memories housed in intimate spaces I hope to create a topoanalysis via a thick description of archaeological materials, including ancestor busts, stelae, and household features (Meskell 1998), and the immaterial aspects of ritual and commemoration, preserved in the texts. From documents and iconographic sources one can demonstrate that the villagers at Deir el Medina had a very limited sense of the past and most could remember scarcely more than two generations back in regard to their own commemorative family practices. There are scant written references to events even as recent as twenty years in the past, yet a handful of examples show a remarkable sense of family history stretching back 100–150 years (McDowell 1992: 105–7). A well-known individual called Inerherkhau proudly recorded some five generations in his tomb, the male line all occupying the same desirable occupation of chief workman. Various individuals retained something akin to a personal archive that was to be consulted in times of need, whether legal, economic or social. From a hermeneutic perspective, the specificities of memory can only endure within sustained contexts (Halbwachs 1992), and memory cannot be miraculously transmitted without continual revision and refashioning. Constructing memory, then, entails diverse moments of modification, reuse, ignoring and forgetting, and investing with new meanings.

What might it mean if personal long-term memory was not generally operative amongst villagers of Deir el Medina? What if forgetting was also a long-term strategy? Hobbes once claimed that forgetting was the basis of a just state and that amnesia was the cornerstone of the social contract. Forgetting is an unavoidable strategy since no individual or community can afford to retain everything. Iterating his theory of habitus, Bourdieu (1977: 79) argued that the "unconscious" was a tactic of forgetting and that amnesia allowed society to imbue myths, rites, law and their attendant discordances with objective status. Forgetting, on a more individual scale, can be more beneficial than bereavement (Lowenthal 1999: xi). At Deir el Medina it may have been necessary to forget past generations or former residents of bygone years as the scramble for ready-made tombs and chapels became more pressing and when accessing available space in the Western Necropolis became vital. A workman named Kenna took over a chapel that once belonged to a man called Pakhal, suggesting that if one could rebuild the structure and there were no other claimants it simply became yours. One could be forgotten even when the name lived on. However, Kenna found it slightly more difficult when the mendacious Merysekhmet claimed half was his and the whole fiasco ended up before the oracle of Deir el Medina, no less than the deified figure of Amenhotep I (see Chapter 4). Merysekhmet's claim was subsequently denied and he was forced to swear on pain of a hundred blows that he would not try to dispute it again. Appropriating tombs against the cultural mores and better judgments of Egyptian society undoubtedly necessitated a form of religious and moral amnesia, or at least a suspension of memory. One such forgettable individual was a guardian called Amenemope who lived in the early part of the reign of Rameses II. Members of his family apparently disappeared from Deir el Medina by the 20th Dynasty when the chief workmen of the village inspected his tomb in the Western Necropolis, before being handed over to the workman Menna maybe a hundred years later or more (McDowell 1999: 71). The inspection consisted of noting the name of the former occupant, followed by a list of items within the tomb. The first item preserved on the list was a coffin, perhaps the most sacred object that held the physical remains of the deceased and acted as a material double for the individual. Underscoring the serious nature of the removal and usurpation, the coffin bore the likeness of the deceased, and provided protection and information vital for traversing into the next world. But with the sweep of a scribal hand Amenemope was thus forgotten.

Recent work in anthropology on the centrality of forgetting ironically comes at the moment when archaeologists are just discovering the place of memory (e.g Chesson 2001; van Dyke and Alcock 2003; Williams 2003). The two are clearly inseparable and both are in dialogue with materiality and specific material objects. Western concepts of memory are inflected with the Aristotelian principle that memory is a physical imprinting. According to this classic view, material substitutes are thus necessary to compensate for the fragility of the human memory (Forty 1999: 2). The contrary position is adopted by Forty who imputes that collective memory does not necessarily dwell in ephemeral monuments. Embodied acts and rituals may be more successful in iterating memory than simply the forging of objects, war memorials being an oft-cited example. Physical memorials supposedly serving as perpetual reminders are typically overlooked and considered less effective iterative strategies than commemorative performances. Material remembering requires spatio-temporal anchoring, since permanence and solidity are important in both the forging of memory and the healing processes of the living. Memory has even been described as an anti-museum that is not localizable (de Certeau 1984: 108). Specific mnemonic monuments have been accused of topolatry; namely, that monuments betray the memory, since memory is internal and subjective and thus incompatible with public display (Huyssen 1995: 258). So what is the status of the object in the role of memory and forgetting? How do we accommodate the impossibility of memory? A dialectic position advocating that both physical manifestation and iterative performance are required for the instantiation of memory is surely preferable. Archaeologists should not assume a universal relationship between memory and the object. And this is complicated by the acknowledgement that in many cultural settings objects do not inhabit their object taxonomies. Materiality is intimately linked to doing and making, the sensuous process of human interactions with things. As Hallam and Hockey state in respect to contemporary practices revolving around memory and materiality:

> Memory is commonly envisaged as both the facility to remember and as the material representation or trace of that which is remembered, both of which are crucially mediated by a variety of cultural forms . . . While they

are attributed something approximating an object status, memories are also routinely regarded as 'static', as imprints retained and fixed . . . They also require contextual and comparative analysis, which reveals their historical and cultural specificity as well as the ways in which memory and death are caught up in processes of personal transformation and social change. Memory practices and experiences shift over time as perceptions of the past are reworked in the context of the present and in anticipation of the future. (Hallam and Hockey 2001: 3)

Susanne Küchler's work in Melanesia (1993, 1999, 2002) forms a central text in the ethnography of forgetting and materiality. She sees that "the place of memory is not in objects, but in the space created by rendering absent the products of memorywork – a place that is substituted by objects." This is a subtle variation of the notion that objects embody memory: rather, that they come to signify the spaces in between states of being, present and past. Her material base is the *malanggan*, a ritually elaborated wooden carving or vine weaving that invokes the ancestral body brought to life as it is placed upon the grave of the deceased. *Malanggan* are wonderful evocations of corporeal memory since their folds and contours mimic those of the body. And like all living things the *malanggan* dies and this process heralds the termination of the mourning period that in some cases may carry forward over twenty years (Küchler 1999: 57). In her account memory is an unmoored and mobile force and the *malanggan* is simply a receptacle for the dead's soul. In many respects its characteristics parallel that of the Egyptian *ba*, often glossed as soul. Both are nomadic, floating memories that are integral components of the deceased and require material anchoring supplied by living descendants. While the creating and dissolving of *malanggan* could be read as material for forgetting in an ongoing process of moving forward, as generative and reproductive sources for society (Küchler 1999: 68), one could argue that their makers still require a material edifice as a second body or locus for the soul. It depends entirely on the ethnographic moment one chooses to focus upon: the fabricating of a material entity or the final disintegration of the object. To my mind, this still constitutes a site of memory, even if short-lived, as much as it represents an active forgetting.

One point of congruence between various theories is that memory is performed. Practices of remembering and forgetting can only come about through discursive bodily actions and performance. Habitual bodily practice informs memory and serves to refashion and reiterate certain aspects of the past. Bodily memory is enhanced through ritual observances, funerals, ceremonies for the dead, festivals, and daily personal venerations. So too effigies and images of the deceased become mediators of memory. Embracing the dead through living practice was equally important for sustaining both collectivities. Material objects reiterate these bodily practices; they tend to mediate the passage between worlds, and act as a buttress against the terror of the forgettable self.

Places of memory serve to anchor the past in the present and, alternatively, the present in the past. The long, interleaved history of Egyptian monuments and cultural landscapes would imply a fruitful context for the analysis of memory and the reworking of memory. Egyptian culture embodied a strong "sense" of the past; people were surrounded by its materiality, but it did not always evoke feelings of reverence (Meskell 2003). Material and emotional indices were entwined. In a famous didactic text, "The Teachings for Merikare" (Parkinson 1997: 217–18), the protagonist advises, *make your monuments last through love of you*, whereas for the unworthy he recommends purposive action, *drive him away from memory of him, and of the supporters who love him*. And there was cause for concern since individuals frequently incorporated older funerary monuments into new constructions and regularly robbed tombs in the process of burial preparations. In the vital area of the world of the dead, they inhabited and aspired to inhabit a doubly dead landscape in which the funerary monuments around them provided a model of achievement, even in their decayed form, as well as a physical environment into which they awkwardly inserted their current passage to a deceased status through destruction, usurpation, and reuse (Baines and Lacovara 2002). In Egyptian culture, death was not considered as the end of one's existence nor of one's effectiveness on earth. As we will see, the dead were powerful beings who could intervene in the world of the living in both benevolent and malevolent ways. Ancestor busts and stelae are testament to this interplay since they provided a focus for these spheres of interaction and attest to the dead's willingness to intercede in the terrestrial. It is often said that the dead kept the living in line. But it is important in this contextual setting not to conflate social memory, which suggests the long term, with commemoration, which refers to short-term practices operating only over a few generations (Meskell 2003: 39).

Housing Memories

One aim of this chapter is to undertake an intimate study of dwelling and remembering. One of the most compelling studies to fuse memory, phenomenology and domestic space was conducted by Gaston Bachelard almost fifty years ago, although it has received little attention from archaeologists. His biographical and experiential approach to interior places, termed a topoanalysis, converges on the sites of our intimate lives (1994: 8). Since memories are motionless, their spatialization transforms them into something more tangible, localizing a memory in time. While his approach could be seen as particular and romantic, it nonetheless offers a provocative way of thinking through the possibilities of Egyptian experience. The house embodies a community of memories in every room and corner, within its fixtures and features. As he famously remarked, the house is lived and an entire past comes to dwell there. Its materiality constitutes a body of images that confer a sense of stability, specifically when one considers the sorts of social and ritual practices that ensured ancestral presence in the New Kingdom. This might be part of the

Figure 3.1 House NE13 at Deir el Medina looking into the first room with painted lit clos (enclosed bed structure). Courtesy of the IFAO, Cairo.

dynamic rivalry between house and universe to which Bachelard refers. It is not simply a day-to-day existence with a narrative thread, but a co-penetrating series of memories about dwelling, about episodes, people and things. For some, houses are also objects through which we are able to trace the passage of thoughts and desires (Gell 1998: 258), and the play of memory that stretches into the past and into the unrealized and imagined futures.

The archaeological focus of this chapter coalesces around the New Kingdom houses at Deir el Medina, their fixtures, decorations, contents and some of the ritual practices that occurred within them. Houses were divided and partitioned into a number of rooms ranging from three to ten, the most common number being between four and six. These strip houses had total residential areas ranging from 40 to 120 square meters (Valbelle 1985: 117). We are fortunate to know the names of residents and their families in over a dozen dwellings due to the wealth of inscribed materials and textual sources. For the purposes of this chapter, I focus upon the first two rooms and their contents, specifically the second room where it is most likely that ancestor busts and stelae were situated. Cultic features like cupboards, niches and divans were crafted in stone and mud brick and remain part of the individual houses that can still be viewed today. And since the residents abandoned the village gradually, many artefacts were left *in situ* allowing for a spatial analysis of ritual and gendered practices across the site (Meskell 1998). As I will argue, these objects and practices are *mnemotechnologies* that direct and train an individual's memories in culturally appropriate ways (Le Goff 1996). They bind the living and the dead in mutually constitutive ways and hold a "fragile connection across temporal distance and to preserve a material presence in the face of an embodied absence" (Hallam and Hockey 2001: 18). Memories are metaphors.

The first room of most Deir el Medina houses was home to features and representations redolent of the female life cycle and sexual identity, whereas the second room's features and finds tended to revolve around elite male identities and their equally elite ancestors. In both spatial settings were shrine-like constructions or niches that were the repositories of ritual stelae, statues of deities such as Meretseger or Hathor, or ancestor busts. As Bachelard hints (1994: 79), every cupboard and niche may have a history, and a mute tumult of memories return throughout temporal interactions with those fixtures. In many daily scenarios the mundane element of household spaces and features would be prevalent, whereas at moments of ritual or commemorative significance time and materiality conjoin to animate such spaces. Textually, we lack the information pertaining to specific rituals or practices that were employed to transform space, if indeed this was deemed necessary. In a house designated NE12 a cultic cupboard still remains, while in house SE6 there is an altar. More frequently we see constructions called "false doors" embedded in the walls: remarkably, red and yellow paint still clings to the plaster some 3,500 years later. A man called Nebamentet living in house SE7 possessed a false door and a wall painting; Nebamun next door in SE8 had red false doors with central yellow bands (Bruyère 1930: 275). Khabekhenet in house SW5 had polychrome false doors associated with a wall painting evincing veneration of the deified patrons of the village, Ahmose-Nefertari and her son Amenhotep I (Bruyère 1939: 68). In traditional mortuary practice, false doors were niched structures through which the spirit of a deceased individual could move back and forth freely, between this world and the next, to receive offerings and supplications. They were common architectural elements in earlier Egyptian history, dating back to the beginning of the Dynastic period, though they were not generally considered part of the domestic repertoire. In Egypt, as in many cultures, the door is a multivalent signifier that embodies both material and immaterial aspects.

In the household context false doors provided a portal between the world of the living and the dead and were an ever-present reminder of their eternal presence. For all their ingenuity and presence, the dead required a material conduit, whether the false door or the ancestral image. Iconographic motifs present on specific stelae are similar to those shown on inscribed false doors where the deceased is the recipient of food offerings (Friedman 1985). Here too the deceased required sustenance of a human variety and of a tangible nature for ongoing efficacy and existence. False doors facilitated contact with the spirits of ancestors; a view reinforced by the frequency of ancestor-related artefacts in this room. Indeed, many cross-cultural institutions and practices hold that personhood is distributed through time and space: ancestral shrines, tombs, memorials, ossuaries, sacred sites, and so on, may all be invoked to engage in the extension of personhood beyond the confines of biological being (Gell 1998: 223).

Inscribed Ancestors

Egyptian religion placed great importance on the power of visuality and giving form to divine beings: the words "image" and "cult" point to the very heart of Egyptian religion. The pivotal focus of religious practice was neither sacred texts, nor shamanic visions, nor ecstatic or mystical experiences, but rather cult practice. This entailed a daily routine of endlessly differentiated service rendered to the deities in the forms in which they were locally resident, their cult statues (Assmann 2001: 40). At a community level, and further into the domain of the dwelling, that principle was manifest in the veneration of statues, stelae and busts. These were dedicated to deities and deified individuals specific to particular landscapes and localities, coupled with deceased ancestors who were tied to households via kin relations. For instance, the villagers of Deir el Medina called upon the deceased members of their own families, now in the realm of effective spirits and known as the *effective spirits of Re*. We know this from the stelae they inscribed and erected in their houses and chapels. Other examples were found in the Eastern and Western Necropolises as well as around the temple precinct. Find spots of the stelae in the Deir el Medina dwellings, in proximity to wall niches in the first and second rooms, suggest that their placement was in ritual recesses such as these. Examples found in house C6 name the men Baki and Mose; in SW5 there is an example naming Khamuy and Pennub; and in SW2 a man named Khonsu and a woman called Sherire are recorded on stelae. They are small round-topped limestone stelae, generally less than 25 cm high. They date from the end of the 18th Dynasty through the 19th and 20th Dynasties, with a preponderance in the 19th Dynasty (Demarée 1983: 238). Apart from the Deir el Medina stelae, examples have been discovered at sites such as Amarna, Gurob, the palace of Merenptah at Memphis, the mortuary temple of Rameses III, various West Bank Theban temples, and also at Aniba in Nubia. They were dedicated to one, two or three individuals, usually without mention of their relationships: in only a few cases do wives or children occur as offerants or dedicators (Demarée 1983: 174). Some individuals had more than one stela devoted to them, suggesting that they were especially remembered or venerated within their respective communities.

The effective spirits were human beings who had been admitted to the afterworld, but more immediately they were deceased relatives who could be called upon in times of need. Egyptologists consider that living individuals transformed a deceased person into an effective spirit through an exchange of ritual acts and recitations: specific knowledge was deemed necessary for the transfiguration (Demarée 1983: 193). Similarly, the effectiveness of the dead was sustained by the ongoing practices of their descendants in the family cult. It is likely that additional offerings were performed on the so-called *lucky days* recorded in the Calendar of Lucky and Unlucky Days (Demarée 1983: 272). Thus a certain performative magical element was necessary first from the living before reciprocal

Figure 3.2 Ancestor stela embedded with two ancestor busts, showing the two as related artefacts within a related suite of practices. Courtesy of the British Museum, EA 270.

blessings might be bestowed: an exchange relationship was perpetually set in motion between terrestrial and divine spheres. These acts of reciprocity may have occurred in the second room or divan room since most ritual finds emanate from there, as do the ritual fixtures and niches into which the stelae were placed. The materiality of the stela acted as a conduit for transactions between this world and the next, establishing contact with family members past and present. Votives can be seen as special types of gifts that create ligatures between individuals and extend into time, forming a special type of ritual credit (Derrida 1992). This is a salient example of where objects merge with people or spirits by virtue of the interwoven relationships between persons and things and persons and spirits via things (Gell 1998: 12). Thus a traditional theory of art or material culture can never suffice for the situated understandings of embodied materials that articulate the permeable nature of people and things and defy Western taxonomies through their very being. Probing the intimate relationship between art and the activation of temporal consciousness is productive, according to Küchler (2001: 74), and grounded in the momentary and in the spatial collapse of past–present and future. Pragmatically, it is also important that we think through how these objects were carved from limestone, in one instance, and then subsequently transformed into a portal between worlds.

Village men appeared to have been the primary "dedicatees" of ancestor stelae, and only a small number include women. This pattern underscores what we already know of the centrality of male power, iterated through their singular accessibility to education, literacy and career opportunities. Individuals needed to call on powerful persons in desperate times, those who similarly had access to power in the afterlife by virtue of the necessary texts and accoutrements of death and passing. For the most part the inscribed evidence suggests that dedicatees fall into the category of father, husband, brother, son, and thus constitute deceased kin within living memory (Demarée 1983: 282). The "dedicators" were not always depicted or named, but could also include women (Friedman 1994: 112). In most instances a seated man is depicted, holding a lotus in one hand. Smelling a lotus flower had many cultural associations for the Egyptians, including breath, rebirth and cyclicality. One could capture the phenomenological power of scent and smelling through visual evocation. The other hand is traditionally outstretched toward a table of offerings or holding the ankh sign, symbolizing life. Actions were rendered permanent through their representation in stone, yet it was the enduring visualization that ensured the ongoing efficacy and power of the act.

Cult activities involving the stelae were enacted in houses, and also in chapels, tomb environs, and temples. Their size and portability facilitated movement from and around a number of contexts. Processions of ancestral images were probably linked to the festival calendar. The Beautiful Festival of the Wadi was a key example of a festival of the dead, which took place between the harvest and the Nile flood. In it, the divine boat of Amun traveled from the Karnak temple to the necropolis of Western Thebes. A large procession followed and living and dead were thought to commune near the tombs, which became *houses of the joy of the heart* on that occasion. It is likely that the images of deceased individuals were taken along in the procession and then returned to the grave. On a smaller scale, family festivals also took place in which the deceased again took part (Bleeker 1967: 137). Festivals involved the group, well attested within the community at Deir el Medina, and such groups "provide individuals with frameworks within which their memories are localised by a kind of mapping. We situate what we recollect within the mental spaces provided by the group" (Connerton 1989: 37). Following

Halbwachs, these mental spaces always have material referents and refer back to the material spaces that particular social groups occupy. Since physical objects change so gradually over time, particularly at the pre-industrial village level, they offer a sense of permanence and stability within the particular spatiality. That illusion of the unchanging, or reinstating the past in the present, is crucial at festival time. Festivals were transitional moments that served many functions: emotional outpouring and remembering, feasting, social interaction, religious observance and communing with the gods. Reinstatement of dead individuals was key through commemorating their lives and their continued presence among the living. Egyptian conceptions of self traversed life and death, since both worlds were porous, such that the contexts of existence had a shared substrate. This set of practices fits nicely with Connerton's (1989: 7) view of recollection as operating in two distinct arenas of social activity: *commemorative ceremonies* and *bodily practices*. Festivals certainly constitute commemorative ceremonies, while the ritual devotions directed toward the cult statue constitute a set of bodily practices for both the participants and the recipient.

Ancestor stelae embodied a knowable, biographic thread that served to link generations and individuals through time. Time, for the Egyptians, was primarily divided into human or divine time, what might be called "here-time" and "there-time." Earthly life could be broken into increments of years (*rnpwt*), months (*3bdw*), days (*hrw*), hours (*wnwt*), and moments (*3wt*) (Bochi 1994: 56). The Egyptians also had a category that encompassed a notion of a lifetime. An ideal life span was considered to be 100 years, with an extra ten or twenty years in order to attain ultimate wisdom (Hornung 1992: 58). The identity of each individual was accumulated through life and was used to determine the deceased's fate at the point of judgment. Materializing the identity and biography, whether in tomb art, tomb biography, monuments or images, was paramount. It was necessary to give life form, but also to be remembered in an ongoing set of ritual observances: speaking the name and offering libations were popular observances. In New Kingdom Egypt social relationships were real and biographically consequential ones that articulated to the subject's biographical life project and often found their ultimate form after death.

Embodied Ancestors: Magic and Memory

If the ancestor stelae we have examined suggest a penchant for the specificities of memory and remembered individuals, it might be said that ancestor busts reveal a certain willingness to suppress memory, to be comprehensive or more encompassing. There is a subtle difference here. Ancestor stelae embody the identity of the individual and similarly act as a conduit for communication between worlds and persons, living and dead, whereas ancestor busts blended the anthropomorphic qualities of the individual with the statue-like qualities of the divine and tended to be more anonymous and less focused upon named individuals.

Ancestor busts (Figure 3.3) were painted limestone or sandstone anthropomorphic votives, often depicted with floral collars around the neck, redolent of festival time and also significations of the blessed dead. Ancestor busts have been discovered in various locations – domestic, mortuary and temple – from the Delta to the Third Cataract. Approximately half of the extant 150 examples come from Deir el Medina, while the rest come from fourteen other sites, including the Faiyum, Gurob, Abydos, Karnak, Sesebi, Saqqara and Sedment (Friedman 1994: 114; Keith-Bennett 1988: 43). A limestone bust of uncertain gender has recently been found in the excavations of the New Kingdom houses at Memphis (Giddy 1999: 43). The fact that several unfinished examples were found at Deir el Medina verifies that they were made locally, perhaps when times of need were greatest. Such objects gather the universe in and around themselves: a past that stretches back generations inheres in the material world, one that is redolent of power and fate (Bachelard 1994: 84). These busts figuratively represented the potent dead who were capable of interceding benevolently or malevolently in human affairs. They were tangible sites of embodied memory that simultaneously operated as a physical channel between worlds. Moreover, they were not art objects or perhaps even *objects* in our sense, and they were ritually activated in much the same manner as the stelae through offerings and invocations of a ritual and performative nature. In practice, ancestral objects required veneration and active participation from the living; they could not be activated in isolation.

Ancestor busts and stelae were probably placed in niches, given the number discovered in domestic contexts. It has also been suggested that their similarity to images in Books of the Dead and Books of the Netherworld implies a more funerary role, or at least multiple usages (Keith-Bennett 1988: 50). They are largely uninscribed, lacking names or titles, yet most scholars assume they are male due to the presence of red paint that characterizes male skin coloring. Red was also a magical color with potent associations, commonly found in the decoration of the first two rooms in the village houses, and also common on female figurines. What might it signify that most of the busts were uninscribed

Figure 3.3 Ancestor bust said to be from Thebes, probably Deir el Medina, 19th or 20th Dynasty. Courtesy of the British Museum, EA 61083.

or unnamed, given the ritual potency of the name in Egyptian ritual practice? One interpretation might be that the busts were generic figures and could evince or manifest any male relative who could be called upon. Multiple memories could possibly reside in their material form. Their lack of specificity might also designate them as objects of forgetting, material places where fixed memory was deemed unnecessary. This potentially would make them rather different to the ancestor stelae. Halbwachs perceptively captures this tension between active memory and a certain inevitable amnesia:

> In remembering, we locate, or localize, images of the past in specific places. In and of themselves, the images of memory are always fragmentary and provisional. They have no whole or coherent meaning until we project them into concrete settings. Such settings provide us with our places of memory. Remembering, therefore, might be characterized as a process of imaginative reconstruction, in which we integrate specific images formulated

in the present into particular contexts identified with the past. (Halbwachs 1993: 78)

Another interpretation, marshaled by Friedman (1985: 97), is that ancestor busts are a visually abbreviated form of the statue of the kneeling man presenting a stela (Figure 3.4) that we witness in numerous niched pyramidia at Deir el Medina (see Chapter 4). They could be moved about the village from houses to chapels and received offerings of food and recitations in the same manner as other images and statues of the deceased. One spell in the Book of the Dead states: *as for him who knows this spell, he will be an effective spirit and he will not die again in the realm of the dead* (Faulkner 1985: 175). Other spells in chapters 100 and 101 of the Book of the Dead allowed the spirit to travel on the solar barque of Re in the company of the other gods. Such spells, spoken by the living, assisted the deceased in the netherworld, and the rewards of their homage would hopefully filter back to those same individuals in an ultimate circle

Figure 3.4 Man with stela, known as a stelophorous statue, from Deir el Medina, dated to the late 18th Dynasty. Courtesy of the British Museum, EA 24430.

of reciprocity. Their efficacy was literally magnified by contemplation. The desire was to facilitate the progress from a deceased state, transforming the individual into an active and powerful being in the realm of the divine. On one stela a man is shown worshiping in front of an ancestor bust, so we can assume that such practices of active supplication were undertaken (Demarée 1983).

We need to rethink the status of Egyptian ancestor busts and whether they operated in the interstices between individual agency and a form of ritualized magic. Agency, according to Gell, is attributable both to persons and things which initiate causal sequences of a particular type, specifically events caused by acts of mind or will or intention, rather than the mere concatenation of physical events. An agent is one who causes events to happen in their vicinity and, as a result of this exercise of agency, certain events transpire. While this looks dangerously close to describing the situation of ancestral objects, the exact relationship of intention and mediation requires interrogation. Gell's formulation of secondary agents, or agents by proxy, must be tempered by the admission that human action and activation is always necessary for ritual activation. The workings of *things* are axiomatically circumscribed and context-driven and there can be no universal claim to intentionality. While individuals may have attributed a certain sphere of agency to ancestral images, whether in this world or the next, that is a very different proposition from asserting that ancestral images had *independent* intentions. And given the nature of Egyptian ritual and magical practice, the intentions and actions of the living seem to be more crucial. Venerating, remembering, libating, and speaking the name were all performative ways of perpetuating the power of the deceased: acts possible only for the living community. In that sense, ritual and magical practice were perhaps the most salient and evocative vehicles for living individuals to actualize their individual agency. Did those same individuals attribute agency to ancestral objects? Perhaps, but they also understood it as a dialogic relationship, that living and dead had interplay and the material presence was also a necessary constituent.

The differentiation between religious and magical spheres is at times problematical to draw and the borders somewhat fluid. Mauss argued that magical life is not compartmentalized like religion and has not led to the establishment of autonomous institutions. Ostensibly it is a division of official religion versus local practice, between communal distance and the possibilities for individual communication. Religious practices are perceived as predictable, prescribed and officially sanctioned. For the Egyptians this sphere was encapsulated by the word *heka*, which had the associations of magic, magician, the deity Heka and the concept of divine manifestation. It could also be understood as the effective power of duplication or empowered images (Ritner 1993: 249). The god Heka was Atum-Ra's first creation, an authoritative, divine utterance that infuses the cosmos with his magic vitality. While he is the son of the creator god he is also the "hypostasis of the creator's own power which begets the natural order" (Ritner 1993: 17). The gods themselves could be frightened by the powers of magic, although they, too, clearly embodied *heka*. Magic was *possessed* as a property, *performed* as a rite and *spoken* in words.

In Egypt there was a sliding scale and the boundaries between official religion and small-scale magic were blurred and certainly intimately related. Practices of veneration for official cult statues undoubtedly had conceptual overlap with those household activities dedicated to the spirits of ancestors, as manifest in their material forms. These heuristic divisions are somewhat complicated in the case of Egypt. For instance, textual documents attest the presence of a scorpion charmer at Deir el Medina who drew official state rations for his services. The overlap between priest and magician must have been considerable. Numerous spells of a protective nature have also been preserved. There were spells to stop nightmares, to ward off the enemy, dangerous beasts, and so on. Some inscribed on ostraca were copied repeatedly and passed from one individual to another and could have been carried as portable protection (McDowell 1999: 117): *Year 3, third month of inundation, day 8. This day, (coming) by the scribe Pahemnetjer to give the spell for catching the poison to the scribe Paneferemdjed of the necropolis in the house of Abimentet.* Mauss was correct in asserting that magical facts defy categorization and thus impel us to think abstractly. Magic is more real than its individual parts and should be viewed in its totality. Magic exists everywhere in a diffuse state, and for those subscribing and participating it has an objective reality (Mauss 2001: 109). Between the extremist poles of sacrifice and evil spells, in the interstices, lies a morass of activities. It is meaningless to try and determine what was real or credible from our own post-Enlightenment perspective and there any many instances of non-rational, non-scientific belief and practice that surround us in our own everyday lives: belief in extraterrestrials, new age spirituality, creationism, and indeed most world religions would inhabit the same category.

Radical in his approach was Mauss's recognition that magic becomes an approximate to the sciences and resembles its experimental research based upon logical deductions. Magic is the maintenance of the world as a play of analogical relations, a cyclical progression where everything is linked together by their signs (Baudrillard 1990: 139). It is an immense game that is inherently rule bound. In Egypt one might say that magic came to resemble technology. It had a genuine kinship with religion on one side and science and technology on the other. Magic assumes a very practical role in quotidian life. Famously Malinowski documented that magic and practical work was inseparable amongst the Trobriand Islanders, yet they did not confuse domains. Here the practicalities of gardening were infused with a sequence of rites and spells that ensured crop success (Malinowski 1935: 64). Essentially magic is the art of doing things; with words and gestures it does what techniques achieve by labor. Yet such practices are not gesticulations into thin air, it has a taste for the concrete. Magic has always dealt with material things, carried out real experiments and made its own discoveries. It is a practical art and a storehouse of ideas: knowledge is power (Mauss 2001: 175–6).

Recentering the material embodiment of the ancestor, we might ask how the technology of crafting, instantiating, venerating and contacting the spirit of the deceased could effect change in the lives of the villagers. How were the stelae and busts enmeshed in a causal web of social relations? Following Gell's notion of enchanted technology, objects can be seen as devices for securing the acquiescence of individuals and entities in a network of enmeshed intentionalities (1992: 43). In Egypt, the living called upon the dead for support and beneficence, facilitated through the medium of such objects. This is not an inference that *objects by them-selves* are working independently of a field of expectations and under-standings, as Thomas makes clear (2001: 3). Technology is enchanted, and thus enchanting, because it is the result of a barely comprehensible virtuosity, a magical efficacy largely unrealizable in other domains. We might think of this virtuosity and efficacy in Egypt as something much greater than the individual stretching out into the divine realm and the cosmos (certainly the individual artist is never named on magical objects). Egyptian magical transactions were inseparable transitions between people and things that could have positive or negative effects, bestow fertility, procure revenge, generate auspiciousness, and so on.

Ancestor busts and stelae evoked a sense of the deceased and invoked their presence and potency to intervene in contemporary affairs. Ritual practice inheres in place. The position of the image, within the house or chapel, localized within the community itself, was crucial to the salience of the devotion and its desired results. Stelae or ancestor busts placed in the house were in the image of the deceased, while representations of the deceased in statue form were traditionally situated at the tomb chapel. Both received offerings and both were associated with a deceased individual and were thus concurrently part of domestic and funerary cult. We should also add to this corpus the inscribed stone libation basins, some of which are also dedicated to the blessed dead, and have been regularly found in the Deir el Medina houses (Demarée 1983: 287). In the case of stelae, they certainly do depict deceased members of the community who were being implored or appeased – not the long dead who had fallen from memory but the fathers, sons, brothers and husbands of the villagers who were part of living memory. The effective spirit could retain human form but could miraculously commune with deities such as Re and Osiris in the netherworld (Friedman 1994: 114). Dedicants would have been keen to propitiate the deceased since their perceived actions could impact the living positively or negatively, particularly since they mingled with such omnipotent deities. When the image was venerated a ritual memory exercise was accomplished, and when this was coupled with larger festive offerings and performances the effect must have been heightened. At their core, festivals were fundamentally acts of commemoration and remembrance.

Ancestor busts, as embodied objects, are evocative examples to think through Mauss's two laws of magic: the law of similarity and law of contiguity (2001: 15). The law of similarity can be repackaged in the dictum that like produces like. In our case the anthropomorphic nature of the image imbues it with power and efficacy, linking directly to specific ancestors. This notion harks back to Frazer's discussion of imitative magic as the "power that the copy extracts from the original" (Taussig 1993b: 59). Alternatively, the ancestor bust may have resonated a permanent presence in the home or chapel. Relevant to the Egyptian process of entreating the deceased for assistance is the principle of like produces and cures like: *simila, similibus, curantur*. Images cross-culturally, whether effigies, dolls or schematic representations (like the bust) or drawings, form the focal ritual pivot (Mauss 2001: 84). It is the act of mimesis or doubling that is key, and it was the pervasive conceptual substrate that underwrote much of Egyptian culture. This desire for doubling and simulation is an embodied element in many cultures and is part of the very crafting of situated identity: "As the nature that culture uses to make second nature, mimesis cannot be outside of history, just as history cannot lie outside of the mimetic faculty" (Taussig 1993b: 136). Moving the discussion away from art-historical approaches toward materiality, Taussig's ethnography outlines that the magically important thing is the spirit of the material not its carved outer form. Resonant with Küchler's work in Melanesia, the container gives form to the immaterial. Reading under erasure in a new light (Taussig 1993b: 136), the question of the content of the image now gives way to further questions: Why make images anyway? Why embody? And in that suite of framed reversals we see that making requires unmaking and embodiment its disembodiment.

In Mauss's second law objects that were in bodily contact, but have since ceased to be so, continue to act upon each other at a distance after physical contact is severed. Here I would suggest that the proximity of the deceased individual during his/her lifetime to either the dwelling or the tomb/tomb chapel formed the significant points of connection. Dwelling and materiality are very much at issue here: the material instantiation of a person's existence in a living context, with all the webs of connection that this entails, is thus transposed into a wider significance for his/her descendants in the next generation. The sphere of dwelling, being, working and communicating are all grounded in the corporeality of one's kin or material possessions and are carried forward into the coming generations in an endless chain. Moreover, the part–whole correlation is mirrored in the association of the individual–embodied object. An object's essence is found in its fragments, almost like a synecdoche: every flame contains fire, any human bone retains the sign of death, one single hair contains the life force, and so on. Underlying the idea of magical continuity relationships between the part and the whole resides the concept of contagion. Personal characteristics, illness, life, luck all transmitted along the sympathetic chain (Mauss 2001: 81).

Bringing on the Dead

Just as the portrait claims a certain power through its historicity, the image of the ancestor also performs as the receptacle of a certain life history. They have both a *presence* and a *history* (Belting 1994: 10). In the Egyptian context such objects were perceived as embodied with appreciable timelines and active trajectories. Ancestral images acted as a mnemonic to reactivate the presence of a known individual and to capitalize on the ascendancy of the "effective spirit." The agency imputed to the ancestor was inherently future-oriented. Just as the mummified body formed the material substance that anchored the ethereal components of the deceased (see Chapter 5), ancestral images also constitute the material repository for the immaterial being. Provocative here is the notion of distributed personhood, that biographical and narrative quality of individual lives that might be dispersed materially through objects, tombs, texts and traces which subsequently accumulate to bolster the identity, deploying it in the present and projecting it forward into the future. Iterating this great Egyptian desire, the biological career may thus be prolonged after biological death through material means. Although far from universal, in specific contexts such as Egypt personal agency generates distributed objects, which in turn extend the limits of the self (Gell 1998: 222–3). These iconic objects in ritually saturated contexts operate in social networks not unlike human subjects, since the latter have mobilized them and imbued them with aura and intensity.

Ancestral images physically mirror an entire genre of writing, called "letters to the dead," that called upon deceased family members to intercede in the world of the living. Some letters were transparently self-serving. Sometime in the 19th Dynasty a man wrote to his dead wife, Ankhiry, believing that she was maliciously interfering in his life (Wente 1990: 216–17). He writes:

> *What have I done against you wrongfully for you to get into this evil disposition in which you are? What have I done against you? As for what you have done, it is your laying hands on me even though I committed no wrong against you . . . I took you for a wife when I was a youth so that I was with [you] while I was functioning in office and you were with me. I did not divorce [you], nor did I cause you to be vexed . . . I concealed nothing from you at all during your lifetime. I did not let you suffer discomfort [in] anything I did with you after the manner of a lord, nor did you find me cheating on you after the manner of a field hand, entering a strange house.*

In concluding his detailed letter, Ankhiry's husband implores her that even three years after her death he had not entered into a relationship with another woman or become involved with various women in his own household. It is the materiality of the letter itself – and its placement undoubtedly near the tomb – rather than simply making a verbal supplication that marks its efficacy. Writing, inscribing, making, and even the physical physical ingestion of those products, were all ways that Egyptian magic was instantiated. Some effective spirits were clearly real personages while others were spectral beings retold in tales that assume a more didactic character. One fabulous story, well known at Deir el Medina and preserved on five ostraca, was the *Tale of the High Priest Khonsuemheb and the Ghost*; the latter might be reconsidered as an effective spirit like those who were venerated through ancestor busts and stelae. Khonsuemheb was undoubtedly a fictional character; however, the story was set in the Theban Necropolis, home to the Deir el Medina community. Khonsuemheb invokes the effective spirit and then asks the deceased individual, named Nebusemekh, what he requires. It transpired that his tomb needed refurbishment, a coffin of gold and wood, and so on. Nebusemekh wept: *I will remain here without eating or drinking, without growing old or becoming young. I will not see sunlight nor will I inhale northerly breezes, but darkness will be in my sight every day* (Simpson, Faulkner, and Wente 1972: 138). This description of this individual's existence in death appears rather gloomy instead of the exalted experience other cultural texts would suggest. Embedded here are the seeds of doubt and skepticism about overarching religious beliefs about the future trajectory of the individual. Both material and ritual practices are necessary to ward off those existential fears of oblivion. Khonsuemheb suggests that he will have ten servants, male and female, pour water libations for him and a sack of emmer wheat offered daily. The spirit retorts that these acts are not ones of extreme permanence and he requires stone that never ages or perishes so that his name will endure for eternity. Permanence, whether material or devotional, was a recurrent and lasting concern for the Egyptians, for how else might one control the future?

Ritual artefacts often serve as a repository for answers about the past and questions for the future, especially the crucial trajectory of the individual after death, whether that be anxieties for loved ones now departed, one's ancestors, or apprehension concerning our own fate, our future biography. Things can legibly help. Rather than succumbing to existential angst alone individuals have often sought material intermediaries to intercede on their behalf, to give concreteness and closure to life's uncertainties. As we have seen, the community and the house form the perfect discursive loci for the processes of objectification and social shaping (Bourdieu 1977: 89) through the mediations and hierarchies of things, people and practices that at times overlap and at others sunder. Yet surely it is not by recourse to religious belief alone that people have always struggled to preserve their conditions of existence, both material and immaterial, to prevent their dispersal, division or fragmentation. By imbuing them with the character of a possession to be kept and transmitted intact, things ensure the survival of the generations to come (Godelier 1999: 45). Religion is not the ultimate explanation for why certain things are necessary for reproduction; it lies at the very heart of sociality and identity for communities and individuals. Constructs of dispersal and survival at the individual and cultural level, coupled with notions of permanence, were central in Egypt and manifest in both physical surroundings and cultural codings.

Rites are mimetic acts that gain power through gestural activity and embodied geographies and attempt to combat life's uncertainties. Every artefact is a performance, as we shall see reiterated in the next chapter, and many perform in the service of memory. Far from being the reliquary of the past, memory sustains itself by believing in the existence of possibilities and vigilantly awaiting them, constantly watching for their appearance (de Certeau 1984: 87). It has been said that rituals take place because they find their *raison d'être* in the conditions of existence and the sentiments of individuals who cannot afford the luxury of speculation, mystical effusions or metaphysical anxiety (Bourdieu 1977: 115). While we cannot always be questioning subjects, such a hard-line proposition reduces agency and the ability to reflect back upon the constitution of the social world, as evinced in the ghost story of Khonsuemheb. But Bourdieu was correct to suggest that rituals are logical and practical simultaneously and that practical logic is inflected with immanent conceptual schemes that serve to make sense of efficacious objects and the rites densely woven around them. For many this forms a suite of non-discursive behaviors. But in a theoretical circumlocution, Bourdieu argued that logic is everywhere because really it is nowhere (1977: 113). Informed by a practical sense individuals construct their own logics, as we have seen articulated by Lévy-Bruhl, Lévi-Strauss and a host of ethnographers. These are culturally coherent universes of discourse where cosmologies, hierarchies, and a matrix of actions and perceptions are sophisticatedly deployed to rationalize the world and the order of things. Egyptian ritual life was neither an absent nor ethereal construct of contemplation; it engaged concrete technologies of action, prediction, supplication and material preparation for the individual's future.

Balancing pragmatism and religious devotion, the Egyptians negotiated their lives and their relations with the gods and the deceased on the ground, and sometimes one side of those relations had to be privileged. In the case of Amenemope it was necessary in the absence of living relatives that he was forgotten, his mortuary provisions dispensed with and his tomb usurped. The sanctity of the tomb and of individual memory and material commemoration had to be forfeited in this context in an environment of ideological ambiguity and community ambivalence. And after this small disruption in the fabric of ancestral relations, the social order was inevitably repaired, or perhaps it was an acknowledged taken-for-granted. Implicit in the mythico-ritual system was the potential to divide as well as unify: these are social as well as political choices. Some individuals are too important to forget and must be constantly rehabilitated, whereas others were gradually forgotten. In the main, most deceased individuals probably shifted from the realm of individuated ancestors to a general ancestry through time, from the sphere of particular memories to the universal otherwordly. Disenchantment was ameliorated by doxic practices and beliefs that the ancestors and afterlife were real and potent and one had to strive toward attaining the favors, and ultimately the position, of the blessed dead through embodied practice during life. Crisis situations may also have been necessary to affirm the status quo. They insinuated the possibility for critique of the natural and social world that could be both aired and concealed within a universe of possible discourse, without directly challenging its pervasive sway.

Statue Worlds and Divine Things

Thus an animating breath blows not through Nature only, but all things; and there is in all dealings, even in the decoration of men and the ornament of things, much more spiritual value and purpose than we fancy . . . In the act of animating is something beautifying, such as on their higher levels of poetry and philosophy strive after.

F. Ratzel, *The History of Mankind*

Desiring the image – and, in turn, the desiring image – forms one of the oldest and most romantic narratives within the literary canon. That the aesthetic work, specifically the statue, could be imbued with life, will and desire, seems to reside at the emotional substrate of fantasy. The iconic tale derives from a Greek myth, or, alternatively, the Roman writer Ovid's classic work *Metamorphoses*. The story of Pygmalion has formed the basis for innumerable stories, plays, films, paintings and other cultural works over the millennia. To recapitulate briefly, Pygmalion crafts a statue of woman from snow-white ivory, surpassing all mortal women, and immediately falls in love with his creation. *The features are those of a real girl, who, you might think, lived, and wished to move, if modesty did not forbid it. Indeed, art hides his art. He marvels, and passion for his bodily image, consumes his heart.* Pygmalion touches the statue, kisses it, speaks to it, furnishes gifts of flowers, shells and beads. He dresses and adorns the statue and *arranges the statue of an bed on which cloths dyed with Tyrian murex are spread, and calls it his bedfellow.* Since Pygmalion has no partner in life, he prays to the goddess Venus for a woman that mimics his ivory creation. Finding him worthy she grants the request and when he returns home the ivory statue *yielded to his touch, and lost its hardness, altering under his fingers . . . It was flesh! The pulse throbbed under his thumb.* They subsequently marry and have a child named Paphos from whom the Mediterranean city takes its name.

Pygmalion and his love object Galatea have had many afterlives and constitutive effects. The Elizabethan dramatist John Marston retold the story in 1598, as did William Morris in 1868 and, famously, George Bernard Shaw in his 1912 play. In the mid-1840s Nathaniel Hawthorne refigured and serialized the tale in *Drowne's Wooden Image*, a story of a young Bostonian wood carver who fabricates a ship's figurehead for the *Cynosure*. A more distant parallel can also be found in the Indonesian folktale of Nai Manggale. In this north Sumatran story Datu Panggana is a famous sculptor who carves a wooden statue of a beautiful woman. After prayers from a holy man called Datu Partoar the statue comes to life and is welcomed by him and his wife as their stepdaughter, Nai Manggale. In each of these accounts the statue is desired by individuals who seek various personal outcomes by means of material manifestation. The statue is a projection of earthly desire, yet through devotional practice the object assumes its own agency and power in the realm of the living. Divine intervention is required in all of these accounts. The gods intercede in worldly affairs when they are petitioned and thus come into the world through the statue substitute. During the manifestation there is a conflation between signifier and signified, where the object status is destabilized as its swerves and morphs between manufactured object and divine embodiment. This is the compelling transformation in the statue's existence, from the mundane to the divine, and from form to content. In all respects these narratives hauntingly parallel the statue worlds of many ancient and modern religions and their devotional practices surrounding the statue forms of the divine. Undoubtedly many of those worshiping religious objects desired their own statues to come alive fully, acknowledging that they were already animated by divine force, if only they would move and involve themselves fully in the world of the living.

The Pygmalion story has an enormous legacy and a cross-cultural appeal: the statue of Galatea is the perfect fetish, an entity crystallized into an object beyond value, possessing an unexchangeable singularity. However, it is also a tale of defetishization, where the statue object becomes flesh and is embodied in female form; thus there is a conflation. The fetish, as a singularity, is a composite fabrication of metonymic materiality with the ability to inscribe or historicize a unique, unrepeatable originating event in a novel form. This capacity personalizes the act in its own material presence, thereby forging a new identity from contingent events. As a unique embodiment, the fetish is the territorialization of a reified entity (Pietz 1993). From Predynastic times the Egyptians depicted deities in fetish form, even the hieroglyph for god, *ntr*, was symbolized by a fetish in the form of a wrapped staff (Hornung

1982: 40, 101). The move from object to fetish involves several stages (Ellen 1988: 220–9): *concretization*, where abstractions assume concrete, effective entities; *animation*, where the qualities of living organisms are imputed to objects, usually anthropomorphic; *conflation*, where signifier and signified, content and form, destabilize one another; *ambiguity*, where control of the object by the person and of the person by the object is unclear. We might witness each of these transformative states in the enlivening of Galatea or Nai Manggale. In his work entitled *Statues*, philosopher Michel Serres (1987) poses the question: how do we describe the emergence of the object, not simply tools or beautiful statues, onto-logically speaking? How does the object come to what is human? What Serres lacks are the experiential accounts of how objects constitute human subjectivity, since our focus has always been the reverse and thus the process has been silenced in history. Here I would assert that archaeology, and ethnography, can provide evocative and sensuous empirical accounts.

Divine Things in Egypt

In order to apprehend the Egyptian material we have to divorce ourselves from Western notions of art as a distinct discursive category. While not eschewing the power of aesthetics, Egyptian representations were not solely "to be looked at." In Egypt, the term for sculptor was *he who keeps alive*, which underscores the significance of the image as a living materiality. In Pharaonic, Graeco-Roman and Late Antique times there was little distinction between the statue of a deity and the deity itself. Artemidorus, in his *Interpretation of Dreams*, argued that it made no difference whether one saw a statue of a goddess or the deity herself in the flesh, since a divine numen was present in both. Spirit animated the statue and thus one could actively petition it (Belting 1994: 37), harking back to the Pharaonic idea that the cult statue was equivalent to, and should be treated like, the divine body of the deity. Some scholars perceive a subtle difference, according to Hornung (1982: 135), between the image and the true form, the latter which is only revealed to human eyes in exceptional cases, usually in the next world. In this sense, the statue is still, and more importantly, the only possibly earthly incarnation of the divine. Such existential musings appear throughout Egyptian texts in varying intensities.

Egyptian religion was believed to originate and exist outside human subjectivity: it was literally god-given. In one account, known as the Memphite theology, the creator god Ptah was said to have made the bodies of the gods, established their divine images, and oversaw their indwelling. Ptah states (Morenz 1973: 154):

He bore the gods, he created the cities, he founded the nomes,
He placed the gods in their cult places,
He established their offerings and equipped their sanctuaries,
He made their bodies according to their wishes.

So the gods entered their bodies,
Of all kinds of wood, all kinds of minerals, all kinds of clay,
And of everything that grows on him (the earth = creator god),
In which they took form.

Here we see a specifically Egyptian vision of divine embodiment and material manifestation. The gods enter their bodies, namely their earthly, manufactured statue bodies. Presumably the Egyptians made a clear distinction between the inanimate nature of the material and the sculpture itself before the necessary rituals of animation had been deployed (Morenz 1973: 156). Assmann argues that "clear distinction is drawn between the two 'natures' of divine images: the gods on the one hand, and on the other, their 'bodies' of more or less perishable earthly materials" (2001: 46). However, to my reading the distinction is not transparent: Divine Ptah created the other gods, sent them to their cult places where they took embodied form. Morenz also seems to argue for a more distributed notion of the divine self. He views it as an iterative practice rather than a one time event, where the gods enter their bodies time and time again. Egyptian thought may not have accommodated two separate spheres of embodiment, one in the heavens as separate from that of earth: one can, after all, be immanent. Assmann goes on to argue that "[t]he statue is not the image of the deity's body, but the body itself. It does not represent his form but rather gives him form. The deity takes form in the statue, just as in a sacred animal or a natural phenomenon" (Assmann 2001: 46). This enforces the notion of the fetish and its concomitant power as a *power of*, not simply *power in*. The Egyptians may have recognized that while the transcendent nature of the gods was not be reducible to any form that could be conceived as material or otherwise, there was also a sense that it was only through the act of objectification that they were empowered for humanity. That objectification imbued them with agency. In a reconfiguration of the fabrication act, the Egyptians considered the statues to be born not made. Inscriptions employ the term *to bear* for the practical and technical manufacture of a cult statue. Similarly artisans claim that in the act of making, they *bore* the statues of deities and even the deities themselves.

In asking why the material image was so integrally potent one might look forward to Christian times, acknowledging its strong Pharaonic inheritance. According to Aquinas, Christian images had three primary functions: instruction for the illiterate who might learn from them like books; iteration of memory so that the mystery of incarnation could be more firmly instantiated in the mind; to excite the emotions which are more susceptible to the visual than the aural (Davis 1997: 32). Yet while the role of images was depicted as strongly didactic, the Egyptian concept of image was an agentic force: what is intended is action, not something static. Celestial activities were thought to be carried out on earth, and Egypt itself was regarded as a temple because it was the land where this is done according to heavenly directives (Assmann 2001: 41). Temples were microcosms and landscape simulacra of divine order. Here visible met the invisible: obelisks pierced the heavens, pylons reproduced the horizon, and sacred lakes copied the primeval waters of creation (Bell 1997: 132) The gods themselves were known as *rich in manifestations* or *lord of manifestations*, suggesting that they could be both multiple and complicated in their embodiments, from divine statues to earthly animals, such as the Apis bull (Hornung 1982: 125, 137). Jan Assmann has set out a useful schema into which one can insert the place of the statue and cultic objects in their active roles and resident, territorialized presence:

> In understanding the contextual construction of Egyptian religious experience one might perceive a conceptual horizon of contact with the divine that worked on at least three levels. At the local level was the *cultic*. In the cultic dimension, deities are resident in a place in the form of their cult statues and, as local or state gods, are symbols of collective or political identity.
>
> 1. The *cultic*, which can also be called the "local" or the "political," for these three aspects are inseparably connected: in the cultic dimension, deities are resident in a place in the form of their cult statues and, as local or state gods, are symbols of collective or political identity.
> 2. The *cosmic,* because to the Egyptians, the cosmos was hierophantic, that is, it was a sphere of divine action and religious experience.
> 3. The *mythic,* by which is meant sacred tradition, "what is said about the gods," the presence of the divine in the cultural memory as set down in myths, names, genealogies, and other forms of tradition. (Assman 2001: 8)

Many years ago Herman Junker coined the concept of installation or indwelling, *Einwohnung,* which expresses the specifically Egyptian concept of the local dimension of divine presence. It is remarkably similar to Hegel's thesis set out in *Phenomenology of Spirit* (see Chapter 1). Junker's notion of indwelling was forged in reference to various texts that described the deity's *ba* as descending from the sky and uniting not only with the cult statue but also with the iconographic representations on the walls. These reliefs depict scenes of the cult and thus the deity descends from the sky as a *ba* to participate in the cult in the form of these images. The gods did not dwell on earth as ordinary mortals themselves experienced the terrestrial. Rather, they installed themselves within in their images, not in a singular, originary embodiment but in a series of events that occurred regularly. The collaboration of humankind through ritual practice and invocation was necessary, and this suite of actions formed the basis of the cult (Assmann 2001).

Divine statues, for the most part, have not survived the ravages of time largely because their precious nature made them violable by human hands. Many are described as being fashioned from gold, silver and inlays of turquoise, lapis lazuli, and so on (Figure 4.1). One need only think of the images of Tutankhamun to suggest a sense of their richly arrayed adornment. Metal statues could have been easily smelted (smaller examples were manufactured from solid gold), while wooden images encased in gold leaf would have been stripped of their finery. One only has to recall the famous description of the gods with their *bones of silver, flesh of gold, hair of lapis lazuli* to imagine their beauty. From remaining royal sculptures, like that of the 19th Dynasty Pharaoh Seti I, we can see the attempts to embody statues in fine Egyptian alabaster with its soft, waxy and vein-like qualities that resemble living flesh (Russmann and Finn 1989: 147). Yet in order to resemble the body of the gods closely, their crafting from precious material was required and each was suffused with meaning (Hornung 1982: 135). Preserved from Deir el Medina is a letter from the scribe Amenakhte to the king, pertaining to the cult statue of Rameses VI. The statue was to be installed in part of the Hathor temple at Deir el Medina where other statues of kings were assembled (McDowell 1999: 94–5). While this was indeed a local temple, it could not rival the lavish displays at other cult sites such as Karnak or Abydos.

The beautiful statue whose name is The Dual King, Lord of the Two Lands Rameses VI, Beloved of Amun, of good nib-wood and persea-wood, the torso colored and all of its limbs of faience like real red jasper, and its kilt of hammered yellow gold; its crown of lapis lazuli, adorned with serpents of every color; the uraeus on his head of sixfold alloy inlaid with real stones; its sandals of sixfold alloy; which will be installed in the House of King Ramesses II, the great god, and also King Merenptah, the great god, and also every king who donned the

Figure 4.1 Gilded silver statuette of Amun-Re from the Temple of Amun at Karnak. 18th Dynasty, c. 1300 BC. Courtesy of the British Museum, EA 60006.

White Crown and whose statue rests here. Three offerings are conducted for them daily, at every rising of the sun over the mountain, and Pre-Horakhty will grant that Pharaoh celebrates millions of jubilees while he is King of Egypt, his statue receiving incense and libations for its god's offerings before it exactly like the lord of this great and holy place.

As part of cultic devotion statues were provided with clean clothes each day, in addition to food and drink offerings in an ongoing daily routine of verbal and material sustenance. If we look at the complex stages of daily cultic ritual, clothing rites alone consisted of some forty-five individual acts and those, too, were increasingly complicated by adherence to the smallest constituent elements or rites. According to Assmann (2001: 48) the first acts of the morning clothing ritual in the New Kingdom consisted of (1) lighting the flame, (2) taking up the arm-shaped censer, (3) placing incense in the flame, (4) going to the sanctuary, (5) breaking the cord, (6) breaking the seal, (7) sliding the door bolt, and finally (8) revealing the god or opening the door-leaves of the shrine. Their purpose was to awaken the god and to wash, dress and feed the deity at the start of each new day in a cycle similar to that of human subjects. Altars piled high with provisions were set up, incense burned and libations poured. The Egyptian word for incense also meant to make divine (Robins 2001: 7), adding another layer upon the dense stratigraphy of ritual devotion. Amongst incense and the recitation of hymns officiating priests approached the sanctuary. The body of the god was then uncovered; he was presented with myrrh, anointed, purified with water and then the sanctuary was sealed, accompanied by spells and hymns. It should be remembered that statues were placed in the inner sanctuary of the temple, within a shrine, and not on public view. Cult statues traditionally dwelt within their shrines inside a small, dark room in the heart of the temple as the focus of cosmic order (Shafer 1997: 6). Daily cult ritual formed a temporal cycle as well as a performative one. There were three elaborate services, at dawn, midday and in the evening, the morning ritual being the most significant. A scaled-down set of rituals were performed twice more throughout the day. There were spells for putting incense on the fire, for placing fat on the fire, putting meat on the fire, for the roasting spit, for a beer libation, and finally for removing all footprints and fastening the door (McDowell 1999). Through ritualized speech and action, priests accomplished the transposition of the cultic events into the divine realm. The cult was essentially performative on the part of humans, whose actions invoked the gods' and goddesses' benevolent participation. Thus the corresponding deities inhabited their cult images, fabricated by human hands after their *ba* had descended from the sky (Assmann 2001: 53).

Once the mouth and eyes of an image had been touched, that image could house the spiritual elements, thus providing the material entity for eternal life (Forman and Quirke 1996: 32). Images were thus called upon to play active roles and filled gaps in the social fabric of daily life. As Belting (1994: 45) contends, "many religions are concerned to make visible an object of veneration, to protect it and to approach it with the same piety that they would lavish on the higher being; symbolic acts toward the image thus reveal one's inner attitude." From an anthropological perspective, a statue in a temple was believed to be the body of the divinity, and a spirit-medium that likewise provided the divinity with a temporary body. Both were treated as theoretically on a par, despite the fact that the former is an artefact and the latter is a living deity (Gell 1998: 7). Whereas this was possible for deified or royal personages, it did not always extend to the representations of the rest of society. In the Ramesside period that availability was extended to ordinary people and could encompass the veneration of ancestral images, as we saw in Chapter 3.

It was largely impossible to see the gods, even if one experienced such visions in a dream, as in the literary tale *The Shipwrecked Sailor* (Hornung 1982: 128). Gods could also manifest as divine aromas, as in the case of the conception of Hatshepsut when Amun materializes to Queen Ahmose through the form of her husband Tuthmosis I. Incense was likened to the sweat of the gods and was thus sacred. In fact the depiction of the gods was not a picture of their bodies, but rather a characterization of their nature or identity that could take the form of a sign or hieroglyph. During great festivals the deity could leave the dark recesses of the sanctuary when a portable image was taken out into the world. It was not sufficient that Pharaoh might travel as a substitute for the gods at festival time, the conditions of possibility deemed that the person of the god was required. On a 12th Dynasty stela from Abydos, an official named Ikhernofret claims: *I made for him (Osiris) a portable shrine to display the beauty of the Foremost of the Westerners, with gold and silver, lapis and bronze . . . I supervised the construction of the Neshmet Barque and made the cabin myself. I adorned the breast of the god of Abydos with lapis, turquoise, fine gold, and all manner of precious stones* (Hare 1999: 38). When the god stepped outside and was manifest he was the present god amidst the celebrations; he was not constrained by the works of men, and his were the utterances of god himself. The image, shrouded and still invisible to the crowds of onlookers, was ferried by priests on a shrine (Figure 4.3),

Figure 4.2 Diorama from Glasgow Museum with a reconstruction of statue-making. Courtesy of the National Museums of Scotland.

while others were carried in sacred boats (Hornung 1982: 136, 139). The boats were made from imported wood and clad in precious metals, and their prows bore the likeness of the deity with which to signal onlookers: a falcon head signified Horus, whereas the ram's head signified Amun. Pharaoh Tuthmosis III claimed that he, as a youth, was elected to office through the agency of Amun's statue at Karnak during such a festival. In his account the god appeared in procession, lingered in his presence and thus designated him rightful ruler (Morenz 1973: 91). This probably entailed the barque swaying at the appropriate moment after a specific question was posed. Yet for ordinary individuals who desperately needed to petition the gods outside the festival calendar it became necessary to find someone, probably a priest, who was able to mediate and enter the sacred precinct (Baines 2002); whether these persons were able to regularly view the statue/body of the god is unknown. In one such letter to the god (McDowell 1999: 110) a rather dissatisfied man wrote:

I was looking for you to tell you some matters of mine, but you happened to be hidden in your sanctuary and there was no one admitted to send it to you. Now,

Figure 4.3 Ostracon from Deir el Medina showing the procession of a deity in its sacred shrine. 19th or 20th Dynasty. Courtesy of Ägyptisches Museum und Papyrussammlung. Staatliche Museen zu Berlin — Stiftung Preußischer Kutlurebesitz. Inv. 21446.

when I was waiting, I found Hori, this scribe of Medinet Habu, and he told me, "I am admitted." So I am sending him to you . . . Now as for one like you, being in the place of mysteries and hiding, he sends out his voice; but you do not send me either good or bad (messages).

Other individuals sought material intermediaries in the form of statues, themselves physical conduits that facilitated communication with the gods and supplication from individual petitioners. Two such inscribed statues of Amenhotep, son of Hapu, were installed in front of Pylon X at Karnak. Inscriptional evidence makes it clear that all that was spoken to Amenhotep, as messenger, would be passed on to Amun so long as people performed the offering spell, invoked his name twice daily, and so on. This is an apt example of the enmeshed spheres of material and immaterial, of concretized and performative memory. Similar statues of living people occupying the rank of "scribe of the recruits" were located in the Temple of Mut at Karnak and in the forecourt of the sanctuary of Isis at Coptos. One inscribed statue reads: *I am the messenger of the mistress of the sky, I belong to her outer court. Tell me your petitions so that I can report them to the mistress of the Two Lands, for she hears my supplications* (Morenz 1973: 102). The centrality of the material image and its agentic force in these rituals has several implications. First, individuals rendered in statue form had themselves represented and invoked in perpetuity; memory of them was constantly brought into the sphere of the living, long after their bodily death. Thus they were actively sustained in the next life through the actions of the living. Second, the role of mediators is underscored: they could be living individuals such as priests or material embodiments of individuals (alive or dead) such as Amenhotep, son of Hapu. Here the materialization of memory may indeed be inseparable from the power of the mediating statue, and hence conjoined for maximum efficacy. Did the Egyptians consider the distinction important and was there a hierarchy of service; that is, was a priest preferable and perceived as more efficacious? To my knowledge we cannot comment on these fine-grained distinctions, if indeed they were salient categorical differences for an Egyptian audience. But clearly the statue as a supra-object was considered an effective and legitimate agentic intermediary. And lastly, if we try to reconstruct the practices surrounding petitioning the gods then we must envisage living individuals relating to and relying on material forms in a deeply phenomenological sense. Ritual practice was intimately woven around the statue as if it were the person; they were spoken to, prayed too, invoked, and so on. Collapsing the contemporary boundaries of subject and object in this context seems inevitable.

Fabrications

In Egyptian thought, humanity was made in the image of the gods (Hornung 1982: 138). Yet what happened when humans resided in the world of the divine? The obvious candidates here were Pharaohs, who were cast as great living gods themselves. Their statues appeared most frequently in royal funerary complexes and temples. Presence in the latter allowed the King to be there in essence through his substitute self and also allowed him desirable access to the gods. As embodiments of the royal *ka*, statues formed a physical focus for the cult, yet as a mediator between human and divine realms the Pharaoh was in a subordinate role to the gods as the performer of their rituals (Robins 2001: 35). At times the Pharaoh assumed the bodily postures of the divine, such as the shrouded mummiform pose of Osiris, while others show him with one or two other deities. In specific instances the King is shown smaller than the gods to reinforce the social hierarchy of the divine and to underscore the protective powers of the gods. Other royals assumed divine status in variant ways, as deified and popularized individuals with intimately close connections to certain places and communities. One famous instance is that of Amenhotep I at Deir el Medina.

The deified royals Amenhotep I and his mother, Ahmose-Nefertari, assumed cultic primacy in the village of Deir el Medina and were probably revered as the founders of the village. They were the divinized patrons of the community whose images were the objects of devotion and supplication (Friedman 1994: 111). Memory of them seems to have extended back many generations to the beginning of the 18th Dynasty. Innumerable statues, stelae, offering tables, and wall paintings attest to their ongoing popularity. Wall paintings in the tomb of the scribe Khabekhenet suggest that the image of Amenhotep was carried in procession during festival time, and festivals dedicated to the royal couple were the most numerous and diverse within Deir el Medina (Valbelle 1985: 322–5). *Year 7, third month of winter, day 29. The Great Festival of King Amenophis, the Lord of the Village was being held. The gang rejoiced before him for 4 solid days of drinking together with their children and their wives. There were 60 of inside (the village) and 60 of outside* (McDowell 1999: 96). Perhaps the statue that now resides in the Turin Museum represents this type of performative cult statue. Amenhotep I had another history within the village: as an oracle embodied in statue form, a sort of afterlife for his divine image on earth. This statue of the dead king performed its oracular functions. Like the ancestor busts discussed in Chapter 3, one can see this as a form of predictive technology. As Pels (1998: 91) would have it, this form of fetish traverses the border zones and occludes the divisions between mind and matter, the animate and the inanimate. Critical of Appadurai's original formulation, Pels argues that we should refigure fetishism from spirit in, toward spirit of, matter. This type of animated entity comes to dominate persons and decide their fate (Taussig 1980: 25). Fetishes can communicate their own messages: this is animism with a vengeance, its materiality strikes back. The physicality of the object, in this case the deified Amenhotep image (Figure 4.4), *Ding an Sich*, carries over forms of signification. Material objects, made by human hands, thus transcend their makers, albeit through human intentionality and artifice. It is not simply the power of the invisible hand to decide fate, since the tacit materiality of the object has a force in itself. Thus it is not a *tabula rasa* onto which signification is assigned by humans: we too are inherently molded and shaped by the matter that surrounds us. Pels (1998: 100–1) sutures these two domains, material and human, through a call for aesthetics coupled with the material process of mediating knowledge via the senses.

Archaeologically, the remains of the cultic and divinatory activity might be located within a chapel at the north of the Deir el Medina village. This represents one of the major buildings devoted to Amenhotep I and Ahmose-Nefertari by virtue of it yielding more statuary than any other structure within the necropolis. Tomb 1244 ran underneath this chapel and its roof formed a slab that could be opened to reveal the tomb underneath and the statue (Bomann 1991: 72–3). The pronouncements of the oracle were taken very seriously, and it could literally decide one's fate, reputation and punishment. That the oracle's actions were humanly mediated was never documented. In one case the oracle ordered the policeman Amenkha to pay for a donkey belonging to Hormin the draughtsman, with serious repercussions if he failed to comply (McDowell 1999: 174):

> *The god ordered the policeman Amenkha [to pay] 9 deben.*
> *First month of winter, day 10. He reported him again and he ordered him to pay*
> *yet again, for the third time. He made him take an oath of the lord, saying, "If*
> *I renege and dispute again, I will get 100 blows of a stick, and the donkey will*
> *be counted against me double."*

Meaningful Objects, Living Images

Perhaps it is appropriate at this juncture to ask when is a statue just a statue? Apparently there are four devices for identifying statues in

Figure 4.4 Fragment of a painting depicting the deified Amenhotep I from the tomb of Kynebu, Thebes. Dated to the reign of Rameses VIII, *c.* 1145 BC. Courtesy of the British Museum, EA 37993.

Egyptian painting and relief (although clearly not in sculpture): context; the use of an approximate profile view; provision of a statue base; and a label that indicates statue-ness, the use of the noun, *twt*, meaning image (Eaton-Krauss 1984: 1263). Exceptions are always interesting. For example, the ithyphallic god Min is traditionally shown on a plinth and resembles a statue in many ways (Meskell and Joyce 2003: 106). There are also linguistic markers: the Egyptian term *twt* may refer to an image such as the royal statue, while *khenty* probably referred to a divine manifestation of the Pharaoh (Frood 2003). There is a great proliferation of representations of statues from New Kingdom times onwards, and one can only speculate as to why there was a general reticence beforehand. Perhaps this too marks a progression toward personal piety and a more active communication between mortals and divinities? There are certainly more preserved votive statues from temples from New Kingdom times onwards as well, and more depicting ordinary individuals within the sphere of religious observance, both in this life and the next.

The Deir el Medina villagers crafted statues both of divinities and themselves to take into the tomb. Although not divine in the sense of deities and royals, the images of individuals would be envisaged to be a substitute for the self and similarly to house the animate constituents of the person after death, such as the *ba* and *ka*. The texts describe the relationship between the *ba* and the image as *uniting*, *fraternizing*, and *embracing* (Assmann 2001). Statue selves have been found in numerous private tombs like those of Kha or Iabtina, and the more famous royal example of Tutankhamun. Since the community was one of craftsmen this is to be expected, yet there are no texts recording how individuals envisioned such fabricated things to move from the world of objects to that of their very own subjects.

In New Kingdom rock-cut Theban tombs it was common to erect a statue niche or shrine where the *ka* of the deceased, a simulacrum of the self, could enter and dwell in the representation and receive offerings, libations and prayers performed by one's living kin. A kneeling statue of the male owner, holding forward a stela, was inserted into the pyramid or a niche in the façade above the chapel facing to the east (Robins 2001: 39). According to one interpretation, the ancestral images examined in Chapter 3 were supposedly a shorthand for these very statues (Friedman 1985: 97). Traditionally the stela was inscribed with a hymn to the sun, dedicated by the named individual, thus conferring upon him the benefits of the cyclical journey of the sun god, his desired companion in the next life. What interests me here is the process of manufacturing a statue or object with supra-object status in a mundane, technical

Figure 4.5 Wall painting from the tomb of
Ipy, Deir el Medina. Photo by the author.

capacity, which is consequently transformed into a resonant being or
embodied object that transcends the initial category. The making of
statues is well documented amongst the villagers. Preserved on ostraca
are a number of such commissions for both men and women at Deir el
Medina, costing as little as between 5 and 12 *deben* (Janssen 1975: 247).
In one complicated instance a carpenter named Meryre sculpted a statue
for a man called Ruty who exchanged with him goods equivalent to
the modest sum of almost 10 *deben*. On seeing the quality of the statue
Ruty objected and sought guidance from the aforementioned oracle.
Amenhotep agreed, when petitioned, that the statue was only worth 8
deben and thus the transactions had to be adjusted. That one can commission a statue as one would an ordinary, utilitarian object is one point
of interest. A second is that parties may quarrel over the quality and value
of such a thing. As we will see with Buddhist statues, is it not uncommon
to query the level of divinity or authenticity of a so-called divine embodiment. In another case from Deir el Medina a workman called Amenemope

bought a statue of the deity Seth from an artisan Meryre (possibly the same man), which was then appraised by another carpenter, Sawadjiyt, who claimed he had been overcharged. Undeterred Amenemope gave it to Sawadjiyt's father to spend a month with them, perhaps to take advantage of the divine power of the piece (McDowell 1999: 84–5). It is unclear from the text whether he received a payment for the loan of the statue. What is striking here is that one might haggle over the price of a seemingly divine and powerful representation and then go about circulating it, believing it to be so powerful to simply hand it over! How did one suspend disbelief and the knowledge of human crafting in Egyptian culture? Again, this rather nebulous set of scenarios is paralleled in the contemporary world of divine statue beings.

One could see the active agents within statuary as following the tropic operations of projection, reprojection, ventriloquism, subject-making, object-making, belief and knowledge (Latour 1996). What we classify as statues could be refigured to accord with an emic view, that these are not simply contained essences of the divine but come to be divine in their own right. Thus what we perceive as statues were not simply vehicles, but the materialization of the gods themselves from an Egyptian perspective. This morphing or crossing of boundaries extends the embodiment of objects and subjects alike in an inevitable fabricating of the world. The fetish is a social fact, one that deserves its own taxonomy, coined by Latour as *faitich,* a parallel blurring of fact and fetish. In English, his neologism *factishes* reminds us that the dichotomy of "facts" and "social constructions" is near useless (2000: 113). "And if religion, arts or styles are necessary to 'reflect', 'reify', 'materialize', 'embody' society – to use some of the social theorists' favorite verbs – then are objects not, in the end, its co-producers? Is society not built literally – not metaphor-ically – of gods, machines, sciences, arts and styles?" (Latour 1991: 54). Whether one thinks of Amenhotep as oracle, the divine embodiments of the gods or simply the polymorphous images of deceased ancestors, we can see how mutually constitutive subjects and objects are and how object worlds impinge on the fate of individuals.

There are additional fragmentary insights into the world of the maker. From the 11th Dynasty stela of a man called Irtisen we get a small window onto the esoteric nature of the craft. Making things is isomorphic with knowledge: Irtisen proudly states that he knows the *secret of hieroglyphs* (Baines 1990: 9). He outlines three forms of knowledge as related to carving, including the execution of specific poses, the manufacture of inlays and work on miniatures. As Baines underscores, secrecy, magic and competitive magic relate to the individual's achievement and thus his art parallels religion itself. Nebwawy, high priest of Osiris in the reign of Tuthmosis III, was also charged with cultic functions surrounding divine statues. He appears to have brought the statue from the temple and claimed to have *directed numerous works in the domain of his father Osiris, in silver, gold, lapis lazuli, turquoise and every fine stone, the entirety of this was under my seal . . . I made stonework for my lord as protection for the domain of his father* (Frood 2003). Some have argued that there was an overt overlap between the duties of sculptor and priest, and that the act of making was itself a ritual, priestly task. We might think of the sculptor here as occupying the ambiguous role of half technician, half priest (Gell 1992: 59), neither being self-contained, bounded categories. And there was no separate priestly class in Egypt. There were, of course, social distinctions between those artisans charged to make divine statues but who could not participate in the ritual of indwelling and could not therefore enter the House of Gold, and those sculptors who obtained access into these sacred places for the purposes of their secret and sacred work. This entailed the real crafting of the world, taking pieces of wood and precious materials and transforming them from inanimate objects into divine, embodied statues. In a Ramesside stela, we confront such an individual, a man called Userhat-Hatiay, himself son of the chief sculptor Ya and chief sculptor to the Pharaoh. He does not use the title of priest yet asserts that he had been introduced to his craft when very small and brought to the House of Gold, or goldsmith's workshop, *in order to fashion the forms and images of all the gods, and none of them was hidden from me* (Gardiner 1947: I, 52). This suggests that in the New Kingdom the forging and placement of the divine image was very much imbricated with the role of the sculptor. He shared with the King and his other substitutes, the vizier and priests, the ability to enter the sacred areas of the temple with its access to the divine. The sculptor of the divine image therefore had to be an initiate of sorts, someone familiar with the sacred mysteries, and so on. And because the sculptor could vivify divine statues, this justified his presence in such a restricted domain, whether working with precious metals and materials, or consulting on the procession of the sacred barque at festival times. He, like the Pharaoh and his *sem* priests, was involved in the rites and rituals of animation and enlivening (Hoffmeier 1985; Krutchen 1992: 118).

From one perspective the Egyptian words chosen for statue creation have been read as *re-embodiment* or *reincarnation*, another defines them as *bearing* or *birthing*. Userhat-Hatiay claims to have been privy to many things, including the statue gods Osiris, Thoth, Khnum, Min, Horus, Sekhmet, Ptah, Anubis, Amun Re, and various others. He says that none of them were hidden from him even though they existed in secret seclusion, that it was he who was responsible for their resting *in their shrines of eternal recurrence, carrying them as leader of the Festival of the King* (van Dijk 1995: 30). He sailed in the front of the royal boat when it traveled with the statues and he claims subsequently to have been rewarded handsomely for his skills by the Pharaoh himself. Userhat-Hatiay, like Iritsen before him, had a magical, secret knowledge and access that was unparalleled, and there is a conscious blurring of representation and reality in his description of the deities and their statue forms. But were any of these men seeing the gods, their embodied forms, or their earthly manifestations?

Since Pharaonic religious practice is no longer a living tradition we lack a comparative ethnographic, or even ethnohistoric, counterpart with which to reflexively dialogue. In this instance the coming of Islam represents a serious rupture within the fabric of Egyptian history. Since the tenets and theology are radically different, very little continuity can be seen in terms of religious observances and beliefs. Much the same could be said for the Coptic Christian religion, with the exception of the Coptic script that derives from ancient Egyptian. It may thus prove insightful to look further afield for ideas surrounding the materiality and embodiment of Egyptian religious images and, more specifically, the worship of statues as the earthly vehicles for numerous deities. Here I focus on Hindu practices involving *murthi* (Figure 4.6), drawing heavily on the work of Richard Davis (1997). His valuable approach also mirrors the current project in recognizing that there are numerous interpretive communities (past and present), entailing multiple readings and craftings, similar to the biography of a literary work.

In 2002 soccer star David Beckham, his wife Victoria and son Brooklyn were controversially depicted as Shiva, Parvati and Ganesh to the outrage of the Hindu community. Twin Sikh artists Amrit and Rabindra Singh created the portrait to celebrate the Commonwealth Games in Britain and argued in the *News India* that "we are using the language of religion, but it doesn't mean we are saying they are gods in a spiritual sense but in a material sense." Davis foregrounds exactly these variant communities of response; the multiple meanings emerge in dialogic relations between image and viewer and the respective interpretive strategies (1997: 9). Indian images and their embodied lives have been at the center of an interdisciplinary focus, from art history and religious studies, to anthropologists and material culture specialists (see Glassie 1999).

In *Lives of Indian Images* Davis outlines how Hindus ostensibly take for granted that the statues they erect in house shrines and temples are

Figure 4.6 *Murthi* of Radha and Krishna by Babu Lal Pal. Khamapara, Shimulia, Bangladesh 1996. From Glassie (1999), courtesy of Henry Gassie.

alive. They believe these objects become infused with the presence of the deity. Hindu priests bring the images alive through a complex ritual establishment that invokes the deity into its material support. Like Egypt, this recognizes the fabrication of the object in the first place, but also its transformation into another sort of non-object category. Priests and devotees in India awaken the statue in the morning, bathe it, dress it, feed and entertain it, venerate it and eventually put it to bed at night. As a divine being it can also be petitioned, as was the case in New Kingdom Egypt. Interactions between statue deities and priests were intimate and corporeal; they would smear it with unguents, bathe it with various fluids, throw flower petals upon it, and so on. Ancient texts state that statues could be bathed with precious gems such as diamonds, as well as powders, food substances, and so on. They would dress the image in luxurious cloth and adorn it with jewelry (Davis 1997: 19)

Images of Hindu gods are not likenesses of the gods and are not intended to represent earthly realities, but rather to present divine realities (Eck 1996: 38). Moreover, the image does not stand between the devotee and the god: because the image is a form of the supreme lord, it is precisely the image that facilitates and enhances the close relationship of the worshiper and deity. This proximity, however, is very different to Pharaonic experience where concealment and distance were powerful forms of reverence and esoteric control. Davis immerses himself in the discursive context and taxa of Hindu practice; he sees the statues as animate beings or social beings whose identities are mutable. Yet he also sees how these images can be invested with meanings of alterity; they become idols, devils, lucrative commodities, sculptural art or symbols for newly crafted meanings. Indian religious images are drawn into conflicts in a modern arena as part of their complex biographies. They are stolen, destroyed, disfigured, bought, sold, labeled, displayed and researched. He takes a processual approach, following Kopytoff, that these objects are repeatedly made and remade though interactions with humans (Davis 1997: 7). Similar to the oracle statue of Amenhotep I at Deir el Medina that moved to pronounce declarations, in medieval Indian accounts we also hear of images that move and perform and that also have the function of adjudication over disputes amongst the living (Davis 1997: 7).

There are also momentary embodiments such as in a festival context where the deity takes up residence in the handmade clay *linga*, formed by the worshiper in the palm of their hands. Shiva is invoked, the worshiper offers prayers, possibly along with a flower or water perhaps, then the deity is given leave to go. Again the lump of clay is but clay and the dedicants can simply discard it (Eck 1996: 50). This highlights the contextual presence of the divine and its material manifestation. This may be plausibly linked to the fabrication of votives in Egyptian ritual practice, whether votive phalloi or other body parts (see Chapter 5) that correlate directly to specific deities. However, Egyptian votives retained their sacred inflection and required burying after massive accumulation, whereas some Hindu votives can be de-sacralized and recycled strictly as materials. In specific moments matter is materialized and contact is facilitated; this would have been heightened at festival time. But when the spatio-temporal setting is changed, votive objects may simply return to their gross materials, devoid of spirit. For Hindus the animated image is a localized, particularized manifestation or incarnation of the transcendent deity, considered to be beyond form, yet capable of inhabiting numerous physical embodiments. A god like Shiva could inhabit many "supports" such as bronze statues, stone *lingas*, drawings, cloths, fires, water and special books (Davis 1997: 21): a sort of promiscuous embodiment. As one contemporary sculptor, Haripada Pal, claimed "sometimes I become part of God. Sometimes God becomes part of me. I feel God in myself when I concentrate" (quoted in Glassie 1999: 22). Every corporeal motion is pitched toward perfection, the power of the sculptor's body infusing the image with creation and force; working in clay is itself a devotion to the deity. Hindus utilize an entire range of intimate and ordinary domestic acts as an important part of their ritual devotion: cooking, eating, serving, washing, and putting to sleep (Eck 1996: 47).

Similarly, in Buddhist thought, images of the Buddha and "other objects that imitate them are created with power and energy because they have undergone a 'life-giving process' that 'animates' them" (Tambiah 1984: 230). Opening the eyes of the Buddha is perhaps the most potent ritual act. Two circuits of ritual practice sacralize the object and transfer potency to the image. The first circuit involves joining a newly cast image to one already sacralized by means of a cord. The understanding here is that one can trace, or tie together, a line of authenticated objects back through time leading to the historical personage of the Buddha himself. According to Tambiah, the second circuit materializes the rite of imbuing the object with life that is performed by the monks through whose hands the sacred cord of transmission passes. Similarly, their bodily performances energize the image. Ordinary people seek to have their personal images of Buddha share in the ritual and bring them to the monastery at ceremonial times. As Tambiah reveals, there are thorny issues to be tackled in terms of authenticity and power: How is the likeness of the image to the original living Buddha reckoned? How does one account for iconographic development? If one can replicate originals, how much of their original power is embodied? Can other sorts of copies and fakes be passed off as originals? What weight is given to the material employed and adornment in any assessment of its virtues? (1984: 231). These queries may mirror some of the apprehensions and dilemmas in which Egyptian individuals found themselves when crafting, exchanging, evaluating and revering the statue of a deity. Through the narrative of a mythic and literal journey of one famous image, the Sinhala Buddha, Tambiah reveals again the importance of contextual or situational understandings in the construction of knowledge, history and embodied experience. The Buddha statue as "a palladium is a product of the circumstances of its making" and the authenticity attributed to it by its makers, sponsors and patrons. As he rightly asserts, "history is embedded and objectified in it" (Tambiah 1984: 241). The sedimented presence of the divine, having its own agency, in turn inflects and influences human actors and events and this is recursively registered in the object.

Statue Lives

This begs the question, how does one make a god? What are the steps in the transition from mere matter to divine materiality? Within the

Hindu world the sculptor makes a bronze following the lost wax method, a priest swaddles the wax model in cloth, places it upon a bed of grain, performs a series of oblations, and recites mantras evoking the deity. The wax effigy is returned to the artisan who encases it in clay, the priest then repeats the process of wrapping and offering prayers. The clay mold is fired and filled with molten metal. Immediately after the bronze image is freed from its mold additional mantras are said that specifically invoke the deity. Consequently there is never a time when the image exists as an unconsecrated object; it enters the world through a series of ritual practices. The next phase involves an awakening of the image that is reminiscent of Egyptian practices directed toward the statue as well as the mummified body of the deceased. The priest "opens" the eyes of the statue with a golden needle and opens the other apertures with a chisel (Davis 1997: 35). These statues are powerful direct instantiations that are both transcendent and immanent. Davis goes as far as documenting

Figure 4.7 Sumanta Pal sculpting a *murthi* of Saraswati. Kagajipara, 1995. From Glassie (1999), courtesy of Henry Gassie.

a fascinating British court case where a stolen Shiva statue (or rather Shiva himself) appeared in court as a plaintiff, acting as a "juristic person" to sue for the return of his image (1997: 223). The defense countered that England, as a Christian country, could not accept the fact that foreign gods could bring suit. Ultimately Shiva won his case and was returned to his native India.

Similar to Hindu forging of the deity, a number of ritual practices unfold at every stage of the manufacture and installation, sacralizing the entire creation of the Buddha. First, the place where the metal is poured must be appropriately decorated and consecrated and a sacralized statue of Buddha himself must be present. Numerous ritual articles are required, as are appropriate chants and astrological alignments. The statue is then refined and polished while monks empower, or *phra khlnag*, the statue through meditation and another group of monks chant continuously. Finally a celebratory meal and gift-giving ensue in conjunction with the last ritual act, the "opening of the eyes of the statue" by either removing a cloth or cleaning the eyes with oil, accompanied by more chanting (Tambiah 1984: 245–6). The opening or outlining of the eyes was a symbolic act (Fischer-Elfert 1998: 60; Helck 1967: 28) also significant in Egyptian practice. This was accompanied in Egypt by ritual purification, spells and sacrifices, some of which linked back to the early Pyramid Texts (Fischer-Elfert 1998: 53–4). Seeing, speaking and breathing were intricately connected to the life of the Egyptian statue. One 18th Dynasty statue of Amenhotep, son of Hapu, seems to have its own rather complicated life history post-dating its making. Amenhotep was a holder of high office in the Egyptian court, and his statue must have been erected at Karnak before being deposited in the famous cache (see Chapter 1). On a closer observation of the face, it is apparent that the nose had been smashed in antiquity, probably as an aggressive move literally to kill the statue. On another occasion the eyes of statues were also hacked, as if to blind the person or deity to the act and its perpetrator. Some indeterminable time later a skilled hand restored the face and a nose was thus recreated for Amenhotep. In mutilating the nose the statue was unable to breathe, and so in restoring it breath and life were thus restored (Russmann and Finn 1989: 107). The overall effect, however, was not an aesthetic one and the work was neither disguised nor repolished to give the impression of a cohesive, original piece. Piety was the motivation for the restoration, not aesthetics, and so Amenhotep, son of Hapu, was restored to life. As a man who had reached the desirable age of eighty he was a revered ancestor who undoubtedly offered wisdom and guidance to successive generations and all those who looked upon him.

Breath and breathing were revered in Pharaonic culture as integral to sustenance: they were likened to communing with the gods and being an active part of earthly life as well as its transcendence. Representations of breath take the form of the life sign, or ankh, being held at the nose often or emanating from divine rays. From this perspective the invisible became tangible, albeit through symbolic means. Breath equaled life. This was particularly salient for the dead individual in mummy form, which also has some striking parallels to the breathing of the statue. Since the living body breathed, the perfected, mummified body also acquired the function through ritualistic practices performed by priests, usually referred to as the Opening of the Mouth (Lichtheim 1976: 120): *My mouth is given to me, my mouth is opened by Ptah with that chisel of metal, with which he opened the mouth of the gods.* Some seventy-five scenes representing the Opening of the Mouth ritual, including the anointed rites of sacrifice and installation in the funerary context, are preserved from the New Kingdom. The attendant rituals can be classified as belonging to three actions: revival, offerings, and reintegration into the cosmos (Fischer-Elfert 1998: 1). In the Theban tomb of Rekhmire scenes include purification with liquids, purification with natron and incense, touching the mouth of the statue with the little finger, then with a sacred adze, polishing by craftsmen, and then final delivery. It is striking that this particular ritual could be performed both on the mummy and on a statue of the deceased, signifying their parallelism as receptacles of the embodied self. The third register displays ritual butchering, presentation of food offerings, and the Opening of the Mouth ceremony with the ritual tool and presenting of the deceased's statue to his son, the father–son relationship forming the crucial nexus within the private ritual (Helck 1967: 29). This conferred power to infuse an image, generation after generation, linking between the notion that both mummy and statue were transformed into entities with potential lives. Once the mouth of an image had been touched, that image could operate as the receptacle of the *ka* and could house the *ba*, thus providing the material entity for eternal life, as did the mummified body (Forman and Quirke 1996: 32). The Egyptian word for sculptor refers specifically to the cult of the dead, *he who keeps alive*; and that used for making sacred images, *ms*, was the same as that used to signify birth. The fourth register in Rekhmire's tomb shows his son, the Opening of the Mouth ritual with an instrument, touching the mouth with the little finger, a second slaughter scene, presenting the heart and haunch of meat, and a final Opening of the Mouth with a sacred adze fashioned from meteoric material (Hodel-Hoenes 2000: 172). All of these gestures ensure that Rekhmire could breathe, that his mouth was symbolically open, after the actual sealing of the body during mummification rites. Both statue and mummy were rigid, impermeable and impenetrable beings, both potent and both in need of breath that had to be symbolically constituted. While technologically replete, both statue and mummy required the requisite rituals performed by initiated persons to bring their next state of being to fruition.

Private rituals, though related, were at variance to royal or divine examples of the ritual (Helck 1967: 28). To the north of the temple of Amun at Karnak, between the enclosure of Tuthmosis III and that of Tuthmosis I, lies an area of rooms and magazines (Traunecker 1989). In the first room of this suite, designated Room 2, the south wall portrays Tuthmosis III returning from the Retenu campaign (Syria), presiding over the journey of a sacred barque and performing the Opening of the Mouth rite upon the divine figure on the prow of the barque. He approaches the ram and holds the adze close to the mouth, as if enlivening it like one would a statue or mummy. Behind him, presiding over events, is the deity Ptah. And behind Ptah are the necessary implements for the rite: jars, presumably of natron or incense, as well as another adze. Here the head of the ram, as the insignia of Amun, is doubling as the deity himself. Thus Tuthmosis III is seen performing the ritual of enlivening upon the god himself – a rare if not unique scene with unique implications. The scene depicted in this hall, giving birth and opening the mouth, was connected with much earlier and non-funereal origins of the ritual. It links to the manufacture of divine and royal statues, in the palace workshop or House of Gold, and the animation of those statues by the king of the Old Kingdom (Traunecker 1989: 106). In the archaic ritual the operation was celebrated at dawn, when the sun illuminates the country and bathes it in gold light. Ptah would have been the deity who presided over such events. Traunecker believes that the rooms uncovered at Karnak are probably an analogue to those early examples where similar transformative rites of animation took place, a view bolstered by the images that decorated the walls – for example, festivals, sacred barques, and ritual scenes. The divine objects used in ritual practices were stored in adjacent magazines. This particular representation of the Opening of the Mouth is, in this context, different to the simple liturgy of offerings or purifications, and role of the king is not limited to that ritual practice of animating the divine object in later times. It possessed a very precise meaning: Tuthmosis III is portrayed as both the author of the divine image (sculptor) and of the ritual that animates the statue – by opening the mouth, eyes and ears he thus activates the divine spirit. Through this act, the king infuses in all divine images of the vessel of Amun, and more particularly in the figure of prow, a fragment of the power of Amun (Traunecker 1989: 107). It has even been suggested that the Opening of the Mouth ceremony could also be performed upon the rooms of the temple (Shafer 1997: 7), imbuing the temple with a life of its own and making it cultically functional.

Returning to the initial question, how does one acknowledge the crafting of a god and embed that praxis within the Egyptian cultural sphere? One cannot simply accept historic or ethnographic accounts as analogues without a deeper probing of devotional practice. Individuals have some control over its deities since they are responsible for their objectification. Even if the god is the ultimate author of his resemblance in representations like statues, human agency is necessary at each step in the sequence of causes, instruments and results. The god's presence can be of course anchored in the works of humans and is nonetheless bound to their intentions and this-worldly prosperity. Human capacity to make their simulacra, to encapsulate their likeness, reflects a dispersal of earthly agency, whether in Egyptian or Christian religions. Numerous literate image-worshiping cultures exist today and thus the practice is not confined to "primitive" idol worship. Our reaction, the negative classification of idolatry, is an artifice of Judeo-Christian religion and its proclaimed abhorrence of the image (with the exception of Eastern Orthodox icons). Whether in India or in Egypt we need to think more deeply about the idea that the devotee knows the image of the god is an image, not fabricated flesh and blood, and if the image speaks or moves then this is indeed a miracle. It is a miracle because it is unexpected, yet true belief can be sustained without such occurrences (Gell 1998: 118). In India those statues that bleed or move are considered miraculous because for the most part they are generally not expected to do so. For statues to act or have efficacy in a human sense is remarkable because they are not alive, through maintaining an enlivened appearance: "The image is worshipped because it is neither a person, nor a miraculous machine, but a god" (Gell 1998: 125). There are automata, real or imaginary ones, an example being Egyptian oracles, who have ritual animacy rather than the presumption of biological life. For those present there is a clear demarcation between the two concepts or categorical understandings. Statues may be social others that obey the rules laid down for statues as co-present gods in material form. The question remains: how does an entity possess an intentional psychology without being alive in a biological sense? Paradoxically, Boyer (1996) has argued that non-living objects may be considered to possess these attributes because this is exactly what sets them apart from the mundane: they are counter-intuitive and spectacular. Attention-grabbing objects and spirits can be conscripted to all sorts of social and emotional purposes, but each requires that anthropomorphic assumptions are made in the first place. Religious ontologies require little social transmission to be reproduced from one generation to the next, resulting in local traditions. He asserts that the contradiction of conflating living and non-living beings and their scope for intentionality is what perforce renders religiosity so potent. This some-what circular argument is descriptive not explanatory. Both Boyer and Gell have a tendency to privilege mind and the encasing of mind in religious imagery, a residual of Cartesianism that had little relation to ancient understanding. The idol–temple–mind–body formula is un-doubtedly inappropriate in this context.

What matters most is the embedding of the thing in a social and material network, in specific moments and particular places. Statues perform intelligibly, and since Egyptian representation was highly iconic (not aniconic) the realistic element was devised to capture and enthrall, to render the object more divine, more interiorized, and open up other routes of access. At each level agentic individuals, namely humans, are required within these social networks to facilitate and anchor the efficacy of objects. They provide a concrete locus of engagement between persons and divinities. Gell suggests that we are all natural dualists with a propensity for believing the ghost in the machine. Yet people can imbue things with human-like qualities without mixing their categorical understandings: this entails a fine-tuning of the notion of agency and a local contextual-ization (Gell 1998: 123). Gell specifically draws upon the example of the Egyptian statue in its temple setting, albeit using some rather outmoded scholarship. He concludes that the daily routines, outlined above, entailed the imposition of human agency in a social setting where statues could be rendered objects and subjects, passive and active. Quite rightly, he asserts that actions were neither make-believe nor purely emblematic; rather these were "life-endowing rituals and thus literal transpositions of the means in which we induce agency in social others, in human form" (1998: 134). They were symbolic actions rendered meaningful, deriving from the real or causal outcome of physical interactions. Whether feeding or clothing the god, the efficacy of the divine was interpolated into the relational texture of social praxis, social relations, language and under-standing. Here the indexical object could be seen to exert agency and engage in a double session of representation, for it both portrays and stands in for its prototype (Gell 1998: 98). Egyptian statues were indeed the gods in material form.

five

On Hearing, Phenomenology and Desire

He is driven not merely to awaken congealed life in petrified objects – as in allegory – but also to scrutinize living things so that they present themselves as being ancient, "Ur-historical" and abruptly release their significance.

Adorno on Benjamin, *Prisms*

Some time during the turbulent reign of Rameses III (*c.* 1187–1156) trouble began to loom in the royal harem. Rameses had failed to appoint a woman to the position of Great Royal wife and had similarly failed to name a crown prince who would succeed him to the throne. Thus a plot brewed. One of his wives, Queen Tiye, mobilized her forces and mounted a conspiracy, involving stewards, inspectors, and some women of the harem, along with more powerful individuals including a general, a troop commander in Nubia, a priest, a magician and other functionaries. What she desired was to murder her husband the Pharaoh and install her son Pentawere in his place. From the documentary sources, we know that their attempt failed and some twenty-eight men and an undisclosed number of women were indicted. The records of the trial reveal that all but five individuals were either executed or forced to commit suicide, four of whom were physically mutilated (Ritner 1993: 192). It is the only Egyptian case we know of that deals with prosecution of sorcery. Interesting for our purposes is the role of the material, specifically material substitutes for the bodies of living individuals and their mobilization in achieving magical ends. In the preserved papyri the defendants claimed that they *made gods of wax and some potions for laming the limbs of people;* another claims that the magician *began to make inscribed people of wax.* The manipulation of these objects, along with spells and potions, was intended to exorcise, disturb, lame and enchant the physical being of the King. Moreover, the magician was daring enough to use magical

117

knowledge gleaned from the Pharaoh's own library. Magic, known in more recent times as "the craft" by practitioners, involves the very fabricating practices of employing paste, clay, wax, honey, plaster, stone, wood, in the play of images for affecting change, just as was the case in ancient Egypt. The magician sculpts, models, forms, draws and engraves, today as in antiquity, whether talismans, amulets, figures or spells. Moreover, magical properties are considered to derive from secondary characteristics or conventions such as an object's shape, color, and so on (Mauss 2001: 127). Mimesis, doubling, and representation are all crucial elements of efficacious magical practice.

This chapter looks at specific classes of material culture, groups of objects that have a tacit connection to bodily being, that are either representations of bodies or parts of bodies, that were magically or ritually mobilized to effect change. It also considers the body in death as a fabrication, the shifting and unstable terrain of subject to object status, again calling into question our traditional classifications. Lived experience was palpably changed, or desired to be so, by the crafting and manipulating both of bodies and objects. As argued throughout, many things were *beyond* objects, and while we may categorize them in our own classificatory systems, their Egyptian taxonomies were undoubtedly different. These were considered efficacious objects, with the perceived power to affect the phenomenological lifeworld. They were also potent simulacra for the real. Simulation was no longer a question of imitation or duplication; rather it was a question of substituting the signs of the real for the real, an operation of deterring every real process via its operational double. To dissimulate is to pretend not to have what one clearly has, whereas to simulate is to feign to have what one lacks. One involves presence, the other absence (Baudrillard 1994a: 2–3). In Egypt the pervasive concept of dualism and the double were structuring tropes of an entire culture and each of the objects and simulacra of selves described below were in some way substitutional simulacra or operational doubles in the experience of an unknown future. As if writing about Egyptian subjectivity itself, Baudrillard argues:

> Of all the prostheses that mark the history of the body, the double is doubtless the oldest. But the double is precisely not a prosthesis: it is an imaginary figure, which, just like the soul, the shadow, the mirror image, haunts the subject like his other, which makes it so that the subject is simultaneously itself and never resembles itself again, which haunts the subject like a subtle and always averted death. (Baudrillard 1994a: 95)

Doubling and mimesis were foundational principles and practices for the Egyptians; the representation was a potent stand-in for the human subject and could extend one's being and existence beyond death and into memory. To copy, to forge, to double, to represent was as if the action or state was always in effect, at least that was the underlying desire. In the Egyptian case the simulacrum was a utopian desire, part of the cultural imaginary founded on an image that was harmonious and optimistic (Baudrillard 1994a: 121). One need only think of *shabti* figures: ceramic or faience human figures that would be called upon to perform their duties in the afterlife. Their name meant *answerer* and their acquiescence was literally inscribed textually on their bodies. Ideally, from the New Kingdom onwards the deceased would take 365 of these statue workmen, mimetic copies, with them to the next world as substitute laborers. Given their possible recalcitrance or resistance some thirty-six overseer figures were also typically included to keep the workers in line. But there were many other, more fundamental doubles: the mummified body itself was a transubstantiated substitute for the living being, the constituents of the self – the *ba*, *ka*, shadow and name were doppelgangers for the individual, and images of people in two and three dimensions were considered material doubles. In much of Egyptian life and death the potency and presence of the double and the simulacrum were never far away.

On Doubling and Bodily Magic

Michel Serres enquires as to the direct constitutive condition, the foundational materiality that forms the basis of the object that we apprehend as tangible, visible, concrete, formidable, and tacit. And no matter how far we go back in history or prehistory, they are still there (1987: 209). Likewise the homology between bodies and objects is not something specific to modernity, particularly in the sphere of construction and consumption. Aesthetics of the body, now and then, are often steeped in an environment of profusion, corporealities teeming with accessories, gadgets, adornments that are required for the liberation and perfection of the body. Replication of bodies and body parts in New Kingdom Egypt created an exact fantasy of what was needed or desired, in this life and the next. Writing on the curing figures of the Cuna Indians of Colombia, Taussig (1993b) comments that it is the spirit within the wood, not the exterior form, that determines efficacy. But to capture the spirit one has to replicate the image in some form, no matter how schematic. This seems also to be the case in Egypt and is common to other forms of magical and ritual practice. Images of Christian saints still resemble their dead human counterparts, voodoo figures are effigy doubles, Hindu and Buddhist deities are most potent in their human form, and so on. Even for that which is feared most such as demons and devils, the power to represent them, their iconicity, means an accruing of power for those who do the depicting. As Taussig notes, much more could be made of the extensive role of mimesis in ancient societies, and this has become a central aim of the present work. Here we enter the sticky webs of contact and copy, image and action.

As outlined above, one salient Egyptian instance of simulation, the fabrication of *shabtis*, was required for the successful afterlife and formed a strategic utopian vision for all those who could afford them. *Shabtis* were simulated workers, they had hoes, grain baskets, a yoke and water pots appended to their bodies, as if always at the ready to complete their agricultural tasks. Beginning in the New Kingdom, *shabtis* were viewed as servants of their owner and when these figures were commissioned and sold they were described in the bill of sale as *male and female slaves* (Taylor 2001: 114). Linguistically the word *shabti* was derived from the verb "to answer" – that iterates the agency, however limited, of the anthropomorphic figure and its embodied state. Apart from their potential animation, *shabti* figures were usually inscribed with a potent spell, an example being that from the Book of the Dead, spell 6:

> *O shabti, allotted to me, if I be summoned or I be detailed to do any work which has to be done in the realm of the dead; if indeed obstacles are implanted for you therewith as a man at his duties, you shall detail yourself for me on every occasion of making arable the fields, of flooding the banks or of conveying sand from west to east; "Here I am," you shall say.*

Here I am also concerned with what Davis (1996: 3) has eloquently labeled the problem of passing from matter to meaning, especially when meaning erupts in materiality. For Davis this exploration requires delving into the replicatory histories within our archaeological grasp that lie at the very heart of culture. Its constitution is no less than the history of a suite of socially coordinated replicatory histories.

Tangible mimetic doubles such as statuettes or images, besides offering substitute labor, could be mobilized within the magical repertoire to exact revenge or desire upon the enemies of Egypt. From early in Pharaonic history the representation of the bound prisoner occupied a particularly volatile category. Predynastic images on stone palettes show bound captives in bodily postures of submission and humiliation, a theme duplicated right through into the famous scenes that publicly adorned New

Kingdom temples in Thebes. Bodies are crushed underfoot, tortured and shackled, foreign bodies mutilated in the act of subduing and counting the corporeal booty (Meskell and Joyce 2003: 149–150). By being materialized these images of the defeated, and of the enemy as a category, instantiate the unequal power of empire and periphery, as well as the ethnic superiority of the Egyptians. It is the power of the copy to influence what it is a copy of. A direct power was extracted from the copy and thus by producing the representation it was thought to transfer and confer a similar potency upon their Egyptian makers, the victors, who were ultimately one and the same.

Figure 5.1 Canes depicting bound African prisoners from the tomb of Tutankhamun. Courtesy of the Griffith Institute, Oxford. Carter No. 048b.

On the domestic front the images of bound captives were common motifs incorporated on royal furniture, ritual objects, luxury goods, and statues, and were represented on public architecture. Many famous examples stem from the tomb goods belonging to Tutankhamun. The enemies of Egypt, glossed as the Nine Bows, represented the traditional enemies of the Egyptian state. Placed at the base of chairs, stools, podiums and statue plinths (Ritner 1993: 120), they were palpably crushed under foot, under the person of the King himself in an ongoing set of bodily postures. This iconographic tradition was pushed further and the same enemies were often inscribed on palace floors or upon the base of the Pharaoh's sandals, physically walking over the presence of his enemies and all iterations of chaos, they were literally under foot. It was said of the Pharaoh that *all foreign lands are under your sandals*. Royal canes also bore the sculpted bodies of enemies at the curved handle (Figure 5.1), specifically Nubians, who could thus be strangled by Tutankhamun as he grasped the cane throughout his official duties. The bodily gestures of control and domination over the material manifestations of the enemy suggest the importance of the representational world as a desired parallel for the experiential world. Returning to our dialogue with Gell and his particular construal of object agency, here materialization would promote the overcoming of difficulty, which dovetails nicely with these specific Egyptian ritual objects. Alternatively it may make for a better description of magical practice through material means; that is, the overcoming of resistance and inertia. Art objects, he suggests, are characteristically *difficult*, they fascinate, compel and entrap as well as provide visual pleasure (1998: 23). Their specificity, intransigence and oddity are crucial in their efficacy as social instruments. Struggles for control are played out in an enchainment of intention, instrument and result through the materiality of the object or its representational qualities.

Egyptian Magic was materialized by overt bodily practices such as licking or swallowing, but also by the physical practices of binding, burning, knotting or smashing. A pertinent example of the materialization of magic, specifically the ritual deposition of objects, occurred in the Middle Kingdom fortress at Mirgissa. The deposit consisted of four separate burials of material: 197 red vases and ostraca, inscribed and broken; 437 broken uninscribed red vases; 346 mud figurines, three limestone prisoner figures and part of a fourth; and the remains of a human sacrifice (Ritner 1993: 153–4). Given that Mirgissa was a second cataract fortress and an outpost for fending off Nubian incursions, the necessity to provide a magical safeguard was paramount. Looking closely at the material, it is clear that some violence was inflicted upon the limestone figures; their heads were subject to blows while others had holes pierced in the head. Finally, one example was reduced to fragments, a total dissolution of bodily being. More potent was the human skull with its missing mandible and around it traces of red beeswax that probably represented the remnants of melted human figurines. Nearby was the abandoned disarticulated skeleton, the remains identified as Nubian in origin, a human parallel to the magical figurines that were regularly used in execration (Ritner 1993: 162–3). What better substitute than the expendable enemy itself? His body served as a metonym for all Egypt's enemies, although primarily Nubians, and he too became an artefact of magical practice, a thing deployed to direct the course of the future.

Representation of the human body in all its corporeal specificity was required for Egyptian magical intercession; one had to materialize or at least speak the name of the enemy or the desired, if one was to legibly control them. One can decipher a similar suite of material requirements and techniques in the mortuary sphere, the crucial domain of ritual practice that extended the existence of the individual into an afterlife trajectory. The attenuated physicality of this world and its concomitant

Figure 5.2 Curse figures from the Middle Kingdom. Courtesy of the British Museum, EA 56928, EA 56912, EA 56913, EA 56914.

physical limitations had to be transcended by magical means, by the instantiation of a new and more durable physicality designed to overcome the frailty of the flesh. I argue that this is a form of transubstantiation, perhaps culturally the originary process that many other religions and cultures have subsequently copied and replicated. Baudrillard takes this transfiguration into the modern period, examining the mummy (both subject and object) of Rameses II that was brought from Cairo to Paris, famously receiving the red carpet treatment at the Orly airport. The Pharaoh's mummy is of inestimable wealth because it guarantees that accumulation has meaning (Baudrillard 1994a: 10). His mummified body required further saving from the ravages of time, and even the West was seized with the panic that they may not be able to save the symbolic order.

Embodied Materiality: Subjects to Objects

Textually and archaeologically we can apprehend constructions of the embodied Egyptian self through the material world. In the New Kingdom images and objects operated as personal biographies for the individual through mimetic and iterative processes. Individuals could be represented or doubled through statuary, images and wall paintings. Mimesis can be read here as the nature that culture uses to create second nature – in this case the living body. This second nature is foundering and highly unstable, spiraling between nature and culture, essentialism and constructionism, forging new identities and offering dramatic new possibilities (Taussig 1993b: 252). We see this creatively concretized in Egypt where the dead individual represented an Osiris – a dead, but deified being capable of being reborn in the next world. In corporeal terms the body of the living subject, through a series of bodily processes, becomes an object – at the nexus between the living world and the next, a type of artefact in and of itself. The body of the dead individual was more than a human carapace; in its mummified state it existed as the physical remains of a human being albeit transformed by technology into an/other sort of product. The body in death and its inherent partibility formed a major cultural focus, explicitly the bodily organs performed as a gestalt for the entire person. In death, the body was a plastic entity that had to be manipulated before its successful entry into the next world since the unique characteristics of the individual and his/her narrative biography also persisted beyond death. The integrity of the bodily self, its material representation in statue or visual form, and the existence of the person were inseparably tied together.

Central to Egyptian funerary ideology was an obsession with preserving the living body through and beyond the zone of death, coupled with an attendant dread of material decay. Decomposition of the corpse is a source of anxiety that lies at the heart of many cultures, requiring the materiality of the dead to be manipulated and made perfect in appearance. In Egyptian language bodily decay was referred to as *transitoriness, to consume, to dry up, to perish, to become maggoty, to go bad, to flow away, and to smell* (Zandee 1960: 56–60). Decomposition and decay voids the corpse of its signs and its social force of signification. It de-personifies the individual leaving it as nothing more than a substance. For the community who countenance that decay, the process reinforces the fragility of life and the existential terror of its own symbolic decomposition. One interpretation posits that the Egyptians sought to abjure or defeat death through artificiality: specifically via elaborate bodily rituals and preparations the elite sought to evade the unbearable moment when flesh becomes nothing but flesh, and ceases to be part of the embodied whole. At the point of death, the motionless body becomes a thing, now deprived of the capabilities of living individuals. Magical spells were required explicitly to bring those functions back to the corpse, to make the dead body akin to its living counterpart. A series of opposition spells in the Book of the Dead were needed to stave off the process of perishing, to confer physical perfection and activate bodily facilities (Faulkner 1985: 153):

> *Such is he who is decayed; all his bones are corrupt, his flesh is slain, his bones are softened, his flesh is made into foul water, his corruption stinks and turns into many worms . . . who kills the body, who rots the hidden one, who destroys a multitude of corpses, who lives by killing the living . . . You shall possess your body; you shall not become corrupt, you shall not have worms, you shall not be distended, you shall not stink, you shall not become putrid, I will not become worms . . . I have not decayed, there is no destruction in my viscera, I have not been injured, my eye has not rotted, my skull has not been crushed, my ears are not deaf, my head has not removed itself from my neck, my tongue has not been taken away, my hair has not been cut off, my eyebrows have not been stripped, no injury has happened to me. My corpse is permanent, it will not perish nor be destroyed in this land forever.*

Thomas Mann's famous description of Egypt was indeed apposite – "your dead are gods and your gods dead" (Mann 1978: 510). Mummies continue to prove powerfully ambiguous entities, they are things and beyond things, subjects and objects, physical and cognitive categories, perceptible and apperceptible (Armstrong 1981: 43). The signifier of the mummy, oscillating between human and object status, has long captured the imagination of cultural theorists. The body is not reducible to a system of signs; its materiality in the mortuary sphere was a source for the extension of individual being and potential biography and ensured that it reclaimed the position of a privileged subject. For Baudrillard (1993: 180), the decayed body was an abject sign of mortality in this world and subsequently the afterlife, and of the non-divine status of the individual. Numerous cultures find it necessary to ward off death, to smother it in artificiality in order to evade the unbearable moment when flesh returns to flesh and ceases to be a sign. And for Derrida (1987: 43), while the mummy bore the trace of the individual, preserved the identity and made it visible and material, it was scarcely readable. It was not a matter of continuing the lifelike body of the original subject, but transforming it into another sort of object altogether. It was eternally self-referential and yet only a trace, a trace soon to be lost, residing at the interstices of subject and object. More negatively, Andy Warhol exhorted that being embalmed, with one's organs separately wrapped and then interred in a pyramid, was the worst of fates – "I want my machinery to disappear" (quoted in Taylor 1997: 234). Through time-consuming practices of encultura-tion the "natural" body with its biological realities had to be transcended through mummification and sarcophagic practices, resulting in a very specific form of transubstantiation. In an Egyptian context the body becomes objectified and transmuted into the divine, but it is not the *thingness* that characterizes the fabrication of statues or stelae, although some overlap in the efficacy of all representations of the deceased might be posited. We see how this ancient fascination with the dead body and its effigies is transmuted into the present, into altogether different spheres of representation and consumption, as outlined in Chapter 7.

Death and its attendant rituals were anchored in materiality. Extended or distributed selfhood was not simply contingent upon arcane ritual practices that inhabited the ethereal, it was reliant on the physicality of the body and its propensity for fabrication and prosthesis. Bodies and body parts in Egyptian mortuary culture could be apprehended as pros-theses, replacing the frailties of the body, and thought of as supplementing the body and co-extensive to it, thereby extending the self through material means. Mummification was tantamount to preservation of the body through its violation: one had to attack the physical fabric of the body before a new permanence could be imparted. The human body was never considered naturally immutably divine and thus required sub-stantive modification or construction. In some myths even the gods were not considered immutable (reflected, for example, in the dismemberment of Osiris), and thus they too required transformative rituals. Egyptian mummies aspired to a perfectly preserved and often embellished image of the deceased, transmuting the body into a simulacrum of itself. The transubstantiated body *was* the person, the self, and yet only a remnant of its earthly being. The final product was a newly crafted corporeality, hermetically sealed, free from imperfections, orifices, openings or fissures that might allow demonic forces to seep into the body and thus the self. This new body must bear no trace of its nature in the realm of death, it must be clean, proper and impenetrable in order to be fully symbolic (Kristeva 1982: 102). In this new guise of perfection it should be presented as free from earthly disfigurement where even the mark of the embalmer is masked. Although many cultural practices were deployed to deflect the force of death, the difficulty lay in reconciling the abhorrence of bodily intervention with the explicit requirements of fabricating a new type of body through artificial means. Egyptian notions of death operated within both monistic and dualistic ideologies simultaneously: the monist perspective regarded death as a necessary condition for eternal existence whereas a dualistic one recognized death as the enemy of life and some-thing to be feared. The first is based on religious reflection, the second grounded in the materiality of death and personal experience of the natural world.

When physicality failed the individual in death and perfection was deemed lacking or called for enhancement, prosthetic techniques were implemented to provide the requisite material effect. In death the corporeal presence of the person had to resemble the ideal living state, devoid of all physical shortcomings or effects of aging. Missing limbs could be substituted, and numerous prostheses have survived. Extreme care was taken to give the body a lifelike appearance even after bodily damage or loss of parts, using wood and other artificial substances. Other individual imperfections could be addressed through cosmetic pro-cedures. Balding could be remedied by interweaving additional hair, hair and nails could be hennaed, and black paint could be applied to hairlines and eyebrows. The corpse was then wrapped, in the sense of making hidden, and the practice itself may have been considered a sacred act, bestowing a mystery and sanctity to the body. Amongst the dense layers of amuletic linen were placed amulets, efficacious ritual materials representing deities, symbols, body parts and the like, usually inscribed with protective spells. The body of Tutankhamun revealed in excess of 140 amulets strewn throughout his linen wrappings (Figure 5.3). The body was then encased in a wooden or stone coffin that conferred protection and rejuvenation, harking back to the myth of Osiris. In one

Figure 5.3 Uncovering the body of Tutankhamun with numerous layers of jewelry, amulets, and ritual paraphernalia. Courtesy of the Griffith Institute, Oxford.

version of the myth, Seth discovered the exact measurements of his brother, made an elaborate box that only Osiris could fit, and lured him to try it out for size. When he was inside, Seth secured the lid and threw it into the Nile, rather than placing it in a tomb. Inadvertently Seth's actions assured Osiris eternal life since the coffin ultimately guaranteed continuous preservation and existence (te Velde 1967: 83). The body of Osiris was later dismembered and dispersed, and numerous spells were needed before Isis and Nepthys could reunite the body parts, underscoring the Egyptian preoccupation with partibility as a route to wholeness. The coffin stands as a regenerative structure, a time machine that defies the limits of the earthly life cycle and promises eternal being. The goddess Nut, depicted arched above the deceased on numerous coffin lids, was also integral to its materiality and power, signifying the daily cycle of the sun reborn through her body as a parallel for the deceased. Nut is the vehicle or womb that births the deceased in a spiral of new becomings. For the Egyptians the living body's cycle was likened to the cycle of the known universe and existence itself.

We have some documentary insight about the processes by which artisans crafted and decorated coffins in the village of Deir el Medina. Demand was obviously high and the skilled workers were well placed to supply the community. Carpenters and draughtsmen like Bakenwerl and Horisheri worked together, the latter decorated wooden objects in return for unfinished furniture and mortuary objects from the former. Some of the finished coffins went to relatives of Bakenwerl, others were sold to ordinary villagers. The carpentry work that the workman Bakenwerl gave to the draughtsman Horisheri is listed below (McDowell 1999: 81–2):

1 plastered, wooden debet-box	*makes 8 deben*
1 afdet-box	*makes 2 deben*
1 coffin, it belonged to me as wood	*makes 15 deben*
1 small wooden bed, it belonged to me as wood	*makes 15 deben*
1 small wooden bed, it belonged to me as wood,	
* the ebony belonged to me via his son, Nebnefer*	*makes 20 deben . . .*
The decoration that is with the workman Bakenwerl:	
funerary couch of his mother (?)	*makes 12 deben*
the outer coffin of An	*makes 20 deben*
the small coffin of An, given to the builder Paaoemone	*makes 10 deben*
again, making another one for her	*makes 10 deben*
the coffin he gave in exchange for the cloak in Thebes	*makes 10 deben*
its inner coffin	*makes 4 deben . . .*

Coffins were clearly alienable commodities, typically made by specialists and circulated through regular exchange processes and networks. Despite their immeasurable symbolic weight and ritual significance, their inherent technical specificity required an expertise that was external to ordinary individuals. Following Marx, coffins came to represent, in themselves, a social hieroglyph. As guarantors of the self and material reflections of the individual and their trajectory after death, they problematize the traditional distinction between commodities and gifts and their respective alienability: Egyptian coffins were dependent, subject-like and strongly demarcated by quality; the notion of the in-dwelling spirit drives them; they were intimately tied to the person, even an extension of the person and their biographical project. While everyone knew and appreciated the manufactured nature of coffins, they retained their supra-object status and, as Godelier would extol, they represent one of the enshrined material foundations for Egyptian society.

Returning to the body itself, Egyptian predilections for duality in the somatic sphere are reflected linguistically in the distinct words for the living body (living form or appearance) and that of the corpse (embalmed body, mummy, or the body after the performance of specific rites). Yet it was not the living body itself that was expected to become life-like again or physically active. Rather, the body provided the place of conjunction for all the physical and non-physical elements of the person (Taylor 2001: 16). All the accoutrements of death, the copies of the individual (statues, canopic jars), representations (wall paintings, texts), assistants (*shabtis*), structured simulacra (coffins, masks, cartonnage), physical enhancements and ritual magic were focused toward physical completeness and material perfection in the next life. If one could copy, simulate, replicate or double through magical and material means, then one could control and direct the potential trajectory of individuals, whether that entailed enemies, loved ones, the deceased, and so on. The desire, indeed bodily desire, to do so was a central component in Egyptian culture, a characteristic that infused much of their quotidian existence and their conceptualization of death and the hereafter. These iterations also spilled over to the divine realm, to the invocation of the gods and goddesses who had desirable powers that were so often needed and called upon in the lives of ordinary people.

Material Listening

Hearing and seeing, in sensorial terms, put individuals in direct contact with the physical world and sometimes beyond its confines, whether connecting to a deity, a thing, or an experience. This connectivity is thus part of the mobilization of specific material objects toward attaining particular outcomes. Yet at the same time an ambiguous power is unleashed; namely, that the power to represent the world is also the power to deceive, misrepresent and mask (Taussig 1993b: 43). This returns to the notion of technology as a strategy for change, and in this specific sense the objects discussed below (stelae, sculptures, votives) are sensuously linked to ancestor busts or stelae (Chapter 3), statues (Chapter 4), and other ritually charged objects and practices combined. Votive objects could be seen as gifts in a Maussian sense, although gifts are not really gifts if a suite of obligations is extended forward in time. Establishing a form of credit between mortals and deities, the votive either materializes gratitude while soliciting ongoing protection, or extols the virtues of the divine and thus invokes these qualities to be bestowed upon the supplicant during their lifetime. The impossibility of the gift is bound in its associations of reciprocity, obligatory fulfillments, and desires. It is a bond without a bond and a bind that entails debt, credit, contract and exchange (Derrida 1992: 27). Votive stelae, the first set of objects that I consider, were dedicated to the goddess Meretseger and come specifically from domestic and ritual contexts in the Ramesside period (Andreu 2002: 275). Meretseger ironically had the epithet, *she who loves silence*, but was also clearly a deity disposed to listening. She was patron goddess of the Theban Mountain and literally personified the Western Peak that surmounts the Valley of the Kings. Deir el Medina residents constructed numerous small shrines and votive chapels from which to venerate her. She could be represented purely in cobra form or as a hybrid body incorporating a female body and the head of a snake. As a chthonic deity, her primary sanctuary was a cave near the Valley of the Queens. Additionally, the villagers of Deir el Medina placed three-dimensional serpents near their doorways, while the inhabitants of Memphis manufactured clay sculptures of cobras with miniature offering bowls for their households (Quirke 1992: 116). Memphite cobra statuettes number forty-six within a small excavation area, most are fragmentary and all but one are ceramic. Given the location of Memphis, they are probably manifestations of the Lower Egyptian goddess Renenutet rather than Meretseger (Giddy 1999).

At some time during the Ramesside period a man called Neferabu commissioned a stela to petition the goddess, in the acknowledgement that he transgressed in some way, and had received what he viewed as a punishment in life. He erected the stela to atone for and, at the same time, display gratitude for the ultimate mercy that he experienced.

Meretseger was an implacable deity who was feared and adored in the knowledge that her dual character was beneficent and maleficent. The stela, now in Turin, depicts the goddess as a beautiful trained cobra with an undulant body, her groomed head sporting a divine crown, and accompanied by several small snake pairs intended to contribute to the efficacy of Meretseger as benefactress. As Neferabu entreats the goddess, *so the Peak of the West is merciful when one calls to her.* He presumably erected the stela in one of her peak shrines, reiterating the mimetic association of the goddess with her sacred landscape. The main sequence of biographic events is as follows (McDowell 1999: 98).

> *Made by the servant in the Place of Truth Neferabu, justified, an ignorant man,*
> *without sense. I did not know good from bad when I made the transgression*
> *against the Peak, and she punished me, I being in her hand night and day. I sat*
> *on bricks like a pregnant woman while I called out for breath without its coming*
> *to me. I humbled myself to the Peak of the West, great of power, to every god and*
> *goddess . . . Beware of the Peak, because a lion is in her. The Peak, she strikes*
> *with the strike of a fierce lion when she is after the one who transgresses against*
> *her.*

The creation of a stela is in part a metaphorical or mimetic act, one of fabricating a material embodiment of supplication and rendering that action permanent in limestone. Metaphor or metonymy is at once a source of clarity and an enigma that has the facility for unlimited semiosis, dependent upon the viewer's powers of imagination and contextual knowledge (D'Alleva 2001: 89). It was deemed necessary not simply to pray to the deity, but to physically establish a permanent testimonial in the form of the stela. Acts of personal piety such as these were popular during the Ramesside period as individuals moved closer to the possibility of contacting and communing with the gods themselves rather than simply being reliant upon intermediaries who might do their bidding in official temple practice. This form of observance and petitioning still went on, as the documents suggest, yet the personal route was obviously more direct and immediate, as Neferabu might himself have testified. Meretseger was indeed a listener.

The second votive stela (Figure 5.4) was dedicated around 1170 BC by a Deir el Medina scribe called Amennakhte. He is pictured to the right, kneeling, while the goddess is seated to the left holding a lotus flower. Neither figure has their eyes depicted, which links oddly to the accompanying inscription (Parkinson 1999: 159):

Praises for your spirit, Meretseger, Mistress of the West, by the scribe of the Place of Truth, Amennakhte true-of-voice: he says: "Be praised in peace, O Lady of the West, Mistress who turns herself into grace! You made me see darkness in the day. I shall declare your power to other people. Be gracious to me in your grace!"

Text and object together may be read in several ways, as Richard Parkinson suggests. A literal reading is that Amennakhte suffered from blindness, eye problems being very common and a constant fear for the artisans at Deir el Medina. Failure to render the eyes, however, may provide a tantalizing clue. Another interpretation is metaphorical, that blindness was a signifier of some other affliction or misfortune. The importance of sensory life is mimicked in concrete terms and the capacity to heal or cure depends on out-doubling doubling. Through the creation of the stela, activated by invocations and prayers, Amennakhte instantiates the doubling by means of mimetic magic, what Taussig refers to as out doubling the doubleness of the world (1993b: 118). Votive stelae were material

Figure 5.4 Votive stela of Amennakhte dedicated to the goddess Meretseger, 20th Dynasty from Deir el Medina. Courtesy of the British Museum, EA 374.

contracts between mortals and gods that replicated present situations, ameliorated those conditions, and speculated on a better future. They were material contracts in a system of exchange between worlds. Via mimesis, they represented the desire for a cultural overcoming of one's natural condition. Mimesis, as "an unadorned human faculty . . . is a capacity that alerts one to the contractual element of the visual contract with reality" (Taussig 1993b: 70), albeit concretely grounded in a specific historicity. As the nature that culture uses to make second nature, mimesis cannot be outside of history, just as history cannot lie outside of the mimetic faculty. This challenges both essentialist and constructionist visions of the world and begs a certain mutual constitution and recursive understanding.

Other Egyptian objects more schematically and literally *doubled* the capacity of hearing. How might one materialize the phenomenological experience of hearing and also of listening? This returns to the fundamental question: when is an object not an object, or, more succinctly, how is the power and character of the original transmuted to the copy? The Egyptian word for hearing, *sḏm*, was written with the hieroglyph of the ear. Hearing was a conceptually significant faculty because it was synonymous to divine responses to human needs. In the Ramesside example illustrated (Figure 5.5), a man called Mahwia commissioned a stela with some forty-four ears arranged in parallel formation, and they were originally painted red and blue. This time the object is dedicated to Ptah (Parkinson 1999: 67): *Praises to the spirit of Ptah, lord of Truth, great of strength, the Hearer.* Found in the temple of Ptah at Memphis, this form of agentic material culture has been found in shrines and temples across Egypt. Other deities known for their listening abilities included Hathor, Amun, Horus, Thoth and Isis (Wilkinson 1992: 45). Some, of course, are uninscribed, which may imply poorer patrons or ready-made pieces. The number of ears depicted could range from one to 376; many examples show paired ears, and many are painted red, blue, green, black, or yellow (Pinch 1993: 248). They were usually installed in the vicinity of state temples, but others have been discovered in household shrines and funerary contexts. The largest group of stelae have been found together in the Ptah temple at Memphis during the reign of Rameses II.

Votive ears often carved in wood were also offered at sanctuaries such as the Hathor shrine at Deir el Bahri (Figure 5.6). At Deir el Medina model ears were found in a cache of votive objects from the 19th Dynasty, other were uncovered in the courtyard of a 19th Dynasty funerary chapel (Pinch 1993: 246). Crude and unpainted, the illustrated example was neither part of a larger statue nor intended to be (Parkinson 1999: 66). Examples

Figure 5.5 Limestone stela of Mahwia with forty-four ears, found in the foundations of the Temple of Rameses II, Memphis, probably 18th Dynasty. Courtesy of the British Museum, EA 1471.

of ears were crafted from stone, wood, faience, metal, and so on. Model ears in blue-glazed materials were common at Deir el Bahri; some were right ears and others left. They tended to be mold-made with few details and some are even shown pierced. Details, like piercing, made the ears more ear-like to look at, more real somehow, and more identifiable. Moreover, their visual power conveyed the message without necessary inscription, which must have been significant for all those individuals without literate skills. Offering of such a fetishized body part might signify a prayer offered in the hope of curing deafness, or an imploring of the goddess to hear a prayer, or even a token of acknowledgement that prayers were indeed answered. Since these classes of objects appear similar, scholarly interpretation of their function and meaning has been collapsed and unitary explanations have been sought. Our two inscribed examples suggest a medical or moral problem for which divine intervention was sought. Neferabu may have transgressed in some moral sphere, whereas Amennakhte (whose problem was eye-related) probably suffered physically. In offering these material devotions individuals may have wanted to retain these faculties on earth and perpetuate them in the afterlife, or ears may have been metaphors for the divine and were thus painted the colors of the gods. One could be shown adoring the ear as one would a divinity, and texts also implore the *hearing ear* of specific deities. A blue ear could represent Amun, a green ear would be a signifier of Osiris or Ptah, and so on. The gods are, after all, the ones *who hear petitions*, as the accompanying texts exemplify. Linking to the subject of Chapter 4, the statue representations of royal individuals like Ahmose-Nefertari, Tuthmosis III, Tuthmosis IV, Rameses II, and Rameses IV were similarly inscribed: *hearing the supplicant* (Pinch 1993: 251).

Looking back to Mauss, one might posit the workings of a form of sympathetic magic: by representing corporeal materiality individuals could evoke the phenomenology of hearing and listening to entice the

Figure 5.6 A wooden ear from the Hathor shrine at Deir el Bahri, late New Kingdom. Courtesy of the British Museum, EA 41077.

deity to both hear and listen to the petitioner. In this manner ears and ear stelae operated as portals, material conduits between worlds and experiences. They could be viewed similarly to a host of other classes of objects, whether ancestor busts, stelae or statues. Of course we should factor in multiple meanings for these potent body parts, since we cannot be sure how all persons viewed the materiality of rendering ears, eyes, and so on. The replication of eyes may have the signification of being merciful or looking favorably upon the petitioner, a direct connection between mortal and divine. Body parts were multivalent signifiers that could speak to the senses, but also to individuals, divinities, properties, and so on. They were objects that invoked action on the part of the divine but cannot be construed as primary agents. They may, however, be considered as technology in a similar vein to the ancestral images. Not specific to modernity, technology is an innovation that signifies creative inventiveness and brings itself into being (Strathern 2001: 259). By imagining entities or containing them one can concretize habitation and dwelling; it is a strategy of making the phenomenal world literal. In Egypt, too, we might think about *inhabiting technology,* the special techniques of habitation and indwelling that serve as augmentation. Statues, stelae, and effigies could be posited extensions of social agents or as innovations that extend and substitute for human actions and capacities. But human intention has to first give them life and potential. Following Gell, the enchantment of technology is the spell cast over us via the power of technical processes (Strathern 2001: 261). Patenting or doubling, as Strathern outlines, is a classic case of this enchanted technology. Patenting requires a body, an originary concept has to be embodied in the artefact or device, a concrete manifestation of the idea or innovation that contains it. The patent protects the idea, the original innovation or being, and is the materialization of an inventive step. Moreover, patents do not simply acknowledge creativity and originality – they transform them into something that works, that is knowledge, by simultaneously attaching them to and detaching them from the originator (Strathern 2001: 266). This is how people essentially fabricate a notion of the world and their place within it.

Body Doubles

Writing this book in New Mexico, it is difficult to resist looking comparatively at a pervasive body of votive material culture, *milagros*, like those donated at the famous pilgrimage site of Santuario de Chimayó north of Santa Fe. *Milagros* depict body parts and increasingly include other objects of desire of modernity such as houses and cars. *Milagro* means "miracle" and these *ex votos* are materialized sedimentations of prayer and petitions that are offered to God. This is a common practice in Mexico and other parts of Latin America (Egan 1991), construed as Catholic, although a clear pagan substrate can be detected. In Brazil, with its African influence, *milagros* are worn as amulets and talismans around the neck or wrist and are considered material intercedents with the saints. In Guatemala they are used as prayer offerings but similarly have a talismanic function and are worn as part of women's jewelry. They are made of numerous materials: gold, silver, tin (see Figure 5.7), lead, wood, bone or wax. Ready-mades are often sold outside the church, although individuals may fashion their own images. As emblems of desire they are attached or tied to images of saints, altars or crosses and thus rendered permanent and ever present. The meanings associated to these body fragments or wholes are multiple and present us with the same

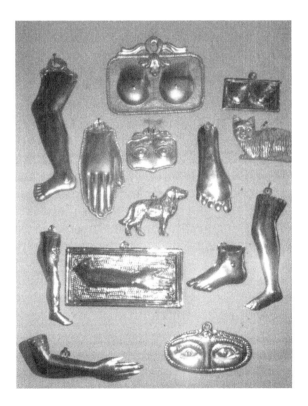

Figure 5.7 Tin *milagros* of body parts, Santa Fe, New Mexico. Photo by the author.

interpretive ambiguity that we face with Egyptian votives. Body parts may be offered in the hopes of attaining a cure, or represent specific characteristics of the part, such as eyes that see, ears that hear or hearts that love or feel, not dissimilar to the Egyptian context previously outlined. Miniatures can perform as a gesture of gratitude for a prayer answered or yet to be fulfilled, they can symbolize hope, thanks for something healed, a desire to be protected, or simply a desire. The materiality of the offering also serves to personalize the dedicant's relationship with a special saint. By directing focus upon the mortification of the flesh, the partibility and frailty of human corporeality, the petitioner contemplates the transcendence of the soul. And by either making or viewing the body in pieces the dedicator is impelled to confront the human anatomy as a landscape of suffering, one that we desire to overcome in this world and the next. One could say that all *ex votos* provide palliatives for the human condition.

The use of *milagros* is an ancient custom in the Hispanic world, and is generally considered to stretch back to an ancient Iberian tradition (fifth to first centuries BC): these are small bronze examples that parallel contemporary examples. Although the custom is not as prevalent as it once was, the use of *milagros* has continued to hold a significant place in folk culture throughout rural areas of Spain (particularly Andalusia, Catalonia and Majorca) and across the Mediterranean, especially in Italy, Crete and Greece where they are called *tamata*. In Greece votives have been traced back to Minoan times to dedications made at Peak sanctuaries (Georgoulake 1997). Reminiscent here are the lead votive miniatures offered to the goddess Artemis Ortheia (Themelis 1994) at her sanctuary site in Sparta. *Milagros* have further attained a privileged position in modernity, whether as a sign of ethnic ritual, diverse Catholicisms, new age affirmation and even in the secular perpetuation of good health. For instance, the breast *milagro*, now patented as jewelry, has attained a life of its own as it symbolizes the spiritual connection between the wearer, health and healing and "represents hope for a lifetime of breast health. For breast cancer survivors The Breast Milagro represents gratitude for survivorship. For all women, wearing The Breast Milagro creates a sense of empowerment, and a manifest connection in our struggle against breast cancer" (http://www.thebreastmilagro.com/ourstory/milagro.htm).

I have often speculated on the connections between traditions, the connectivity between wider Mediterranean practice and its later Christian derivations. The donations of Roman anatomical votives (*donaria*) at cult sanctuaries such as Latium and Campania from the fourth to first centuries BC reveal very large numbers of eyes, ears, limbs, and so on. Votives were donated for reasons of curing, as petitions or thanks, gifts to the gods, symbols of devotion, representations of specific qualities, or desire for well-being (Turfa 1994). So much of Egyptian thinking about judgment, heaven and hell, and so on, have later parallels in Christian belief systems (Meskell 2002). Yet perhaps this is simply the intense desire, common to many cultures, to represent the body and its parts materiality in the hopes of bodily integrity, wholeness and the evasion of aging and mortality. Other hopes, such as that of fertility and sexual potency, have similarly long-lived histories. Egyptian individuals were no different in their specific concerns, bodily and socially, to produce offspring, have successful unions and to be sexually active – in this life and the next (Meskell 2002). It is to these concerns and their material manifestations that I now turn.

At Egyptian shrines such as those of Mirgissa and Timna votive offerings to Hathor, goddess of sexuality, include numerous natural objects that mirror or double for human bodies and their parts. Specifically these are pebbles and fossils that resemble images of women with large breasts or representations of mother and child together. Similarly, in the temple of Satet at Aswan numerous pebbles, mainly in phallic form or resembling pregnant and nursing mothers, have been found within the environs (Dreyer 1986; Pinch 1993: 210). Other forms of natural doubles have been found at Deir el Medina, where numerous limestone nodules have been painted to accentuate the sexualized nature of the shape and intent (Keimer 1940). Here we see another salient blurring of category, that of the natural and cultural, the found and the crafted. Nature itself produces evocative similarities and we, as humans, possess the highest capacities for mimicry and simulation (Benjamin 1979: 65). Some of the reworked nodules exploit the characteristic rounded natural protuberance to accentuate the rounded stomach of the female subjects, making them appear pregnant (generally a taboo representation in Egypt). One evocative example illustrates a nude female with her hands close to the clearly demarcated pubic triangle. These quasi-artefacts are often crude objects, uninteresting to many, yet their importance rests on their mediatory function in a specific ritual context (Gell 1998: 68). While these pebbles and fossils may have existed a priori, they are not embraced within the symbolic realm as such without detailed contextualization and transference of meaning. Performing in another mode of mimesis, we perceive and internalize which forms the basis of the imitation and so we become and create what we apprehend (Benjamin 1968, 1999). By enhancing the natural emulation we produce what we perceive.

Unmistakable models of breasts and genitalia were also offered as votives. Some, in faience, have finely carved detail. Parallel ceramic models of female genitalia have been found in houses at Deir el Medina (Pinch 1993: 211). However, many more votive phalloi have been discovered primarily dedicated to the goddess of sexuality, Hathor. As to why the phallus accrues such power, Lacan argued it was the most "tangible element in the real of sexual copulation," as well as the most symbolic in the literal sense of the term. By virtue of its turgidity it also serves as the image of vital flow as it is transmitted in generation (Lacan 2001: 318–19). Whether we can rethink its power within Egyptian culture is of course debatable, but nonetheless provocative. Ancient Egyptian phallicism was materialized in the everyday, a salient reminder that sexuality infused many aspects of ordinary life, challenging our notions of the discrete taxonomies and sexual semantics that characterize modern Western culture. Phallic objects modeled in clay, wood and stone were common votive offerings in the New Kingdom at sites across Egypt at Deir el Bahri, Deir el Medina, Mirgissa, Timna, and so on. For prudish reasons the early excavators failed to properly document these finds; however, they collected them nonetheless. At Deir el Medina the 19th Dynasty scribe Ramose offered a votive in the form of a stone phallus attached to a plinth dedicated to Hathor in the vicinity of her temple (Pinch 1993: 235). At Deir el Bahri many basket loads of wooden phalloi were found, whereas only three were officially recorded archaeologically. Those many examples now in museums are roughly hewn from acacia wood, approximately 12–20 cm long, and some have traces of red paint. That paint signified potency and ritual power, but also may have indicated the fleshiness of the male member. Others are painted with bands of red and blue, the latter possibly representing veins, while some are mysteriously yellow (Pinch 1993: 236). Many are carved in enough detail to show that they are circumcised, and on one a scrotum was attached. Male figurines have been recorded from the settlement at Memphis (Giddy 1999: 48). One clay example appears to have been wheel-turned, finished by hand and painted red; others have been created in blue faience. Several of these body parts were found in the royal tombs of Amenhotep II and Tuthmosis IV. While these objects of material culture are clearly venerating specific aspects of the male body, they are votives prepared in service of a female deity, Hathor. Interestingly, it is the phallus that was offered not the depictions of female genitalia: perhaps appeasing Hathor required the offering of her sexual opposite.

Phalloi were offered by a wide cross-section of social strata in Ramesside times and their donation was perhaps linked to specific festivals like the

Beautiful Festival of the Wadi only to be later removed by priests after they had accumulated: at the time of excavation they literally covered the shrine floor (Pinch 1993: 244). Displays of sexual organs were probably considered apotropaic, and this harks back to the humorous myth of Hathor distracting her father, the god Re, through display of her own genitals. The materialization of the phallus operates as a metonymic signifier for the male identity, specifically his sexual identity (Meskell and Joyce 2003: 103–111). One interpretation is that offering the votive phallus was a way of overcoming male impotence, as an offering to the goddess in exchange for sexual activity. Or they may represent a material gratitude for the curing of impotence: all of these interpretations, for example, are operative for *milagros* that depict male genitalia. Alternatively the phallus may have been cast as the prime signifier for the desire to bear children for those who were rendered childless. These votives may have bestowed blessings upon the sexual union of individuals, their family lives, and so on. Men and women probably offered these objects with no social stigma attached. Mimesis here is the actual production of images whose salient prototype (the god, goddess or their potent characteristics) is the visible resemblance to the original and within the sphere of material culture. By that mimetic virtue to the original deity or concept (Gell 1998: 100) images were accorded a separate and empowered status. Benjamin argued that mimetic genius was a life-determining force for the ancients, whereas we moderns seem to have reflexive capabilities for apprehending these formations (1979: 66). A necessary opacity is required to mobilize the magic that inheres in these object doubles. But what if the magic of doubling appreciably failed, if simulated votive offerings faltered and life's uncertainties held sway? Do people *know otherwise* and merely choose to ignore the facts, or do they operate within other schemes of understanding, other logics that make the materiality of magic and ritual inherently comprehensible and believable? Can individuals oscillate between positions, entering a form of critique and self-reflexivity into the equation? The last question will be fleshed out in the following chapter; the others will be interrogated below.

Suspending Disbelief?

Origins and craftings of particular ritual objects can be forgotten or concealed, blocking off abduction leading from the existence of the material index to the agency of the artist. How is this chain of intention and fabrication effectively masked? Gell's work is informative here as he re-examines the contributions of Fraser and Tylor and their configurations of sympathetic magic. He argued (1992: 59) that magic haunts technical activity like a shadow and is the negative contour of work. If those who practiced magical acts perceived this object-forging as embedded in the trope of simulacra, would they have disengaged from the practice? In teasing out this principle, from emic to etic understanding, one moves from the experiential world of *doing*; one erases the possibility of empathy. Taussig too argues that this is a tragic misunderstanding of the physical causality of these symbolic and expressive performances. This harks back to Lévy-Bruhl's attempts to understand the emic system from an interior rationality and to probe cultural logic contextually rather than impose a system of scientific epistemology. Magic is considered possible because the intentions of human subjects cause events to happen in the vicinity of objects, things, places, and so on. One might say that agency here is perceived as distributed, but it is a very different construal of causation. It is not an inevitable scenario like Gell's (1998: 101) examples of the sun rising and setting. His contemporary analogy of these two forms of causation is explicated in the following, albeit tongue-in-cheek, question: what causes an egg to boil? First, our natural response is to argue that it's all tied up with physics; the egg in the water on the stove is heated by a flame. Secondly, one could equally answer that it happens because I decide to choose the egg, place it in water, light the flame and boil it because I fancy eating it. But what if we look deeper: these second-order causations are complicated. Using Gell's example, historically individuals have to first desire eggs, chickens are then exported to England, suitable cooking materials are required, and so on. So despite the seemingly straightforward explanation of physics, the real causal explanation for boiled eggs is that individuals *intend* that they exist. Thus one can detect the internal logic, the personalized vision of how things come to be, whether mechanistically or magically. This may accord with Lévy-Bruhl's notion of pre-logic in "primitive" contexts, which he argued was every bit as logical as our own explanations under the veil of post-Enlightenment thinking.

The question remains, do individuals suspend disbelief in their negotiations between the physical and existential worlds or are there contextual understandings of experience that cannot be encapsulated within our own taxonomies? How do we balance the cynicism of the first proposition with the romanticism of the second? I would suggest that Egyptian culture, much like our own, is a fragile and unstable combination of both. The human dialectic is first manifest in socio-cultural structures and reflected materially in its use-objects, but these would not be as they are if the same facility for their originary crafting did not also allow for their rethinking, rejection or superseding (Merleau-Ponty 1963: 176). How are we to understand someone else without sacrificing our own logic to them? There is little difference, as Dewey once said, between magic and science in the manner that they each "serve to protect us from the perilous, aleatory character of life by making the unknown appear to be determined by the known" (quoted in Jackson 1996: 5). Magical spells seek to impose the order of words onto the chaos of the world, not unlike our own notions of universal progress, inherent rationality, modalities of cause and effect, and the uniformity of nature. Lévi-Strauss (2001: 13) said equally that both scientific and indigenous explanatory models seek to impose order upon chaos, control nature and identify the hidden causes or events underlying the phenomenal world. Both attempted to make sense of the world and both suffered from the illusion that they were successful. For Leroi-Gourhan (1993: 338) religion and science have, since antiquity, been rivals in explaining the world and attempting to strike a balance between safety and freedom. Given the collapsing of taxonomies we need to relinquish the sterile antinomies of rationality versus irrationality, science and magic, and to redefine the discourses of ritual, totemism, witchcraft, and so on (Jackson 1996). The residual impact of such vocabularies has epistemic weight, although I have found it difficult throughout this book to bypass the language of magic and ritual and replace it with less laden terminologies.

The ways in which individuals reflect, analyze, and rationalize the world around them self-reflexively are seldom commensurate with the attitudes they embrace during day-to-day life (Jackson 1996: 2). Egyptian literature reveals an element of doubt, dissent and skepticism that is not prevalent in official discourse. While not necessarily countercultural (Parkinson 2002: 145), the inclusion of such sentiments and the facility for reflexivity is significant, irrespective of our difficulties in tracing the outcomes. People are not, and have never been, automata. All cultures are capable of disinterested and intellectual knowledge, allowing them mutually to reside in a coherent cultural frame. In the famous Middle Kingdom text, *Dialogue between a Man and His Soul*, we see a well-articulated discourse that might be described as skepticism and pessimism toward the pervasive Egyptian world-view of the afterlife and the permanence of one's historical presence: *They who built in granite, who constructed pavilions in fair pyramids, as fair works, so that the builders should become Gods – their altar stones have vanished, like the oblivious ones who have died on the shore for lack of survivor, when the flood has taken its toll* (Parkinson 1997: 157). Reflective and doubtful, the protagonist questions the very bedrock of Egyptian religion, its promise and delivery. When writing on myth, Lévi-Strauss pleaded for a more qualitative analysis that would allow us to understand others, rather than dismissing their lifeworlds as irrational or meaningless. Between life and thought there is no absolute gap as positioned through the lens of Cartesianism: if we eschew those dualisms and accept that what takes place in the mind is not substantially different to the experience of life itself, then we open up the possibilities for enhanced understanding (Lévi-Strauss 2001: 19). As academics we tend to reify theoretical knowledge, yet in most societies it is not ratiocination but rather commonsensical, taken-for-granted knowledge that informs the fabric of daily life (Jackson 1996). In crisis situations people tend to assent to the absolutism of authority and objective knowledge when they realize that such beliefs are instrumentally necessary and existentially true, in order to regain meaning and control of their lives. In this regard ancients and moderns have much in common. And abstract or intensely philosophical discourse may in some cases be superseded by experiential practice, when ordinary people call upon ritual or religious forms in their daily lives.

Discourses common within Egyptian literature belie this tension between the facility to question and doubt, yet detecting the socio-political ramifications of such sentiments is difficult. Dissonance between the expression and the practice of dissent should be expected. Parkinson, following Goody, accentuates these ambiguities that are themselves constitutive of cultural transmission. Rather than reductive socialization akin to more extreme forms of habitus, there are always elements of doubt and critique that lead to oppositional practices – what one might position as cognitive contradictions. Parkinson notes that ideologies of absolutism tend to deny that a state can suffer internal conflicts or faultlines and proffer a vision that the elite is unified and coherent in its aims. Disruption is often imagined as coming only from outside (Parkinson 2003). The concept of *Lebenswelt* is useful here; namely, a theory of the lifeworld that effectively bridges anthropology and phenomenology. This entails engaging with the world by acting and changing it through those actions; we are impelled to address life's conditions, its pre-given social and natural realities with which we struggle and cope. Presaging Bourdieu, the lifeworld is the province of practice; but this is not tantamount to a world of dogma and repressive generative forces, it is a world where the possibilities for reflexivity and modification take shape. This is developed further in the following chapter. We should not forget that ancient subjectivities were not simply focused upon power and cultural negotiation, but upon the experiential, the exuberant, critical, and frivolous (Parkinson 2002: 288). Meaning lies in relationships as they are lived rather than in the hollow structures and systemic properties that subjective analysis may yield. We must be less wed to our theories and more in love with the sensuous materialities of lived experience.

Sketching Lifeworlds, Performing Resistance

You are like the story of the woman blind in one eye who was in the house of a man for twenty years, and he found another, and he said to her, "I will divorce you! Why, you are blind in one eye! And she said to him, "Is this the discovery you have made in these twenty years that I have spent in your house?" Thus am I, and thus is the joke I have made with you . . .

New Kingdom Egyptian joke[1]

Many artefacts of homo ludens may entertain, but are also deeply serious.

Richard Parkinson, *Poetry and Culture in Middle Kingdom Egypt*

This chapter explores the performative elements of one class of material culture and its circulation in the Egyptian community of Deir el Medina. While the previous chapters have addressed the performance of ritual life, this chapter grapples with one aspect of civic life within the same community. Such categorical distinctions undoubtedly falter, so that one might say that the material actions discussed here are more subversive or counter-cultural in terms of their social critique, but draw nonetheless on religious subject matter. They remain reflective of worldly behavior and similarly seek to affect change, but in subtle and different ways. One might say that they offer a counterbalance to previous pictures of

---

1. Pap. Bibl. Nat. 198 from Deir el Medina, translated by A. G. McDowell (1999) *Village Life in Ancient Egypt: Laundry Lists and Love Songs*, Oxford: Oxford University Press. This chapter is a revised version of "Egyptian Worlds-turned-upside Down: Parody and Performance on a Small Scale," a paper delivered in a SAA session entitled "Spectacle, Performance, and Power in Premodern Complex Societies," held in Denver in 2002.

Egyptian practice, yet existed side-by-side and were not seen as revolutionary or heterodox in a cultural sense. My aim is to reinstate the sensuous qualities of New Kingdom life, its resistances and playfulness, but also emic attitudes to the workaday grind away from the official gaze. Using the mechanisms of material resistance, specific individuals mobilized a precocious satire of social hierarchy and launched interventions that instantiated serious social critique. In the theater of the powerless, rumors, gossip, folk tales, gestures and jokes are all vehicles that insinuate a critique of power while hiding behind a certain anonymity. Our Egyptian evidence takes the form of hundreds of illustrated ostraca, either excavated from Deir el Medina or imputed to be from the site by virtue of craftsmanship and uniformity of canon. The satirical and politicized images are materialized, and thus rendered permanent, on potsherds and limestone flakes, the by-products of the workmen's labor in the crafting of the royal tombs in the Valley of the Kings. On average the ostraca were palm-sized (Brunner-Traut 1979: 2) and perfect for painting and later hand-to-hand circulation. The limestone chippings were the excess remnants from carving the subterranean tombs into the natural bedrock, so that the materials for ostraca were readily available, literally cost nothing, and practicing illustration on such objects was very much part of the workmen's stock in trade. Moreover, producing these chippings was part of the physical labor that separated the classes and subsequently marked their physical location on the West Bank as separate and different.

Ostraca are both representational and physical objects that could also be seen as magic doubles that encapsulated images of individuals and scenarios. In that way, they may be viewed similarly to other magical things such as stelae and votives, yet they were probably not considered to exist within an official repertoire. Examples of figured ostraca have been assembled over the decades and comprise artists' sketches and trial pieces for sculptures. Most come from the village of Deir el Medina as a result of the 1922 excavation, specifically dispersed in the debris of houses; others were discovered in a heap of rubbish accumulated outside of the village, at the foot of the southern enclosure wall and among remains in ruins of the votive chapels (Vandier d'Abbadie 1946: 1). In most instances, exact provenance is sadly lacking. Some depict religious scenes while other numerous examples have recently been considered together as exemplars of Egyptian humor (Houlihan 2001). That these images have seamlessly been read as humor fails to theorize satisfactorily the vast sweep of motivations and meanings conveyed through the very act of performance, of crafting and circulating these ironic and parodic renderings. Bergson was correct in stating that humor needs to be recontextualized to understand its social function fully; it is not a universal presumption. Humor plays an important function in social movements, often by setting out to criticize the social order.

At the outset, it is necessary to acknowledge the spatio-temporal hermeneutic gulf that renders problematic the direct reading of ironic practices in New Kingdom Egypt. In general, and specifically in Egypt, these sentiments were expressed in words, gestures, images, attitudes and contextualizations that may not have conveyed the same meaning to everyone. And certainly the unbridgeable cultural divide undermines our ability to hear all the words or see all the actions in their momentary performance which is, after all, so crucial in the crafting of meaning. These material and transitory statements are always already embedded in various world relations. Egypt was rather different to other ancient cultures such as Classical Greece, where theater, plays and public performances provided powerful vehicles for social comment and humor. We can speculate that during Egyptian festivals or community celebrations such moments of satire and humor were indulged, perhaps accentuated by the powers and pleasures of intoxication. Communicative action relies on a mutual process of interpretation in which participants relate simultaneously to something in the objective, social and subjective worlds. At each action, such as the crafting or circulation of satirical images, individuals were determining their own position in regard to external nature, society and inner nature, three worlds that inform each other within an intersubjective frame. The individual horizon shifts with the theme and the context: nothing is set or predetermined (Habermas 1987: 122).

Performing Ancient Egypt

Archaeologists and anthropologists alike have considered the domains of performance and spectacle as residing in real-time theatricality, focusing primarily upon those activities with a public face, a medium with a powerful message in the Foucauldian sense. Yet as Searle, Goffman, Scott and Bourdieu have all argued, these performances are also tacitly enacted at the level of the quotidian, the mundane and everyday activities that constitute and instantiate identities and communities. Anthropologists like Victor Turner (1969, 1982) directed disciplinary attention toward ritual and deep play, as the most obvious and often elided examples of social performance. Archaeologists, by virtue of their data and desire for Bataillean excess, have ostensibly been drawn to state level societies and their more glittering examples of public ceremonies and rituals: sacrifice, rites of kingship, parades and festivals, propagandistic displays, and so on. Yet we have only the carapaces of performance in most instances, the frameworks and *mises en scène*, rather than the windows into daily action and lived experience. The crafting of a visual repertoire at Deir el Medina provides a counterpoint to the elite vision, an active challenge to the standard narratives woven around ancient societies and top-down approaches to social life. These are heterotopic spaces, where counter-culture is forged and instantiated by individuals in specific discursive moments. In so many of our archaeological accounts, human agents are missing from our visions, the end products of their actions are simply taxonomized, yet all such data become meaningless when disconnected from the human agency that lies behind them (Torres 1997: 18).

The artists and scribes charged with constructing and decorating the royal tombs in the Valley of the Kings formed the backbone of the community at Deir el Medina. Many of the inhabitants were literate and skilled artisans, although the mixed community also included illiterate men and women of varying social statuses, including those of servile or "slave" status and foreigners. We are on relatively safe ground in asserting that the majority of the images were produced locally on the basis of artistic parallels with official or royal art: this is further reinforced by the documented examples excavated by the French Institute at the site. More than 1,400 ostraca decorated with scenes from Deir el Medina have been published so far (Houlihan 2001: 73). Painted ostraca are usually executed in black paint, more rarely red, and only a minority were polychrome and these tend to bear religious scenes. Primary colours were employed to indicate artistic complexity and to underscore contrasts such as emblems, symbols, the specificity of ethnic identity, and so on (Brunner-Traut 1979: 3). The coherence in subject matter and general themes is also consistent with those known examples from Deir el Medina. And while the radical subject matter represents a clear disjunct with officially sanctioned imagery, many scenes focus heavily on ritual, religious or royal domains. The artists were clearly individuals with some knowledge and experience of these acts and had the intellectual capabilities to invert the order of things cleverly: the occupants of Deir el Medina certainly found themselves in such a position by virtue of their very *raison d'être*.

The iconographic material outlined here forms a hidden transcript, an alternative and parallel discourse that subverted social structure and hierarchy through the use of skill, humor and narrative. The hidden transcript characterizes discourse that takes place offstage and beyond the official gaze: performances such as "speeches, gestures and practices that confirm, contradict, or inflect what appears in the public transcript" (Scott 1990: 4–5). These were practical activities, involving bodily skill and dexterity, and were inherently performative in the doing as well as the sharing of the production that undoubtedly took place. Mimetic faculty is also deeply associated with play that was directed to sociality and cohesion. The inherent mimesis in these visual scenarios serves to give pleasure to spectators and participants: a practice termed "play-excitement" by Elias (Dant 1999). Humor tears asunder our presumptions about the empirical world, a world where the causal chains are broken, where social practices are turned inside out and rationality is left in tatters (Critchley 2002: 1). As Hobbes made clear in his epic *Leviathan*, we find humor in comparing the infirmities of others, thus making ourselves feel superior, a form of *schadenfreude*. Given the numbers of ostraca and their find spots we can assume that there were many makers and many more viewers and participants. Although we cannot be observers in an ethnographic sense, I think it is safe to say that these images were circulated and viewed throughout the community, and instances of their final placement within the royal tombs might suggest a longer-term subversion, a social comment that extended from this life to the next. The play of meanings in this context involves the reversal of hierarchical orderings of values and social statuses. Through deep play the limitations of the social condition and of the lifeworld appear to be overcome, if only momentarily. By attempting to analyze and interpret the gestures, emotions, perceptions and actions of community members at Deir el Medina, we see reflected different practical logics that deepen our understanding of actors' interventions in their everyday lifeworld or *Lebenswelt*.

The lifeworld, as it is applied here to Egypt, manifests as a reservoir of taken-for-granteds and unshaken convictions that participants draw upon in the cooperative process of interpretation. These social networks of meaning are culturally transmitted and consist of a linguistically organized stock of interpretive patterns: language and culture are constitutive. As evidenced at Deir el Medina this stock of knowledge supplies members of the community with common background con-victions, such as the inequality of social life experienced by the elite as opposed to the villagers themselves, and it is from these contexts that consensual understanding is shaped. Moreover, such contexts provide the testing ground where new definitions are negotiated. The lifeworld is the transcendental site where speaker and hearer meet and where they can criticize and confirm validity claims, settle disputes and arrive at agreement (Habermas 1987: 126). In this manner it provides a potential framework for change or modification in belief or attitude about the world. It is that process of sharing and viewing the material culture of resistance and subversion that reshapes the lifeworld of a community like Deir el Medina. It cannot simply be mobilized at an intersubjective level, although that is where inspiration may emanate, it must be shared or performed communally in an external sense. Through the materiality of the visual corpus, processes of communicative action transmit cultural knowledge, facilitate as social integration, establish solidarity and forge personal identities. Material reproduction takes place via purposive activity undertaken by socialized individuals who intervene in the world to realize their aims (Habermas 1987: 138).

The Ironic Turn

Determining whether the ancient Egyptians had a term or expression coinciding with irony or parody is a rather dubious enterprise, although the corpus of images under investigation suggests that there are elements of overlap between cultural perspectives that are provocative and worth exploring. The most recent study of Egyptian "humor" purports an unproblematic relationship between moderns and ancients, and I am skeptical that the imagery can simply and reductively be read as "rollicking good fun and laughs" (Houlihan 2001: 61). A more theorized analysis of satire and parody, specifically its dark side, and the contextual elements that reside at the heart of these material images, is clearly required.

Relevant to Egyptian political satire is the centrality of aggression and small-scale social resistance. Since Freud scholars have characterized humor as a vehicle for ridicule that thinly masks aggressive behavior – an attribute that meshes well with the ancient materials at Deir el Medina. The corpus contains pointed messages about power, hierarchy and reversed roles: the images portray assaults against real individuals within a particular experience of the social world. Yet socially such aggression and resistance is harmlessly masked as play and can be cleverly performed as a non-threatening genre, as opposed to the more militant action taken by the workmen during the reign of Rameses III. Yet from a psycho-analytic perspective all rituals, myths, tales, and so on serve to disguise hidden impulses that can then be performed in socially acceptable ways. Psychoanalysts have formulated much of these reversals under the rubric of incongruity theory, the perception of appropriate interrelationships of elements derived from implausible domains (Oring 1992), as elucidated by Kant, Schopenhauer and Kierkegaard. Ambiguity is key in these constructions so that distinct categories are brought into incongruous oppositions. This is eloquently demonstrated in the Egyptian repertoire where impossible world-views or experiences collide, what I would term the world-turned-upside-down genre: animals assume the behaviors of humans, predators become prey, the lowly assume the highest roles, and the elite are reduced to cowardly retreat.

All humor depends on intellect for its creation and appreciation, but this is not to deny a pervasive emotional substrate. The manufacture of these material images should be read as an open-ended action that allowed for the possibility of multiple meanings and readings. Individuals may of course attack specific institutions and individuals that nonetheless form important and serious elements in their respective lives. For the community of Deir el Medina, priests and royalty constituted the main subjects of parody, and such elites undoubtedly assumed various levels of importance and warranted different levels of respect and veneration. In recentering the social aspects of this political production, the parallels between the ancient data and contemporary ethnography are implicitly underscored. First, we need to consider the social universe of the image, to historicize the socio-political context of production. Second, what is the relationship of these images to established social stereotypes, drawing upon textual and historical data to sketch the contours of Egyptian culture? Third, we might examine the differentiation of social identities and demarcate whether those portrayed are the same as in life or are oppositional. Fourth, we should evaluate negativity as a form of aggression perhaps mirrored in the visual renderings of reversals of power. Next we should question the truth of images: are serious messages encoded and can we assess social risk? And finally to understand the transcendent function of humor, that despite the provocations of reality, the inescapability of suffering, and the traumas of the external world the triumph of self-serving prevails, since such charged social moments are no more than occasions to gain pleasure (Oring 1992: 125–34). Social critique through parody, irony or wit is ultimately inflected with the indomitability and resilience of the human spirit.

In contemporary culture, irony and parody are slippery terms. That lack of precise specificity leaves an important interstitial space where humor, play and politicking can easily maneuver. Irony is a capricious term. In literary terms it means the discrepancy between what is said and what is really meant and may impinge upon the realm of sarcasm. In a more general sense it can mean the discrepancy between expectation and outcome. The word itself derives from the Greek *eironeia*, referring to feigned ignorance and dissimulation. Irony underscores the subtly humorous perception of inconsistency in which an apparently straight-forward statement or event is undermined by its context so as to give it a very different significance (Fernandez and Huber 2001: 2–3). Richard Rorty (1989) regards irony as continuous doubt about people's final vocabularies – the words they use to justify actions, beliefs and, ultimately, their lives (Torres 1997: 20). In the face of life's uncertainties and con-tradictions, many people have found "irony a valuable resource for inciting the moral and political imagination against whatever is given, assumed, or imposed" (Fernandez and Huber 2001: 1). Irony has a dark side, what Kierkegaard (1968) posited as an enthusiasm for destroying.

Moving beyond the trope of irony, parody takes this form of insurrec-tionary power to a more intense level of sarcasm, mockery and political critique. More specifically, it uses mimicry as a vehicle for comic license and can easily slide from burlesque into travesty. Given the rich political and social critique materialized in the ancient community at Deir el Medina, and presumably in other towns across New Kingdom Egypt, it seems appropriate to use the terms "irony" and "parody" as they inform each other. Perhaps parody is more applicable to the visual repertoire of the New Kingdom that played upon physicality and corporeal satire to invert the status quo, whether inverting the human and animal worlds, or the domains of societies most powerful against the disempowered.

The connected tropes of irony and parody are intimately linked to human agency, specifically at the small scale, and individualized experi-ence of social life. Agentic individuals mobilize ironic statements or gestures in the pursuit of political aims, even if they are minimal, or even unrealizable. Political satire can operate as everyday forms of resistance in the process of ordinary undramatic change, as famously outlined by Scott (1990). In New Kingdom Egypt these are best described as a series of reversals, revealed in the iconographic record, deployed as a direct challenge to the infallibility of the Pharaoh, the power of the sacerdotal classes and the privileged position of the elite. The villagers of Deir el Medina clearly exercised their political and aesthetic imagina-tions when constituting these powerful visual narratives. Such micro-level analysis illuminates how politics, power differentials, social conflict and local community identities coalesce in specific circumstances, without assuming these to be objective, universal phenomena (Torres 1997: 205). This form of analysis more closely mimics ethnographic accounts of everyday life and resistances whereby human subjects evince the capacity to bracket and challenge the quotidian world. Questioning subjects can construct alternative worlds and possibilities, interpolating ironic and satirical gestures into the realm of imaginative techniques through the mediums of play, paradox, ritual, art, myth, and folktale (Fernandez and Huber 2001: 4–5). The extraordinary becomes possible in the midst of ordinary life, fantasy is indulged and deployed to constructed imagined worlds that simultaneously proffer critique of those who impose strictures upon individuals and groups, by their very place in the world. Of course situations change and individuals are key in directing and forging change. Every step taken beyond the horizon of a given situation opens up access to further possibilities and complexes of meaning. The taken-for-granted can change from situational context to context and thus must be open to revision and reformulation. The Deir el Medina artists were both *products* of the New Kingdom cultural tradition and similarly *initiators* of accountable actions (Habermas 1987: 135).

Victor Turner (1982: 40) was one of the first anthropologists to take seriously the power of parody in its critique of the profane through myth and folk tales where individuals reveled in the grotesque, sometimes reconfiguring them in experimental combinations. His insights are particularly salient for Egypt, especially his observation that artists, entertainers and "makers" form a counter or underground culture by multiplying specialized genres of artistic and popular entertainments that are highly critical of the status quo. Satire reveals and attacks the vice and abuses of those in power positions: I argue here that in the New Kingdom royalty and religious and political elites bore the brunt of these attacks. In many respects this appears somewhat familiar, and one need only think of caricatures or effigies crafted to satirize political leaders today. Artistic media are still the most powerful for attracting, drawing in and entertaining the widest majority due to their immediacy, accessibility and humor, rather than being tacitly laden with obfuscating political or exclusionary rhetoric. Turner likened these practical and political distortions to a hall of mirrors where the reflections are multiple – some magnifying, some diminishing, some distorting the faces peering into them – thus provoking not merely thought, but also powerful feeling and the will to modify everyday matters in the minds of the gazers. There is an element of reflexivity within this mirroring, since no one likes to see themselves as ugly, ungainly or dwarfish (1982: 105). The distorted, parodied bodies that formed the objects of critique for the Deir el Medina artisans were directly opposite to the idealized, perfect bodies that they were employed to create in their everyday work. In the context of the royal tombs their renditions of the Pharaoh and his priests were without even a hint of derision or resistance, and similarly they accepted commissions for colleagues and relatives that also were constructed within this perfect frame of reference.

Local Performances, Unflattering Portraits

As stated, the artistic corpus left to us was illustrated on ostraca and, to a limited degree, on papyrus, the former being naturally available and ubiquitous whereas the latter was in itself a cultural production and more expensive. Hundreds of ostraca have been found in the Great Pit adjacent to the settlement site where they were dumped along with thousands of other objects at unknown periods in the site's history. Since drawings on ostraca were both crude and cheap, it is not surprising that they were often discarded in this manner. Examples of papyrus scrolls, whether the Book of the Dead or literary texts, have commonly been located at Deir el Medina and some bear the traces of having been passed down from one individual to another. The scribe Kenhirkhopshef, a notable man in the village, kept quite a number of these texts, including his famous Dream Book (McDowell 1999: 110–13). We know that it was passed down two more generations to his grandson. The circulation of such works in daily life were likely to have been regular events and reflected well upon a man's status within the community. I have suggested similar mechanisms of performance with love poetry, also known from Deir el Medina (Meskell 2002; see also Parkinson 2002). We might expect other forms of small-scale performance associated with the circulation of these images: jokes, gestures, laughing, debate, storytelling, and so on. And while the illustrated papyri were undoubtedly important and valued as permanent (or valuable) objects, the specific versions that appear on ostraca may represent more informal, temporary actions where the very "doing" constituted the performance. Both media could easily be circulated amongst individuals and also easily hidden or disguised if need be.

Many authors have explored the relationships between ironic or humorous behavior and workers' routines of alienated labor. Anthony Giddens suggests that to understand power relations fully we have to interrogate the notions of autonomy and dependence from many different directions. Scott argues that the greater the imbalance in power between dominant and subordinate, the more the public transcript of the dominated will assume a stereotyped and ritualistic cast: the more pervasive the power, the thicker the mask (1990: 3). It is only through assessing the discrepancy between hidden and public transcripts that one can begin to judge the impacts of power upon public discourse.

Performative acts like those of the Deir el Medina workmen represent a
hidden power, mobilizing fugitive political narratives that insinuate a
critique of power into everyday life. Some are direct challenges to royalty,
priests and elite men, while others are more subtle social commentaries
on the inequities of quotidian life. Humor and overt parody, as we see
in the ostraca, are powerful vehicles for social criticism, since they
reinforce the skepticism that makes us see everything as less divine and
more human (Torres 1997: 188). Several Deir el Medina representations
evince these dangerous sentiments, specifically those that launch attacks
on royal individuals. In one sketch, a female in royal regalia looks
sideways, as a lion or wild beast pounces above her head, threatening
her very life (Figure 6.1). She is ignorantly unaware and gazes aside as
the lion confronts us as viewers. Furthermore, the frontal style makes a
break with elite iconographic tradition, iterating that even the semi-
divine can be rendered vulnerable. As with all political gazes, we the

Figure 6.1 Limestone ostracon depicting a queen being attacked by a lion or
hyena. Probably from Deir el Medina. Courtesy of the Medelhavsmuseet,
Stockholm. MM 14069.

Figure 6.2 Drawing of a limestone ostracon showing the Pharaoh as a lion being pursued by a smaller animal, possibly a hyena. The hieroglyphs represent the title, "King of Upper and Lower Egypt." The ostracon was found in KV9, the tomb of Rameses V and Rameses VI, and dated to the 20th Dynasty. Cairo Museum CG 25084.

viewers have the benefit of knowledge and power, while the viewed clearly lacks knowledge and agency.

Metonymic mockery seems to be at the heart of another image portraying a lion, a powerful symbol of kingship, fleeing from a smaller, less powerful animal in close pursuit (Figure 6.2). To omit any confusion over the nature of the intended satire, the draughtsman has included a hieroglyphic text above the lion stating he is the King of Upper and Lower Egypt. The travesty is clearly enunciated: the most powerful man in the land is weak, cowardly and impotent. This ostracon was found, and probably intentionally positioned, in debris within tomb KV9, the royal resting place of 20th Dynasty Pharaohs Rameses V and Rameses VI (Minault-Gout 2002: 155). This purposive placing ensured that this social criticism and blatant taunt would plague the Pharaohs in this life and the next. It similarly evinces the impudence of the Deir el Medina workmen, who lacked the requisite reverence and fear of the reprisals following from such a subversive challenge to authority.

What does the image as an example of visual humor trigger in the creator and the participants? Certainly the visual pleasure of consuming and circulating such images within close proximity to a royal installation must have been quite titillating. Both danger and excitement must have accrued to those audacious enough to craft and possess these materials, for they were tangible expressions, not simply verbal gestures. Since most illustrated ostraca are lacking in textual notations we can assume that this opened out their interpretation to a substantially wider audience, namely the entire Deir el Medina community. Illiterate men, women, foreigners and servile individuals could all appreciate the visual text. Critically, Egyptian culture placed enormous stock in the materialization of the image and the text it was imbued with life, potency and a certain agency, as previously highlighted. It is also noteworthy that the artistic skill that honored and immortalized the Pharaoh, by the very same workmen, could conversely craft his theoretical downfall, diminution, and his eternal humiliation. Material acts such as these violated all categories of expectation; they sought to subjugate, degrade and even feminize the great living god.

Less aggressive themes are evidenced in the numerous ostraca that depict imperfect and unsightly individuals – a characteristic that would never have been permitted within the official canon. Hence the workmen parodied their own appearances: there are several evocative examples of unshaven, paunchy, balding men on ostraca and papyri. These were in direct contradistinction to the youthful images of perfection that mark the traditional canon of representing the elite in every artistic medium. To represent perfection was a vital step on the trajectory to attaining it, so these seemingly minor subversions could be read as bold dissensions and refusals. So that even if the workmen knew little would change in their own lifeworld, and they may not have subscribed to the attendant religious dogma, there was still space for joy, resistance, or at least rebellious behavior. We should not entirely rule out the possible readings of self-mockery for the Egyptian materials, that the village men were also parodying their own position as lower status, or at the mercy of the elite. As Torres demonstrates in his Mexican fieldwork, irony helps workers to recover their dignity against the stereotypes and prejudices of their employers, the state and other workers, especially in the face of group anonymity. He argues there is never total subordination, since all the flows that constitute the collective profile of power cannot be specified because they are concealed under various appearances of (in)subordination. Adopting a Foucauldian stance, one could say that the power of the (in)subordinate is as complicated as any other type of power and requires an equally complex conceptualization (Torres 1997: 168).

Let us examine the context of production more closely, specifically the social, political and economic situation in which the workmen found themselves. While the Ramesside period was an age of personal piety and wealth of empire, it also ensued as a time of economic hardship for the community, of large-scale robbery, defiance of the Pharaoh, foreign incursion and civil strife. Ideally, the community should have exercised great loyalty and respect, yet members of the Deir el Medina ranks went out on strike, were accused of slander, stealing, and some were prosecuted for the capital offense of royal tomb desecration and theft. These are all examples, in varying degrees of severity, of challenging the autocracy of the Pharaoh and the state. These acts represent a further step from the *arts* of resistance, to *acts* of resistance.

In the first example, slander could be used as a device for persecuting one's fellow workmen, as in the case of chief workman Hay, who was ambushed by his colleagues. Consequently, he took them to court: *I was lying in my hut when Penamen came out together with his people. They mentioned an accusation concerning the greatness of Pharaoh involving Hay, that he uttered a curse against Seti.* In court the defendants claimed they did not hear or say such things and received a hundred severe blows of the stick for their accusations (McDowell 1999: 184–5). The serious and official nature of the charge and the penalty suggest that slander could be treated as a criminal offense.

In terms of strictly work-related strategies, pilfering, foot-dragging, and dissimulation are all part of the suite of practices that Scott (1990) labels the *infrapolitics* of the powerless, the unobtrusive realm of political struggle. Workmen took numerous days off for drunkenness, for brewing beer, festivals, fighting or, more legitimately, illness, and their fearless recording of these excuses was extremely common (Janssen 1980). They also skipped work to pursue their own private commissions such as making tomb goods or furniture for private sale. More seriously there were several times when the workmen actively went out on strike when they felt their rations were insufficient or delivered late. A famous strike occurred during year 29 of Rameses III's reign and is recorded in a document now known as the Turin Strike Papyrus (McDowell 1999: 236): *The chief workmen Khonsu said to the gang, "Look I am telling you: take the rations and go down to the riverbank to the Enclosure. Then let the children of the vizier tell it to him."* And further, *Year 29, first month of summer, day 13. The gang passed the walls saying "We are hungry!" Sitting at the back of the temple of Merenptah. And they called out to the Mayor of Thebes as he was passing by.* Other protests continued into the reign of Rameses IV, with demonstrations taking place at night by torchlight.

Apart from striking, one could take matters into one's own hands and recoup directly from the Pharaoh. Nebnefer, a Deir el Medina workman, charged his colleague Huy with stealing three copper chisels obviously belonging to the state and used for the construction of the royal tomb. These might be seen as the actions of the disgruntled or perhaps simply the greedy. A notorious man called Paneb was accused of various crimes against the Pharaoh's property, although some scholars argue that a more personal and political motive lay at the heart of this legal action. Nonetheless the purported crimes are telling: stealing stone from the royal tomb, redirecting workmen from the royal tomb to his own private tomb (Janssen 1980: 144), and using state equipment. On another document Paneb is charged with stealing an ox that has the royal brand of the Ramesseum. Determining the facts are beyond our abilities some 3,500 years after the events. However, the specifics are salient examples of thefts and affronts against the Pharaoh (or the institution of the Pharaoh) that undermine his power and stature as the great living god. The most evocative of these incidents occurred on a much larger scale in the late 20th Dynasty; it has subsequently become known as the Great Tomb Robberies. During that time systematic looting of the Theban Necropolis plagued the authorities, and testimonials of the accused were acquired by torture and make for riveting reading.

The people of Deir el Medina were similarly implicated in these criminal ventures. Papyrus Abbott is the document from the site dated to year 16 of the reign of Rameses IX, detailing the commission of inspection and the outcome – that of the ten tombs inspected, only one had been violated. The commission gave the vizier a list of suspects who were apprehended and interrogated within hours. However, when they were brought to the Valley of the Queens, specifically the tomb of Queen Isis, wife of Rameses III, it was clear that they had given false confessions, and all charges were dismissed. While we cannot be sure of guilt or innocence we know that this incident triggered additional crimes and punishments. Within fourteen months this very tomb had been violated and robbed by eight workmen from Deir el Medina (McDowell 1999: 194–8). Their expert knowledge made it relatively straightforward, as the testimonial from the thieves, Nakhtmin, Amenwa and Penteweret, makes clear:

"Go to this tomb and break through the corner stones of the tomb," so they said to us, "You will go up and hack away opposite the corner stone of the tomb." So they said to us. We went up to the tomb and we reached the proper place, and we opened the doors, and we entered.

Another group of men robbed the tomb of Rameses VI aided by at least one Deir el Medina workman, who was then hastily murdered so that he kept the crime and their identities secret. With little respect for the Pharaoh's body or his possessions these five men entered his tomb and ransacked it. The Valley of the Kings was situated further out into the desert than the community at Deir el Medina and was thus more vulnerable. Apart from the threat of punishment at the hands of the authorities, demonic deities in their statue form protected royal tombs, particularly those in the Valley of the Kings (Figure 6.3). Several of these disturbing figures have survived and are testament to the belief that the

Figure 6.3 Demon with mask from the Valley of the Kings, wood coated with resin. 19th Dynasty. Courtesy of the British Museum, EA 61283.

statues themselves were apotropaic (see Chapter 4). Unfortunately for the Pharaohs, their demonic magic failed and fear of them was not a sufficient deterrent for the inhabitants of the West Bank.

These robberies may be situated within a larger context of unrest. The situation was deteriorating and Thebes was under threat; there was fear of attacks by Libyan nomads coming in from the west. As the first settlement at the desert edge, the people of Deir el Medina gradually abandoned their village and sought refuge elsewhere in Thebes. At the close of the Ramesside Dynasties civil war effectively ensued. What I am suggesting here is obviously not that images of subversion or reversal heralded or caused the downfall of the Ramesside Dynasty, but rather that individuals were involved in their own infrapolitics and strategies that legitimized their respective social and political critiques. That critique was mobilized within the village tells us various things about notions of royal dogma, dissenting actions, and individual agency, as well as emic structures of satire and parody. What, if any, punishment would have been meted out if the ostraca had been detected by an over-zealous official it is almost impossible to say. Deir el Medina was also not policed and the workmen led a fairly autonomous lifestyle, conducting their private commissions and engaging in agricultural pursuits free from state incursion (Meskell 1994). In some sense we must acknowledge that the context is rather different to early modern Europe or the Communist era, where political humor was used to incite opposition to the ruling authorities. The Deir el Medina community was not vying for a separatist state and certainly did not run off to join the invading Libyans when they encroached on the Theban West Bank. They were Egyptians after all. That being said, a hidden transcript was, in all its performative spectacle, clearly in evidence at Deir el Medina. And the shared, experiential nature of that satire may have had a galvanizing effect on the community as a whole, although with such a broad cross-section there must have been many diverse subject positions. At this very local level, through the iconography presented, we have gained access to a possible world of rumor, linguistic tricks, metaphor, euphemisms, folk tales, ritual gestures, grumbling and dissent that, in itself, formed an ideological war (Scott 1990: 137), albeit waged on a fantastic and often anonymous battlefield.

Reversals of Fortune

Popular to many of these local depictions at Deir el Medina is a genre one could call the world-turned-upside-down, made famous by historians and literary critics such as Bakhtin. Foucault famously captured this ethos, exhorting "let us pervert good sense and make thought play outside the ordered category of resemblances" (1970: 898) The Deir el Medina corpus is replete with many evocative examples of perverse resemblances and reversals, specifically of human–animal transpositions, suggesting it was considered incongruous and humorous, despite the particular complex envisioning that was clearly possible. Moreover, the rules of the animal world were also reversed, compounding or doubling the effect of incongruity so necessary for parody. Following Douglas, these parodies and reversals are anti-rites, yet they are connected, in that both genres gather resonance from a cluster of socially recognized and compelling symbols.

Instructive here is Bakhtin's famous study *Rabelais and His World* (1984) since it foregrounds communal places and celebrations that offered anonymity and encouraged forms of discourse typically excluded from the world of hierarchy and its preferred etiquettes. Rabelais's sixteenth-century prose occupied the ritual location of uninhibited speech and in some sense represented an ideal speech situation, although clearly all utterances are politically saturated. His work seriously examines parody, ridicule, blasphemy, the grotesque, scatology, and ultimate revelry by looking at patterns of speech and gestures that existed outside the realm of sanction. Gossip is perhaps the most familiar and elementary mode of disguised aggression or sedition. Sadly this immaterial mode is lost to archaeologists, yet perhaps the material renderings we see in ancient Egypt are a kind of ideal speech act in themselves. In Europe, as in Egypt, the arts of resistance often took the form of culturally elaborate disguises of symbolic inversion, whether in oral or pictorial culture. Importantly, the Deir el Medina craftsmen were in the business of image-making, specifically image-making of the Pharaoh and his immediate kin. Ironically, they were still fulfilling their function by practicing their art. But by manipulating the realm of the quotidian, of their very livelihoods, they were recoding it with political meaning and demonstrating in a fashion that was difficult to surveil or suppress. In one ostracon the human and animal worlds are reversed in a scene of grooming that would have been very familiar to an audience embedded within a domestic settlement. Implicit in all such images is the disproportionate hierarchical status of master and servant. Various human scenes of grooming have been discovered at Deir el Medina, both in wall paintings located in the front room of houses (Meskell 1998) and on informal ostraca. In one example the main subject appears to be a mouse, dressed in the style of linen customarily worn by elite men, who sips wine from a jar through a straw. The mouse is attended by a feline, who appears to be fixing his hair or wig, as was customary for servant girls to do for their elite female mistresses. This scene also has a gendered subversion coupled with the obvious human–animal inversion. Other felines are seen to the right of the wine jar and a duck is positioned in the left corner. Cats and ducks betoken female sexuality in general iconographic terms, stressing the importance of feminization as a strategy for subversion. The exact nature of the scene is unclear, but the irreverence to the elite class is largely transparent.

At one level these performances could be read as all residing in the realm of fantasy, that the fictional animal scenarios reflect the creative imaginations of a community of artisans. At another level they could be read as muted social critique for the groups of insiders who understand the specific images and can translate the textual notations. This was all couched in metaphorical communication and may not be perceived as militant protest. At a third level creation of a caricatured reality has a pointed political agenda and subversive threat that plays into already established norms of resistance, and even criminal behavior such as the ability to strike or steal from the tombs, whether supplies and equipment or actual royal burial paraphernalia. The cumulative power of numerous petty acts of resistance can have political and economic effects.

Apart from attacks on royal personages, subjects of a religious nature were also popular targets for satirical attack since they already constituted actions that were arcane and performative in character. One famous ostracon depicts a religious festival or ceremony featuring a statue of a deified mouse or rat processing in a portable shrine carried by four jackals as priests. This is exactly the form of procession that would have featured deities like Osiris or Min at specific festival times: numerous representations of such events cover the walls of the New Kingdom Theban temples. The villagers of Deir el Medina and the residents of Thebes witnessed and participated in these events at various times in the yearly festival calendar. Importantly, no rodent was ever deified as a god and this constitutes a particularly vicious attack on Egyptian religiosity and ideology at all levels. While the scene invokes all the accoutrements of ritual and devotional practices, the central figure is mobilized as a motif of derision that marks a serious transgression. This is not an isolated instance. Other images parody religious scenes such as the sacred judgment scene (Chapter 125 in the Book of the Dead) or mimic devotional practices inserting animals such as dogs, cats and mice into the roles of human and divine actors. This reversal from the sphere of the human/divine to the lowly domain of the common animal marks the profanity and debasement upon which the parody is founded. The incongruity of the reversal, its unlikely occurrence, and the stark contrast it provides with ordinary life, provide a source of amusement and wishful thinking on the part of the artists and viewers. Reversal is the crucial narrative device.

Cultural negation has taken similar forms in later history. Many historically documented groups have chosen the animal world as a source of mirroring for the foibles and frailties of human society. These scenarios provide a breathing space where the categories of order are less than completely inevitable. Scott recalls a popular series of prints called "The War of the Rats Against the Cat" produced and circulated amongst the broadsheets in eighteenth-century Europe and considered particularly subversive. French revolutionary troops occupying Holland seized both the prints and the publisher. In 1842 Tsarist agents apprehended all known copies of a print depicting an ox slaughtering the butcher, a direct attack on Peter the Great (Scott 1990: 168). The world turned-upside-down genre deploys playful fantasies involving our animal counterparts and functions to both mask and materialize, in a creative double play, the dangerous and vindictive desires, conscious or unconscious, that inflect these impossible reversals (Kunzle 1978: 89).

Egyptologists have long realized the satire of these reversals operate on at least two pragmatic levels. On the first, the human, cultural world is inverted into the natural and lesser animal world, a distinction clearly understood by any Egyptian viewer. On the second level, within that specific animal world the natural hierarchy and order is inverted, so that predator becomes prey, larger animals are terrorized by smaller, aggressive animals become passive, and so on. In one vignette of the Turin Papyrus we see an image of a warrior mouse or rat (mimicking images of Ramesside Pharaoh warriors) in a chariot drawn by dogs, attacking a fortress guarded by cats (Houlihan 1996: 62–3). On the reverse of the papyrus are the parodic sexual scenes, discussed on pp. 169–174. The image of the mouse/rat as deity or Pharaoh is a common reversal, taking the most powerful being known to the Egyptians and reducing it to one of the weakest and most timid creatures on earth: the Pharaoh shifts from the royal symbol of the lion to the position of a rodent. Thus Pharaoh can be parodied in numerous ways: one is to reduce him to a powerless creature; the other, as noted above, was to mock his own metaphorical power in the form of a fearless lion, that in turn is reduced to a state of cowardice and impotence. The end results are commensurate.

Both are strategies that displace and disguise reality, a reality that might be considered too dangerous or alternatively too predictable, in favour of a creation that is intellectually savvy, humorous and ambiguous. Affirmation, concealment, euphemization and stigmatization, coupled with the "appearance of unanimity seem central to the dramaturgy" (Scott 1990: 45) of hierarchical power in evidence in Egypt. Overt references and realistic rendering may have been considered too volatile or risky. However, the mode of doubling or producing a parodic simulacra was deemed effective. Just as royal and administrative "art" in the New Kingdom used its immense power to broadcast messages of sovereignty and imperial force over its neighbours, the "arts" of the non-elite tend to offer the same challenges on a smaller, more private scale. Representative schemas provided powerful domains for assertion and resistance. The power of the subordinated is no different from other kinds of power, because it only has diffuse signs that are easily confused with the complexity of everyday circumstances. We cannot in any way measure this power in living or ancient communities, but this does not preclude analyzing its interventions (Torres 1997: 188–9). From a Habermasian perspective, through the actor's agency such iterations and performances (intentionally or unintentionally) change and recreate the external world and thus the personal lifeworld. In a local community such as Deir el Medina at any juncture in time there were an indefinite number of shared lifeworlds. Individuals and groups share accumulated knowledge, practices, material resources, values, norms, discourses and expressions that overlapped with other individuals or groups. This means that during every communicative action an individual may for some reason feel the need to demarcate the boundary of the lifeworld they assume they share with others or the boundaries between this shared lifeworld and what are considered other lifeworlds.

At Deir el Medina we can be fairly sure that there existed a shared lifeworld where the mockery of authority was enacted and indulged, and that the concomitant satirizing of their fellow villagers and their shared conditions was equally acknowledged. We cannot be certain how either of these sets of performances were perceived by discrete individuals; however, the ubiquity of the images suggests a certain common appreciation of the genre. If one were able to conduct micro-scale ethnography of the community it might be possible to determine how such performances migrated across domains and influenced the structure and formation of individual lifeworlds. This would also be situational in regard to gender, age, status and individual life experience. Ethnographers have certainly conducted relevant fieldwork to explore the relationships between structure and action and investigated how structural constraints either obscure or enlighten the meaning of change (Torres 1997: 200). As with all archaeology, in either text-aided or prehistoric situations, the contexts of action, the effects of agency on the practice of everyday life and the implications of changing individual lifeworlds unfortunately elude us.

Upside-Down Sex

The world-turned-upside-down genre, so popular with Egyptian audiences, clearly exhibited a jagged social and political edge. The frame of reference was the social elite for the most part: orientation and subject matter change somewhat when sexuality enters the frame and scenes of parody and excess become the central focus. Many ostraca from Deir el Medina, and one notable papyrus, form the corpus under investigation here. Using the Turin Papyrus as a pivot point, specifically its composition and the very crafting of it as a material object, one can demonstrate how these various ludic genres of reversal and parody are intimately entwined. The entire papyrus could be read as an example of comic heteroglossia *à la* Bakhtin, where multiple readings are possible and probably encouraged to allow for maximum impact and communication, *sensus communis*.

The Turin Papyrus was executed some time during the 19th or 20th Dynasties in the Theban region and probably emanates from Deir el Medina (Omlin 1973). Unfortunately no provenance for the papyrus was ever noted (Russmann 2001: 167), although it is generally agreed to come from a trained scribe in the community. It presents viewers with a striking example of parodic representation from two distinct perspectives. On one level, and on one part of the papyrus, we see the familiar genre of the world-turned-upside-down with animals in human attitudes and activities: mice attacking cats; birds attacking cats; mice in chariots led by lions and dogs; monkeys, lions and donkeys playing musical instruments, and so on. On the other level and portion there is a satire on human sexual relations, with people burlesquing human practices. The entire piece can be read multiply as a social and sexual critique of human follies and vices.

On the animal portion we see a lowly donkey, dressed in the types of expensive linens typically associated with elite men. The donkey carries the insignia of office, a long staff and crook, and is perhaps in the position of passing judgment on the bound captives brought before him as might the Pharaoh or a high official. A tall pile of offerings is placed before him. To his left a goat has the job of punishing the guilty (Houlihan 2001: 71), most likely a biting commentary on the justice of the Egyptian legal system and those that carry out its penalties. Alongside, animals are performing as musicians while a cat is ensconced in the process of making wine. Below these scenes is another popular vignette: an army of mice attack a fortress manned by cats. The now familiar Pharaoh mouse/rat shoots arrows from his chariot that in turn is drawn by a pair of dogs, which were clearly meant to mimic the common representations of royal horses as depicted on New Kingdom temple walls. In fact, this entire scene is reminiscent of numerous Ramesside depictions of the Pharaoh storming enemy citadels in Syro-Palestinian territories.

On another papyrus from the British Museum, a vignette features animals adopting peculiarly socialized human activities, most pointedly a lion and a gazelle playing senet – a board game popular in the New Kingdom (Figure 6.4). The lion has his paw in the air holding a gaming piece and looks confident and excited, mouth agape. Further on the right of this scene we encounter a lion, possibly the same animal, on its hind legs with a grinning face having sexual intercourse with a hoofed creature, possibly the gazelle again, that is prostrate on a bed. While some have denied the sexual nature of the activity, the artist took some care to indicate the lion's penis and show an almost x-ray image of the penetration of the gazelle's body. Was the game played with a wager in mind, and was this act of sexual intercourse a celebration of victory? Of course this interpretation would be diminished if these were all different individual animals represented. Some doubt has been raised since the colourings of the two beasts are somewhat different (Houlihan 2001: 66), as is the drawing. And perhaps this is much too modern a reading of the scene. Unfortunately, so much is lost on the modern viewer and the precise details of the papyrus are somewhat obscured. Moreover, there are no written stories about animals that would parallel this visual repertoire. The fragments may or may not be correctly placed in their original order, and the length of the lacunae between them is uncertain. Yet this action further mimics the human sexual behaviour we see on other sections and it, too, may or may not involve a financial transaction.

In turning to the human sexual aspect of the Turin Papyrus, a series of sexual encounters is depicted between short, aged men and young, hyper-sexualized females. We cannot say whether it is simply a pair of individuals represented in a series of vignettes or a number of people. Some scholars have suggested these scenes represent a brothel. To date, no unambiguous archaeological evidence for such establishments has been recorded, and it is not known what such a place would look like archaeologically. These are problematic Western assertions influenced heavily by presentations of prostitution and brothels in the Classical world, such as at Pompeii. While such activities undoubtedly took place in Egypt they may have been conducted in indistinguishable domestic dwellings. Leaving aside the issue of prostitution, both in formal or

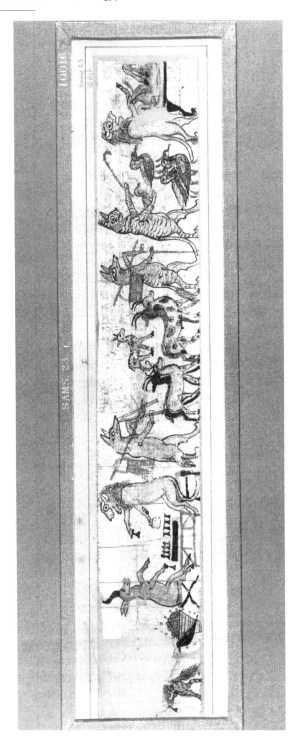

Figure 6.4 Painted papyrus depicting animals engaged in human activities, 20th Dynasty. Courtesy of the British Museum, EA 10016.

informal settings, we might question the nature of the play of human corporeality, as set forth in the vernacular imagery of these ostraca and papyri, and why these imagined and desired bodily performances were rendered material.

The papyrus appears to parody a central Egyptian myth: the nightly travels of the sun before the dawning of a new day and its attendant discourses of rebirth and resurrection (Assmann 1993: 35). If this inter-pretation is correct, it reveals another critique of a fundamental element in Egyptian religious ideology. Some of the poses do indeed appear remin-iscent of religious mythology, such the sky goddess Nut arching over the ithyphallic earth god Geb, who supposedly had sexual intercourse according to the tale. Richard Parkinson has pointed out, however, that all of our recorded examples of the sexualized Geb and Nut scene in Egyptian visual culture actually post-date the Turin Papyrus. He further suggests that the vignettes are related to festivals or festive mood rather than a traditional satire on official life (1999: 171). Cross-culturally there are well-documented linkages between festivals and the satirizing of established authority as can be seen in classic Maya images, often referred to as ritual humor (Taube 1989: 351), or in early modern Europe (Davis 1978). Or perhaps quite simply the main thrust of the Turin Papyrus is of an overtly sexual set of pairings with attendants and props to heighten the salaciousness (Figure 6.5).

The first element one notices is that the male figures are shown with inordinately long penises – to the point where they are clearly comical; where they become obstructive. Sometimes these penises have added red detail signifying potency, ultra-masculinity and even associations with the deity Seth, also known for his sexual proclivities. Irrespective of the male's stature, short or tall, the penis remains wildly out of proportion. Secondly, the female figures adopt various contorted and acrobatic poses in the throes of sexual intercourse. The men do not achieve such feats, although the raising of such large erections must have been viewed as quite a physical exertion. Women are shown bent over, standing on one leg with the other in the air, upside down, over a chariot, and posed against a sloping wall or ladder. Beside one scene a fragmentary text says: *Behold, come behind me with your love.* Another states: . . . *because of the movements. I make the work pleasant.* Next to a woman we read, *your phallus is in me, see, you don't bring me a good reputation.* The theatrical nature of these corporeal acts might well have added to the viewer's entertainment and titillation. Thirdly, the women bear all the visual cues signifying sexuality, and each of the elements harks back to the goddess of sexuality, Hathor (Derchain 1975; Pinch 1993; Robins 1996): lotuses,

Figure 6.5 Scenes from the Turin erotic papyrus, thought to come from Deir el Medina. Redrawn by the author.

hip girdles, make-up, kohl jars, musical instruments, convovulus leaves, sistra, *menat* necklaces, and mirrors. In one scene a woman and some young helpers carry an exhausted man with a flaccid penis. Men are shown in active sexual mode, whereas women are shown as passive, uninterested and often preoccupied with other things while actual penetration is taking place (Meskell and Joyce 2003: 115). I would argue that the papyrus was crafted by a skilled and literate man for other men's viewing pleasure, most likely one of the scribes at Deir el Medina. It is an eruptive and disruptive form of comedy based upon corporeality and the lower body functions transposed into visual humor, reminding one of the ludic world of Rabelais. The papyrus fits well within the schema set forward by Bakhtin (1984) to analyze humor and parody in the Renaissance and Middle Ages. His study converges upon the symbolic iconography of the grotesque body and its sexual functions, which finds its ultimate display in fornication. He argued that such representations were in flagrant contradiction to formal literary and artistic canons: in these the body was a finished product where all apertures were closed. Conception, pregnancy, childbirth and intercourse were not displayed, as was true of elite Egypt iconography. In both contexts, then, one could argue that parody and humor defied the status quo and were linked to other cultural practices that challenged the constraints of everyday existence.

The workmen themselves presumably painted the other ostraca that bear informal sketches: many of them are satirical or ironic pictures of everyday life. While some show men in older age, fat, bald and very much at variance with the canonical renderings of the human body in elite Egyptian art, contrastingly the depictions of women are generally consonant with the ideal. Several ostraca show scenes of sexual inter-course where the woman typically adopts the passive role. A number of less well-known examples show penetrative scenes and men with inordinately long penises. Many examples show women reclining on beds with elaborate drapery and surrounded again with erotic signifiers: these images often parallel the sorts of tropes we hear portrayed in love poetry (Meskell 2002). Another group shows a specific genre of women, those associated with music and dancing and possibly sexual activities (Manniche 1987). These young women were typically depicted wearing only a hip girdle, performing acrobatics or playing musical instruments. From a male perspective these were inherently sexualized activities that also hark back to the elaborate bodily postures assumed in the Turin Papyrus.

An interesting parallel is provided by another ancient culture, the classic Maya. Specifically their representations of anthropomorphic figurines and images on ceramics demonstrate a pairing of young, attractive female and aged, grotesque males. Similarly these scenes have an overt sexual nature and conform to Bakhtinian notions of parodic corporeality (see also Lyotard 1993). As in Egyptian representations, these were unlikely pairings. Lecherous men or animals coupled with young women was a favorite scene, yet it was not the subject of official art. There was also a tradition of exhibiting anthropomorphic animals (Taube 1989: 367–71). Many of the male subjects have been described as clowns, their key characteristics being ugliness, old age, drunkenness, wanton sexuality, animal impersonation and shabbiness. As in the New Kingdom, these characteristics and bodily features were in striking contrast to Maya rulership (Taube 1989: 377). Many Mayanists have perceived this visual corpus in the realm of humor rather than tacit political commentary. However, given the insights of archaeological and historical case studies, perhaps this view might be revised.

And finally, we have to consider why the Turin Papyrus was created. Some scholars focus on its uniqueness, yet we have scores of ostraca and even some graffiti that mirror aspects of its ideological construction. Admittedly, it is a particularly fine example, much superior to the hieratic sketches and caricatures so often confined to ostraca. A wealthy male individual probably owned the object since it was executed on papyrus, itself an expensive commodity usually confined to significant texts such as the Book of the Dead. The workmanship also suggests a skilled artisan, working in various colors, and the overall project must have been costly. To compare, documents from the village record the sale of a Book of the Dead papyrus for somewhere between 60–100 *deben* (Janssen 1975: 246), roughly the same price one might pay for a finely decorated coffin. This was certainly a longer, more detailed piece requiring more work, but nonetheless we can be sure that such an object was considered a luxury item (Parkinson 2002: 84). One must then ask: why make such a piece? The motivations are of course lost to us, but we may speculate that the Turin Papyrus was a more expensive version of the informal sketches that became so popular in the community. Owning such an entertaining piece may have conferred a certain status and notoriety upon its owner. Linked to that is the power of its performativity, the papyrus could be dramatically unrolled as the narrative unfolds and, combined with an oral component, the effect must have been heightened. Its quality and the permanence of the papyri suggest that it could be looked at and used again and again. It is likely that it was both handed around and handed down.

Silent Witness

Like ethnography, archaeology has the potential to reveal how material mediation might mobilize and transform social critique and how the inherent concreteness of the material offers a grounded and active resistance to the status quo. The embodied acts of making and performing instantiate theatricality in the heterotopic spaces of everyday life, challenge the seeming intractability of order of things, provoke dissension and potentially change the lifeworld. As has been argued by Rosaldo and others, human agency always transcends conditioning. Even in the 1700s Vico had suggested that "irony could not have begun until the period of reflection, because it is fashioned of falsehood by dint of a reflection which wears the mask of truth" (1984: 131). As Ortner (1996: 2) argues, such "studies of the ways in which people's resist, negotiate, or appropriate some feature of their world are also inadequate and misleading without careful analysis of the cultural meanings and structural arrangements that construct and constrain their agency and that limit the transformative potential of all such intentionalized activity." The challenge will be for archaeology to elucidate the processes that critique and defy the intransigence of social ordering. Such musings are active, if hidden, resistances that revel in the pleasures of utopian thought and expression, both in the procedures and the narratives of the quotidian life (see Torres 1997: 184). In the words of the poet and politician Václav Havel (1969: 33), "Like Sisyphus, we roll the boulder of our life up the hill of its illusory meaning, only for it to roll down again into the valley of its own absurdity . . . manipulated, automatized, made into a fetish, Man loses the experience of his own totality."

The materialization of parodic image-making, and the images' concomitant social commentaries, embodies a narrative, storytelling inflection that is in itself a form of social theater. And like theater, we should expect a juxtaposition of varieties of material, stylistic discontinuity, and expressive diversity (Pearson and Shanks 2001: 25). We can expect the presence of stylized inverse behavior in the form of poetics, lyrics, in-jokes, and sayings with a range of performative actions, including what we could now classify as song, rhetoric, comedy, direct address, and so on. Hidden transcripts or arts of resistance hold up a mirror to social hierarchy, inequality and the status quo. There is the physical action of making, the performative corporeal style of public enactment, coupled with the public participating in circulation, viewing and responding in a variety of forms. All entail permutations of theatricality. We may not be able to reconstruct the sequencing of events at Deir el Medina and I do not propose that we bracket these activities from the more quotidian happenings in the village. That they represent a distinct genre is very much our taxonomic view, and we need to further contextualize both the iconographies and practices within everyday Egyptian life. I am drawn to the recognition of hybrid performances in heterotopic spaces or counter-sites. Following Freud, life's repressive tendencies are effaced through laughter; hence we let the unconscious bubble its way to the surface, to the conscious world. Transgression, liminality, manipulation, humor and shared competence are all themes intimately tied to material biographies.

Object Lessons from Modernity

You know that we are living in a material world
And I am a material girl.

Madonna, *Material Girl*

Many of the themes outlined in the first two chapters, and interwoven throughout the following four, are also crucially linked to representations of Egypt under the sign of modernity. Throughout the book the nature of materiality, replication, objectification and agency have been explored, largely through excavating the archaeological remains, in order to gain some sense of how the ancient Egyptians implicitly worked with a theory and practice of materiality. The effect of this exercise is to inject a certain relativism into our current theories of materiality. As stated at the outset, no single theory or understanding of materiality will suffice. Any philosophical theory of materiality that assumes its own universality invites critique since there may be critical differences in the way peoples of one period or region understood and lived the consequences of their relationship to their object world. It follows that we also have to pay respect to their philosophical beliefs that may have been constructed through practice, rather than through abstraction. That relativism, or better, contextualism, implies an attempt to pin down both the differences and similarities between two distinct communities. In turning our attention to *others,* namely the people of New Kingdom Egypt, it would be easy to make the contrast crass and glib. People of the distant past can be used to create a kind of Occidental myth. The point is not so much that they are rendered authentic, religious, mystical and profound, but that we render ourselves superficial, inauthentic, and lacking in any such qualities. Instead of *real* statues and monuments, we portray ourselves through the images of excess, speaking to our materialism and superficiality. Museums, casinos, collectors, scholars and ordinary people alike invoke the powerful physicality of things Egyptian for personal or

177

economic enrichment. A Maussian system of magic is prefigured whereby the ancient ritual power of Egypt and its antiquities are transmuted in new configurations for their contemporary possessors. Via homeopathic or imitative magic (reminiscent of ancient practice), elements of ancient Egypt that are designated salient are integrated into the present and selectively form ideas of the future. This process reflects a two-way relationship where individuals and groups treat *certain pasts* as a locus of authenticating myths and futures (Douglas and Isherwood 1996: 23–4). Importantly, this does not automatically render those practices meaningless or superficial, devoid of cultural capital or personal fulfillment, simply because they occur in the present.

Egypt's aura, manifest through its enduring materiality and aesthetic force, is commanding today as in antiquity. Ostensibly the materials that moderns desire of Egypt have not changed, they remain ancient, aesthetic, ritually saturated objects: images of gods, Pharaohs, elites, and symbols redolent of religious devotion, power and beauty. Many people revere them with a quasi-ritual piety, reflecting through them our own situational contexts and mortality. Yet the seminal connection between their makers and their beliefs has been severed for us. These potent signifiers of ancient Egypt are detached from their original signifieds: the implications of those significations greatly affect our own scholarly preoccupations as well as common contemporary interest in Egyptian culture. Importantly, new significations are woven around ancient goods and their copies in contemporary culture, as we will see. But superficial comparisons between ancients and moderns tell us little about either population. The earlier chapters of this book have tried to first break apart any simplistic representation of the ancient world. The quintessential symbols of Egyptianity (pyramids, monumental statues, votives, mummies, etc.) do powerfully communicate relationships of considerable emotive and spiritual force. These were the material forms through which religious life infused the sensibilities of peoples, each of which was shot through with inflections of afterlife scenarios. Yet in Chapter 6 much more quotidian artefacts were explored, demonstrating that there existed material much closer to our world of mass consumption. This genre of artefacts appears to have been constructed more in terms of play, irony, and political satire. Moreover, through this materialization the Deir el Medina community forged and aligned itself with the "mass," in part by its clear distanciation from the world of the elite and the sacred.

Let us now consider the other side of this coin, the actual mass consumption within contemporary secular society. Have we replaced a philosophy of materiality with mere materialism, the significant construction of images with mere fakes, the real with the hyperreal of modern consumerism? Is there anything of what was analyzed in Chapters 3, 4 and 5 that accords with our own world and our own concerns with the relationships to the material construction of presence?

Object Lesson 1

In London one can visit a monument whose size speaks to the same issues of monumentality and scale, whose mandate is no less than a global repository of world culture, within which every object speaks to this collective effect of homage to the transcendent possibilities of objects. I am referring to the British Museum, a site that with its new Great Court strives for some archaic sense of awe and grandeur. A superb monument to the ideal of authenticity, it is the locus of *original* objects of the ancient world and, therefore, at one level a sanctuary of the *real*. Like all modern museums, the British Museum is also a machine for the construction of replicas that turn these original objects into their commodified copies to be sold at a dozen locations inside and outside the museum itself. As with many museums, we shall see that the shop may become as important, if not more important, a site for visiting as the objects whose copies it sells. Throughout this chapter I explore the overall significance, indeed dominance, of Egyptian material within this process of commercialization. But here I want to uncover some of the modern meanings and resonances around one specific object, to take seriously modern consumption of things ancient and Egyptian, rather than reducing such practices as simply postmodern gloss. Rather than simply addressing the consumption of Egypt as a undifferentiated sign of modernity, what can we learn if we are prepared to focus upon the specific act of generating buying and consuming a single statue, in the same way that we considered particular statues of the ancient world? And if there is one object that dominates – not necessarily in the arena of the originals and their authenticity displayed within the museum, but rather this ability to transform them into the commodity – it is a statue: to be precise the statue of the Gayer-Anderson cat (Figure 7.1).

What does it mean to buy the Gayer-Anderson cat today? If we examine the website for the British Museum shop one finds two extremely contrastive forms by which this image can be purchased. Described as "one of the greatest treasures of the British Museum," consumers can purchase a fine replica in bronze, cast from the original, for £2,250. Alternatively, there is a range of Gayer-Anderson cat kitchenware "based on a Pop-Art treatment . . . for a fresh contemporary look." These

Figure 7.1 Gayer-Anderson cat and friend, courtesy of the British Museum.

simulations apparently demonstrate precisely the lack of any genuine sense of the authentic, spiritual or dread nature of that act of ritualized replication, that was described for the making of a statue found in Chapter 4. However, if we subject this material to the same suite of questions that are posed throughout this book and analyze them in relation to developments in material culture theory, and ask what forms of objectification and agency are implicated here, then a different narrative emerges. First we might question, given all the potential Egyptian material for replication, why the one object that seems to entrance those wishing to buy images is a cat deity. What then is the meaning of a statue of a cat within contemporary Britain? The British are renowned for their love (some might say devotion) for pets. Cat-lovers are particularly staunch in this regard. As an index, *The British Museum Book of Cats* is a notorious best-seller, with some 40,000 sold to date. For many people dogs are generally viewed as relatively servile to their owners, whereas cats are renowned for their relative autonomy. A cat may exist as your pet but it is definitely not to be taken for granted. Miller recently discussed his ethnographic experience of shopping with Londoners for their pet cats. He notes: "when informants talked about their pets in relation to shopping, it was with a strong emphasis on the recalcitrant nature of their pet as refusing to conform to the wishes of the owner" (Miller 2001b: 49). Miller articulates that cat-owners happily project a powerful sense of agency upon their pets. It is as though by demonstrating their obduracy the cat demonstrates that it has character and personality and is not merely an animal. As such the owner can feel they have a relationship, and the fact that they have to work excessively for their cat becomes labor that they believe to be appreciated, because their cat therefore loves them as an individual. Many owners allude to their felines as character-istically dignified, mystical, spiritual, and so on.

Returning to the Gayer-Anderson cat, consumption stands not simply as a general sign of our modernity or postmodernity but as a very specific act. From my experience, many people assume that cats were worshiped in ancient Egypt. However, worshiping the cat deity Bastet was a very different proposition from revering domestic cats, which the Egyptians patently did not. Despite this conflation, many people find a connection between the intrinsic quality of divinity embodied in the statue and their personal convictions about their own cats. The Gayer-Anderson cat, as a sacred animal adorned with gold and silver, replete with graceful, elegant lines, is not just a cat; it is an embodiment of that which must be recognized as a sign of the cat's divinity. Here we can see examples of what Miller (1987) termed the process of objectification. The relationship of these consumers, both to their actual cat and to the statue of the cat, is not simply one of subjects and objects. We project qualities onto the cat; the more we insist that it is obdurate and difficult, the more we are claiming that the cat possesses agency in the sense employed by Gell. If this is possible for a living cat, we can take this one step further and project an idealized image of what this agency entails: the transcendent spiritual ideal of not just our cat, but *The Cat*. The vague sense that cats are special crystallizes in the replica of the original divine cat and further suggests that we feel the ancient Egyptians understood properly some-thing that we only half comprehend, and that they were prepared to make explicit what we are only prepared to make implicit by purchasing these replicas.

From this perspective, replica cats sold by the British Museum are not simply reflective of the materialism of crass consumerism. Rather they may mirror the subtle process of materiality that echoes the original con-struction of these statues. Those processes reiterate the means by which we give form to our system of beliefs, thus transcending and reinforcing the relationship between the everyday objects and the invocation of an almost Platonic essence. One could even incorporate the kitchenware with Warhol-inspired cat images: as a set of images they are a replica of a replica of a replica, at one level thrice removed from this object of veneration. Yet they also signify a marked democratizing of the image and a creative re-contextualization. Consumption may to some degree cheapen the grandeur of religion but commodities can also democratize the spiritual, allowing it to be grounded in the quotidian: something the ancient Egyptians certainly appreciated. At this juncture it is central that we remember the contextual or relativist dimension of analysis. A contemporary experience and philosophy of materiality is in many respects entirely different from theirs. Nonetheless I would argue that we cannot dismiss our own philosophy, and we might productively explore this in our own relationships to ancient materials; namely, to excavate that philosophy from the practice of others and the particularities of the objects they appear to venerate. Part of that undertaking is an analysis of why Pharaonic Egypt exudes a certain aura for us today, thousands of years after its passing, and what it is about contemporary culture that actively desires and reifies its vast materiality.

Auratic Egypt

Ancient Egypt is the apex of civilized culture and the province of mystical practice, to be mined by moderns and coveted through feelings of nostalgia, loss and mourning for its passing and, inversely, for our own mortality. It occupies the classic position of a culture with auratic appeal. Aura has been defined as the unique phenomenon of distance (Benjamin 1968), but can also more generally refer to a perceived emanation that engulfs people and things, an essence that one experiences as mesmerizing. For aura to manifest itself, the presence of the thing, or the original, is required. The superlative survival of Egypt's antiquities and their superior age are all factors that augment the effects of aura. Egypt is ripe for the technologies of simulation that we have come to witness in the overlapping spheres of education, entertainment, leisure and consumption (Meskell n.d). Mimesis and replication lie at the very heart of the transference from auratic objects to copies and doubles in the age of mechanical, and now electronic, reproduction. Landscapes and artefacts can all be reproduced as Benjamin foretold, complicating notions of authenticity while simultaneously enhancing their inherent aura. Authenticity is akin to the transmittable essence of a thing, including its substantive duration and its biographical history (1968: 221). Egypt is, by these definitions, eminently auratic; it is supremely distant in temporal and spatial terms, it is culturally distant and different, and it remains mysterious. The past does not exist as such, although its material residues surround us. Egyptian antiquities belong intensely to this world of tangible things, and their staggering durability reflects an immunity to the corrosive effects of nature, giving a spectral illusion of immortality, of something eternal achieved by mortal hands, to be seen, to be heard, to be read (Arendt 1958: 167–8). Archaeologists have long argued that the past is mediated through material objects, although not transparently or objectively: they come transformed by audience and context and consequently require historical reconstitution (Davis 1997: 85).

When an ancient artefact is placed in a museum, privately collected or endlessly reproduced artificially, it is detached from its spatio-temporal context, changing its physical conditions and spheres of ownership. It is alienated from its traditional context, as archaeologists have long been aware. Many Egyptian antiquities could be considered subject-like and should thus be inalienable, yet are manifestly not, despite their illicit substrate, and are bound within a system of limited circulation. Replications, such as the Gayer-Anderson cat, are the subjects and objects of endless commercialization and make Egypt more available to the senses, more attainable but no less desirable. Contra Benjamin, the domestication of things Egyptian has not fundamentally diminished our fascination with its cultural specifics; rather, it has opened it up to new and more complex levels of desire, as I will endeavor to demonstrate. On the other hand, this domestication does accord with Benjamin's notion that the contemporary masses wish to bring things closer spatially and humanly, with the will to apprehend the unique and the permanent. Egypt excels in both qualities and, since we cannot fully know Egypt, it remains mysterious Egypt: our very failure to unlock its secrets forms part of our underlying fascination. That secret is largely a religious one that feeds further into the construction of aura, since aura is inextricably bound to ritual function (Benjamin 1968: 224).

Works of ancient art are auratic because they have cult value and exhibition value, historically both salient properties of Egyptian things. Through a very specific construction of aesthetics, Egyptian art has been construed as an ancient apotheosis of sophistication and brilliance that has accrued cultural capital through the Western artistic canon transmitted via later Mediterranean and European cultures. Representation of the human body is one obvious orbit of appeal (Meskell and Joyce 2003), but no less significant are Egypt's sophisticated development of hieroglyphs and architectural achievements – whether the sphinx,

pyramids, Temple of Hatshepsut or Valley of the Kings. Bodily permanence in the shape of mummies (see Chapter 5) and monumental forms
play into etiological narratives (whether human or extraterrestrial),
cultural endurance and immortality. Objectively, we might ask if Egypt
was any more fascinating or mysterious than its neighboring contemporary cultures? Probably not, yet many people perceive it to be so through
our own desires rather than any projection of the ancients. And this
perception has a long history in the Western canon beginning with Greek
and Roman peoples that sought to tour and collect Egyptian things and
experiences (Foertmeyer 1989). Given the Egyptians' predilection for
eternal presence, one might suggest that they have unwittingly succeeded
through their vast project of materiality and that we too have subscribed
to their wishes.

Digging deeper we might ask why Egypt speaks to moderns; why does
its materiality give us reason to pause and contemplate? Some argue that
ancient artefacts exercise a form of irradiation and fascination (Baudrillard
1997: 15). They are reborn as material evidence, as fetishes exuding max-
imal intensity. By possessing them, some trace of their original fetish power
remains and is transferred to the possessor. As a storehouse of contagious
magic, antiquities impart their luminous magic to new recipients in culturally specific ways. In a Maussian sense, collectors operate on a part–whole
notion of magic, whereby possessing a relic from antiquity imbues them
with a connectivity to ancient power, ritual knowledge and utopian
wisdom. Another perspective would posit that the nostalgia with which
we encase objects represents our own mourning for the impossibility of
mythical return to an enchanted world where the social order and belief
system are meaningful and certain. This is a secular expression of spiritual
longing, "a nostalgia for an absolute, a home that is both physical and
spiritual, the eidetic unity of time and space before entry into history"
(Boym 2001: 8). Loss is both spatial and figurative. Our mourning for a
past lost, phenomenologically, intends or anticipates the fullness of the
lost object, and implies a narrative cohesion and completion that remains
elusive (Butler 2003: 471). Egyptian things evoke three key registers of
loss that are sites of remains: bodily remains, spatial remains and ideal
remains (Eng and Kazanjian 2003: 3). The past is neither fixed nor
complete, but open to a series of creative reworkings. For Benjamin, it
was construed as an "open relationship with the past – bringing its ghosts
and specters, its flaring and fleeting images, into the present" (Eng and
Kazanjian 2003: 4). Encountering the silence of a long-dead civilization,
we search in vain for memorable signs, desperately misreading them.
These reworkings of the past may employ a restorative nostalgia manifest

in the total reconstruction of monuments of the past, whereas a "reflect-ive nostalgia lingers on ruins, the patina of time and history, in the dreams of another place and another time" (Boym 2001: 41). Less ethereally, artefacts are mediators and conduits between the past, future and distant cultures. They are congealed memories and symbolic storehouses of human contemplation, devotion and emotion; they are receptacles of feeling and focus and perspectival points of meditation. Significantly, we require a visible material past for that meditation, not simply a textual account but a visible continuum, a tangible myth of origin that reassures us about our end. And Egypt presents us with the perfect time machine.

Egyptian objects, specifically those designated as art or monumental, reside at the very apex of fetishization. They are entirely removed from their lifeworld and their non-use value accrues joyful excess and luxury for the possessor. The once-hidden objects of ancient times are even more prized now since their languished confinement is at an end. This enhances our desire for them because:

> We desire objects only if they are not immediately given to us for our use and enjoyment, that is, to the extent to which they resist out desire. The content of our desire becomes an object as soon as it is opposed to it, not only in the sense of being impervious to us, but also in terms of its distance as something not yet enjoyed, the subject aspect of this condition being desire . . . the possibility of desire is the possibility of objects of desire. The object thus formed, which is characterised by its separation from the subject, who at the same time establishes it and seeks to overcome it by his desire, is for us a value. (Simmel 1979: 66).

The salience of this statement is self-evident for Egyptian antiquities, characterized as they are by the properties of distance, scarcity, non-utility, and ultimately value that inhere in their ancient physicality. Through various historical epochs, including Classical and Renaissance times, Egypt has occupied a recurrent site of Western desire. And today, Egypt continues to exert a massive cross-cultural appeal, from Art deco to Afrocentrism.

Ancient objects, as inherently collectible things, reorganize the world in ways very different to functional objects. For the most part, ordinary artefacts fulfill practical goals and satisfy our external, outer physical being. Our engagement with the ancient object or artwork is certainly not utilitarian. Auratic things must be carefully removed from the mundane contexts, excluded from the exigencies and wants of daily life, carefully curated, and restricted from contact with other things, to attain their place in the world (Arendt 1958: 167). Collectors destroy original contexts, they wrest the object from its greater living entity and destructively cleanse and reclassify (Arendt 1968: 45). As evidenced with Egyptian antiquities, many are explicitly linked to a higher, religious purpose, even if they are now dramatically severed from the original spheres of religion, magic or myth. Removed from domains of ordinary utility, this implicit non-usability serves to accumulate aura. Every ancient object is revered and considered exquisite because it has survived the ravages of time and comes to embody times past (Baudrillard 1996: 83). "As islands of legend they carry people back in time, to a completely different understanding of subjectivity" (Baudrillard 1996: 80). These are not trivial associations or valences. Antiquities are mediating objects that carry communications between people, but also between deities, spirits, ancestors, and so on. Many revere Egyptian objects just as the Egyptians did, albeit with an encrusting of new, modern and reflexive devotion.

The past's materiality assumes supra-human importance and meaning because it transcends our own individual lives and histories. Archaeological objects witness our passing, as they did their makers'. They impel us, as individuals, to reflect upon our own mortality through the lens of archaeology. The world of things fabricated by *homo faber* through artifice, forges a home, a lifeworld whose stability will endure and outlast the ever-changing movement of individual lives and actions (Arendt 1958: 173). Being central, time is fantasized and romanticized, futures are imagined, and futures and personal identities are reframed in this reflexive dialogue between past, present and future. As locus of space–time compression, an imagined past is recruited as a remedy for the uncertainties of modern life (Attfield 2000: 222, 224). Attfield astutely recenters the intrinsic comfort derived from the past's familiarity, its ability to fuel desires for fantasy pasts, for unreality and hyperreality, for nostalgia, and a general evasion of mortality. Egyptian cultural specificities, whether religious beliefs, optimism for eternity, focus upon permanence, cultural resilience, aesthetics and particular representation of the body, etc. mesh completely with Attfield's suite of characteristics, providing the ancient complement for a very modern set of concerns. But what came first? Is it simply that Egypt fulfills numerous innate human fantasies of the past and future, or did our fetishization of Egypt initially create and foster those desires? One need only recall writings by Freud, Lacan, Kant, Hegel, Bataille, Derrida and Baudrillard that foreground the specificities of Egyptian culture, its strangeness, exoticism, excess and, critically, its originary status and primal influence upon us as moderns.

Collecting Fantasies

Returning to an earlier theme, it is classification that must precede the collection – a system that purportedly goes back to Adam and Noah (Elsner and Cardinal 1994)! Collecting is all about passion and desire rendered material. It connects to materialism on the one hand, and immaterial needs and emotions on the other. That dualism was manifest in New Kingdom Egypt, as the earlier chapters illustrate; however, individuals did not assemble specific collections of objects in the ways obsessive modern collectors hunt and amass things. While a type of consumer culture was operative in Egypt, it varies considerably to the practices witnessed in nineteenth-century Europe with the rise of Romanticism (Campbell 1987) and the proliferation of objects made possible by the Industrial Revolution. Romanticism was rooted in the dynamics of desire, acquisition, use, followed by disillusionment and renewed desire. Under its sway collectors saw their practices as achieving a sense of completion or perfection, and these associations continue to permeate contemporary collecting (Danet and Katriel 1994). The search for a transcendent magic has thus shifted from religion to science to consumption. Collecting in this milieu can be read as the "process of actively, selectively, and passionately acquiring and possessing things removed from ordinary use and perceived as part of a set of non-identical objects and experiences" (Belk 2001: 67). Egyptian artefacts (and often even their replications) fit this schema: they are by definition rare and difficult to assemble; they require knowledge, judgment, taste, and significant amounts of money. Collecting them accordingly operates as a transformative experience, not only by collapsing the time–space separation and displacing real time, but also by constituting a culturally enriching and uplifting endeavor. One need only recall Balzac's character Pons who

> kept his museum, with the intention of deriving from it hourly pleasure; for those minds Nature has endowed with the power of admiring great works of art, possess the sublime faculty of the genuine lover. The object of their passion yields to them the self-same pleasure yesterday, today, and forever. Satiety is unknown to them; and masterpieces, fortunately, are perennially young. (Balzac 1844–46: 13)

As a practice, collecting has been linked developmentally to our social evolution, evidenced by our survival as successful hunters and gatherers, or as an index of high intelligence, first observable in the collecting practices of children (Belk 2001: 79). Einstein was apparently just such a child.

Walter Benjamin knew well the intimate desires of the collector and spoke passionately of his book acquisitions, the chase rather than the purchase being most highly prized. He likened his passion for collecting to that of the revolutionary who dreams his way to a bygone world, a better world in which things are liberated from the drudgery of usefulness (Arendt 1968: 42). The profound relationship of owning is unlike any other. Benjamin considered collecting a redemption of things and a renewal of the old world. Oscillating between order and disorder he exhorted that "[e]very passion borders on the chaotic, but the collector's passion borders on the chaos of memories. More than that: the chance, the fate, that suffuse the past before my eyes are conspicuously present" (Benjamin 1968: 60). Even the famous *flâneur* was a collector of sorts: a collector of visual pleasure, of aesthetics and sensual engagements. Benjamin was certainly not alone. It is now estimated that around one-third of the people in affluent Western nations collect something (Pearce 1998: 1). Sigmund Freud was another legendary collector: by 1939 he had amassed over 3,000 objects and the collection encompassed items from the ancient Near East, Egypt, Greece, Rome and China (Forrester 1994: 227). "All the Egyptians, Chinese and Greeks have arrived, have stood up to the journey with very little damage," he wrote to his friend Jeanne Lampl de Groot after months of anxiety over their fate. He was known to stroke his ancient statuettes while consulting with patients. Despite this avowed connectivity, Freud readily de-sacralized and de-accessioned the Egyptian deities in his collection, giving them away to friends and colleagues. His famous patient the Wolf Man observed that Freud's Viennese consulting rooms were reminiscent not of "a doctor's office but rather of an archaeologist's study. Here were all kinds of statuettes and other unusual objects, which even the layman recognized as archaeological finds" (quoted in Bowdler 1996). Collecting is an abstractive operation that pieces together a personal microcosm for the collector. It proffers a paradigm of perfection through which we can concretely achieve our ambitions (Baudrillard 1994b: 8). Freud's collections were a natural history of civilization, yet his collection was more entangled with desire than historical specificities. So fascinated with archaeology and its effects was Freud that he used its language and principles as metaphors for uncovering the unconscious and indeed the entire process of psychoanalysis: "cleaning away the pathogenic psychical material layer by layer, and we like to compare it with the technique of excavating a buried city" (quoted in Forrester 1994: 226).

Egyptian and Classical antiquity was by far the most influential upon his own psyche and he poignantly referred to his famous *The Interpretation of Dreams* as his Egyptian dream book. Indeed it was a childhood dream of his mother being carried by Egyptian animal-headed gods that was to initiate his entire Oedipal theory; perhaps, for that reason, he desired to own the gods themselves.

Reflecting back to Mauss's formulations of embodied objects and connective magic, one can see both coalesce in the practice of collecting antiquities, especially Egyptian ones. These are, by definition, embodied and subject-like things, rare and difficult to obtain, spiritually inflected and, as such, theoretically inalienable. They are objects on the brink of extinction. Antiquities in many respects are illicit things, they should not be privately owned or circulated, yet they are and, because of the webs of differing legality woven around them, desire for their possession increases. By owning antiquities, we own the past. These are precious possessions that can be savored, handled, treasured and protected from loss or neglect (Belk 1991). Collecting is then about desire, excess, fetishization and ultimately sacrifice. In Henry James's *The Spoils of Poynton* (1987: 53), Mrs Gereth exclaims: "there are things in the house that we almost starved for! They were our religion, they were our life, they were *us*! And they're only *me* . . . There isn't one of them that I don't know and love – yes, as one remembers and cherishes the happiest moments of one's life. Blindfold, in the dark, with the brush of a finger, I could tell one from another. They're living things to me; they know me, they return the touch of my hand." Ancient objects are also indices of cultural capital serving as pathways for individual identities; they operate as a locus for a distributed self and we extend ourselves into objects while they extend our own personal trajectories. The articulated notion that materialism enhances, bolsters and maintains a positive self-identity goes back to Henry James (Belk 1985: 266), if not to prehistory itself! Redolent of the pervasiveness of consumerist culture, buying, shopping and consumption have become the vanguard of subject-making (Miller 1997, 1998b). Dense objects such as antiquities have myriad valences for buyers and onlookers, and our unchecked inhibitions and unbridled desires to read into them what we please, their frequent lack of independent didactic force, render them mutable, porous, reflective things. Lack refers not to the apprehended object but to the mobilized strategies of subject-making (Bal 1994: 106).

Networks of ancient objects are enmeshed in logics of their own and our desires for them elicit a great deal of commitment, often to the limits of our economic potential. Yet these practices cannot easily be subsumed

under a determinist, economic calculus: individuals also desire to live
with ancient things, and thus we need to foreground the social dimen-
sionality. Some may cast the social towards a theory of the fetish, since
the exceptional character of the fetish can take any one of a variety of
extreme forms from the basest to the most sublime. An extreme example
is Baudrillard's thesis on the nexus of collecting, seduction and fetishism.
Ultimately over-determined, Baudrillard apprehends the fetish in its
purely sexual guise, rather than looking toward the spiritual and cultural
roots of its potent materiality. He exemplifies the collector's passion as
an attempt to circumscribe and immobilize seduction before transforming it into death energy (1990: 128). Collecting shares an antagonistic
affinity with seduction, perhaps because both involve a game with rules.
It is also a passionate game, a way of classifying and mastering the world
through strategies of possession. It invokes a zeal for abstraction that
defies every moral law in order to maintain the rigid ceremonial of a
closed universe (1990: 122). To seduce, according to Baudrillard (1990:
103), is to make the figures and the signs play amongst themselves.
Seduction is never simply the result of physical attraction, a conjunction
of effects or an economy of desire. For Baudrillard, collectors are ultimately possessive, and their objects seductive. They seek exclusive rights
over the dead object through which their fetishistic desires are sated:
"Reclusion and confinement: beyond all else he is collecting himself."
This love of the object and its attendant amorous stratagems does not
simply reflect upon the seductiveness of the object, but upon the constitution of persons themselves (1990: 122). While undeniably provocative,
Baudrillard's oeuvre is ultimately un-anthropological and unconcerned
with the practices of real people and the valences they accord to objects.
In an extreme post-structuralist vein all personal meaning is erased in
favor of a displaced sexual and economic mastery of the world.

There are certainly poignant embodied aspects and parallels between
persons and things which make the collection of the latter more meaningful. However, these do not have to be sexualized explicitly. There are
three relevant time-frames within the object life cycle: the history of its
production and reception, the subsequent aging of the object, and its
revaluation. The fact that an object passed through the hands of a person
long dead, perhaps a powerful individual, is alluring. Even more fascinating is the recognition that the moment of creation can never be reproduced,
iterating our mourning for lost time. Collectors and archaeologists alike
search for all traces of creation, the actual impression of the hand, use
of tools, marks of identification, which amounts to a search for lineal
descent and paternal transcendence (Baudrillard 1996: 76). Even more

corporeally, things can parallel human aging, going through a cycle and evincing the signs of wear and patina (Dant 1999: 151). This forges a palpable link between human corporeality and the physical manifestations of an object's life history. Ancient objects and collections possess an heirloom quality, albeit not of our own direct ancestors or lineage. They are inscribed with someone else's memory and genealogy, of the numerous hands that touched or held a piece. That embodied connection serves as a temporal linkage and a recollection of our shared humanity. It is through the sensory qualities of touch that we *feel* the compression of time and space, and why all of us desire to touch in the restricted zones of museums and archaeological sites.

Redemptive Things, Transfigured Objects: Commodification and Consumption

Collecting is ultimately a world-making practice that both appeals to our fantasies and acts as a redemptive strategy. Explaining this phenomenon within a crude dualistic framework, Pearce (1998: 16) suggests that collections embody escapism, fantasy, the familiar, community, certainty, control, cohesion, permanence, and a known, safe past. Alternatively, real life presents us with entrapment, facticity, alienation, atomism, doubt, transience, lack of control and the burden of unknown futures. Undoubtedly the materiality of the collection, its tangible being, is very much part of this positive equation. Given the "positive" characteristics of collecting it is not surprising that Egyptian objects, real or replicated, are ripe for accumulation. Things Egyptian are immediately recognizable, unlike, for example, material products of the myriad cultures of Europe or Latin America. They are considered knowable and readable, benefiting from the early decipherment and popularization of hieroglyphs. Everyone can have his or her name reproduced within a royal cartouche – an iconic sign of desire and fantasy substitution. The buyer thus transliterates the presence of the original from the orthography of its native accents (Armstrong 1981: 9). Coupled with the auratic specificities of ancient Egypt, collecting as a practice can be viewed as idolatrous in that it involves the worshiping, revelation and supplication of certain things (Danet and Katriel 1994: 47). Since most Egyptian collectibles have a connection to the religious sphere, this linkage is further strengthened. Historically, Egypt has been perceived as possessing an inexhaustible supply of treasures characterized by superb craftsmanship and embedded within a known, literate and sophisticated society. Alternatively, Pearce (1995: 347) argues that our attitudes are simultaneously undergirded by a sense of revulsion: the statues are too large, the temples too vast and the pyramids lack subtlety. She contends that their paintings are inhuman, their society was ostensibly a slave state and that they were preoccupied with death. Despite the antiquated, incorrect, and largely subjective nature of these interpretations, such characteristics would remain intensely appealing to a large sector of the public. Pearce imputes that this "strong distaste" has been compounded by subsequent collecting practices, including theft and fakery. Fakes are positioned as a type of tourist art and all such copies and reproductions are in-between things that manifest collusion between creator and consumer. They are "allographic" objects whose value does not rely upon historic uniqueness or authenticity: the latter are considered "autographic" (Douglas 1994: 12). In Egypt today tourists are well aware of the fakes and copies they acquire, both in archaeological settings and in bazaars, and seem perfectly happy possessing them.

Why do so many of us want to live with ancient things, or, if that is beyond our reach, fill our world with duplicates of them? This requires interrogating the connection between the real and the copy. One interpretation would posit that the copy is a poor substitute, whereas another would argue that it attracts other valences to itself, and that there are other pleasures encapsulated within the copy. One cannot simply cite economics, or the limited strategies of appropriation, for their popularity. Clearly many people desire the replication or hyperreal in their efforts to navigate and domesticate ancient cultures. Through mass production we, as consumers, can take copies of royal, divine and sacred goods and copy them into the realm of everyday life; they are democratized and become accessible things to enjoy. Consider the particular objects of desire, statues of gods and Pharaohs, pyramids, obelisks, jewelry that are subject to our visual pleasure and are the hallmarks of contemporary trends to collect ethnic and ancient exotica. There is effectively a transference of spheres. The popular appeal of certain forms of heritage gave rise to invented styles based on historic periods and cultures – Victorian, Deco, 1950s, Classical, Oriental, and so on. One need only recall the popularity of Past Times stores in Britain, or Euro-American museum stores whose commodities add to a common bank of historic memories. Egyptian theming is used in marketing in mass media and styling of commodities for fashion, interiors, home wares, beauty products, etc. (Attfield 2000: 225). Attfield defines them as "things with attitude" or rogue elements that invade the well-ordered home. Most fail to fit into the category of "good" in her view, but are a disreputable bunch of objects that talk back or are in bad taste, fancy goods, kitsch, the domestic, the decorative, the feminine, bric-a-brac: all are unashamedly material (2000: 33). One might also regard the proliferation of Egyptian-themed New Age paraphernalia as a concomitant phenomenon: tarot cards, statues, stone pyramids and obelisks, posters, candles, jewelry, etc. While these are evocative examples of "bad taste" in Attfield's schema, they are for their owners deeply symbolic icons that potentially enhance and channel the resonant power and religiosity of ancient Egypt. One can easily decry such collecting, but one cannot elide the significance of the meanings attached and transferred by individuals.

Ancient objects are time travelers – intercessors between worlds that primarily the rich can afford. The buying of antiques or antiquities allows social mobility, another traversing of the fixed world where the object's physicality demarcates the taste and class of the owner. Such objects are thus situating devices. Delving into the murkier depths of websites such as Ebay (see Chippindale and Gill 2001), it is possible to quantify and compare sales of Egyptian artefacts and copies as opposed to other ancient cultures and discern trends in consumption. For Ebay, Egyptian artefacts are second only to the combined sales of Greek and Roman antiquities (Elia, pers. comm.). Several hundred real and fake objects are regularly listed for sale on-line. Many of these objects are of poor quality and subsequently cheaper than high-quality antiquities (*shabtis*, coins, amulets, statuettes, scarabs), opening their markets to a wider swathe of society. They range from only a few dollars to thousands. Overall, over 6 million items are offered on an average day on Ebay, and upwards of 600,000 new items are offered every day (Chippindale and Gill 2001). The thousands of antiquities sold on Ebay reflect the democratization of collecting, that it is no longer simply the purview of the rich.

Theft and circulation, the international traffic in Egyptian objects is also well documented, with Switzerland being the great clearing-house earning over $2 billion annually in stolen artefacts (Greenfield 1989: 247). Foreign buyers, predominantly North Americans, constitute the major players since the sale of illicit artefacts is not heavily monitored in their home territories. Lacking their own tacit connection to ancient culture on their own soil, that of others must be procured. Recently the successful prosecution of New York antiquities dealer, Frederick Schultz, former president of the National Association of Dealers in Ancient, Oriental and Primitive Art, was a first step in an ethical direction (Gerstenblith 2002; Watson 2002). Schultz was involved in the disguising and smuggling of Egyptian antiquities, claiming their provenance from an old English collection: a head of Amenhotep III fetched US$1.2 million. Between 70 and 90 percent of antiquities sold in auctions fail to list a provenance, and these objects are bought by *knowing* individuals and institutions such as the Getty Museum (Elia 1995, 1997, 2002). These are illegal and inalienable goods that, in theory, should not be wrenched from their cultural and national contexts. For many they are supra-objects, non-things, which might exist as entities and deities for their respective cultures, as Davis (1997) documents with Hindu statues. Australian Aboriginal, Native American and Pacific Islanders are other groups who recognize the embodied, subject-like qualities of their fabrications, challenging the containment and musealization of their creations. Beyond the collectors themselves, Western museums are clearly reluctant to give up the old symbolic order, to return Egyptian treasures to their original home. In the early 1980s Egyptian officials sent out letters to thirty foreign museums requesting the return of artefacts. Of the thirty museums contacted only two replied, apologizing for being unable to comply with the request (Wood 1998: 190).

It is often said that museums are the churches of collectors, and it is to this particular connectivity that I now turn. With the proliferation of objects (and objects of study) and the denigration of the written word as a communicative vehicle in the museum sphere, many patrons are now abandoned to the objects themselves (Harris 1990: 146). This could also be read as a redemptive strategy where the purity of the object and its pared-down explanations allow the viewer to apprehend objects directly through the senses. According to statistics gathered in Britain, about 82 percent will visit a museum in their lifetimes. Much of that behavior is class- and education-related as Merriman (1989) documents, with recourse to Bourdieu's structure of habitus. Some see visiting a museum as a means of emulating the upper classes by partaking in an activity that is deemed high culture, rather than leisure (see also Pearce 1998; Price 1989). Museums themselves are status symbols and their visitation is a public display of conspicuous consumption, whether symbolically or literally (Kelly 1987: 2). Museums imbue the visitor with prestige, class, and confer educational attainment, thus facilitating possible forms of social mobility (Bourdieu 1998: 272–3). Visiting the museum could be read as one of the newly constituted fields of "serious leisure" or "meaningful leisure" (Danet and Katriel 1994: 26). Reinforced by the widespread practice of the museum membership, certain individuals are deigned to be in a privileged status group set apart from the general public; they receive exhibit previews, guided tours, special lectures, members' lounges, and discounts at museum stores (Kelly 1987: 28). However, in contemporary culture all purist or unilinear interpretations of the museum as a cultural space are likely to founder, given the manifold complexity of the interocular field that is the museum.

Museum and Mausoleum Culture

Andy Warhol famously said, close a department store and reopen it in a hundred years and you instantly have a museum. His astute comment exposes a long history of overt collaboration. Museums and department stores have always competed in terms of display, architecture, merchandising and patronage (Harris 1990). Although modern museums have their roots in freak shows and *Wunderkammern* rather than in the world of retail, it was not long before the two became indelibly entwined. Indeed architecture and display in nineteenth-century museums and department stores often look interchangeable. It has been said that department stores are the true museums of everyday life. For each location the reordering of time and space forms a necessary conjuncture. Just as the rise of the department store shaped the exhibitionary regimes of the museum, the popularity of the fair and the amusement park became influential in the nineteenth century. Fairs, museums and exhibitions had close formal interactions from the outset: many major metropolitan museums received their collections from exhibitions, crowd control developed in exhibitions and was imported into theme park layout, and natural history museums acquired specimens through the same circus routes used by P. T. Barnum (Bennet 1995: 5). This was also a sphere deeply preoccupied with changing reflections on classification and taxonomy, a major theme of the current project. Museums in the nineteenth century went through various programmatic transformations: they were a social space rather than a private one, they were representative spaces to enhance cultural knowledge and enlightenment, and they were disciplinary spaces where the body was shaped in accordance with cultural directives. With increasing technology, museums and recreation sites became parallel sites of social control and, while the clientele may have been different, the disciplinary strategies were not.

Spearheading a new alliance between museums and big business, a new breed of curators at the American Museum of Natural History (AMNH), the Brooklyn Museum and the Newark Museum each imitated Fifth Avenue display strategies in their exhibits (Hannigan 1998: 98). The great urban museums of the nineteenth century were moving ahead to place both their expertise and their collections within the realm of mass-market manufacturers and retailers (Leach 1993: 164). Archaeology's development in the nineteenth century, specifically the struggle for excavations in civilization's centers such as Egypt and Greece and the booty they yielded, also impacted upon museum display and the politics of presentation. These collections were mobilized to produce a linear narrative presenting the outcome and culmination of the universal story of civilization's development (Bennet 1995: 77). Encountering the Egyptian galleries at the Metropolitan, strategically placed on the ground floor to the right of the main foyer, one first meets the "Line of Time," outlining 3,000 years of art and history (also sold in the store) (Errington 1998: 26). Exactly what has changed? Where museums once fashioned themselves as bastions of elitist culture many scholars now ascribe a closer alignment to populist culture (Boniface and Fowler 1993: 152). That transformation goes hand in hand with new forms of consumerism.

Back in 1880 Joseph Choate, first president of the Metropolitan Museum of Art, urged wealthy merchants to convert pork into porcelain, ore into marble sculptures and stocks into canvases that would endure for centuries and extend individual glory into the memories of future generations (Belk 2001: 116–17): a perfect example of the distributed self and the extension of the embodied biography. The narrative of art's redemptive value, its purifying, sacralizing and elevating qualities were thus fixed. Bataille described the museum as the lungs of a city: people passed through it and emerged refreshed and renewed, like blood (Hegarty 2000: 131). Art occupied the role of religion in a secular modernity, it was the demarcator that defined humanity, especially in monumental form, and was a reflection of our engagement with death (Leach 1997). Ancient objects, severed from their ritual state and relocated in museums, still invoke visual respect and attentiveness, a form of quasi-religious devotion that enhances the experience of the viewer (Davis 1997: 50). Museums are the new temples of authenticity and through our contact with their contents we appropriate their authenticity, interpolating their magical proof of existence into our own life experiences and constructions of self (Handler 1986: 4). Given this history and complexity we need to recalibrate our views on viewing more finely, since ancients and moderns are both revering the images of the gods, for example, although in remarkably different ways. Cartesian in their outlook, Western museum-goers view ancient objects from the past as inanimate fallen idols. Yet as fine art objects from the distant past they were worthy of another kind of religious reverence and regard. As Gell retorted in his intensely reflexive mode: "I know perfectly well that the Egyptian art in the British Museum was never intended for my eyes. This art permits the vicarious abduction of its original, or intended reception, as a component of its current, non-intended reception" (1998: 24).

Museums are vast storehouses of materiality, archiving a permanent record of humanity's engagement with the physical world, its myriad craftings, spiritual fabrications and quotidian needs. Archive-memory relies on recording and amassing documentation to capture the past. It depends heavily on the materiality of the trace and the visibility of the image comprising a giant global repository of the past and all its object species. Archived in storerooms or displayed in glass cases, thousands of things have been transformed from their enchanted contexts and relegated to the signs of culture and otherness. Reminiscent of Borges' Chinese encyclopedia, the Smithsonian in 1982 warehoused 100,000 bats, 2,300 spark plugs, 24,797 woodpeckers, 82,615 fleas, 12,000 Arctic fishing implements, 14,300 sea sponges, 6,012 animal pelts, 2,587 musical instruments and ten samples of dinosaur feces (Belk 2001: 147). Institutions dedicated to the preservation of past materialities – the museum, the library, gallery, and archive – provide the exterior scaffolding for nostalgia and cultural memories. Contemporary desires to collect and retain everything possible are a response to instability and uncertain futures. As Benjamin experienced, a passion for the past often reflects an escape and contempt for contemporary society. Ironically, this sentiment is juxtaposed with modern throw-away consumer culture that treats our everyday objects as disposable and readily replaceable. Today there exists an archive culture where the disinclination to destroy anything in material form, whether documents, speeches, testimonies, or images – in fact any visible sign of the real – is paramount (Hallam and Hockey 2001: 33). Some fear that we are running out of the past, perhaps because we continue voraciously consuming it at a staggering rapidity. Throughout the 1980s in the US an average of 230 museums were opened annually, while in Britain museums are emerging at a pace of one every two weeks. Museums in France, Germany and Japan are similarly burgeoning (Belk 2001: 110).

Museums today offer new, creative recontextualizations, a different sort of object entanglement (Thomas 1991: 5). As Adorno pointed out, museum and mausolea share more than a semantic overlap since both entomb dead visions. Following Adorno, Baudrillard (1994a: 9) exhorted that the confinement of the object is akin to the confinement of the mad and the dead. The museum as the new entertainment palace has been likened by many to an asylum, not simply for objects but rather for the experience of memory and gallery-going rituals (Harris 1990: 81). Using the example of the Lascaux caves and an exact replica constructed a few hundred meters away, Baudrillard claims that while the memory of viewing may be imprinted upon generations to come there is no longer any difference: the duplication suffices to render the *real* artificial (1994a: 9). Many of Baudrillard's examples are archaeological and many are pitched against the increasing musealization that would render them artefacts of science and technological aesthetics.

Museums are intensely auratic spaces, surrounded by guards and glass cases that preserve some order of the real. They instantiate distance and, unlike in the private collection, visual consumers must refrain from touching the objects. That physical contact allows a provisional participation that only intensifies the longing for actual possession (Belk 2001: 128). According to Kopytoff, the non-saleability of the object in the museum adds to its special aura of uniqueness and apartness from the common and mundane. However, old and new forms of consumerism that are subtly dependent upon museum profile and contents are burgeoning in the museum. In the natural history museum there are no guards but plenty of photographic opportunities, children, toys and games in the shops and hamburgers in the restaurant. Alternatively, the fine art museum boasts "plenty of guards, silk scarves in the museum shop, quiche and radicchio salad in the restaurant" (Errington 1998: 28). In New York one need only compare the AMNH and the Metropolitan. The museum store in the Chicago Field Museum boasts 6,000 square feet of merchandise, beginning with Egypt and Africa, vaulted ceilings, custom chandeliers and floor mosaics. The main store is a breathtaking tribute to design and function, and has three awards to its credit so far: from *Chain Store Age* magazine, *Visual Merchandising and Store Design* magazine and the National Association of Store Fixture Manufacturers (www.fieldmuseum.org/store/store_fmstore.htm). The situation is no different in France. The Louvre is a prime tourist attraction that is critical to the Parisian economy and, apart from offering culture, it must also "cater to crowds of hungry, credit-card bearing consumers in search of souvenirs and gifts" thus necessitating "spacious new restaurants and a monumental shopping mall" (Duncan 1999: 315).

Moving further into the museum, the exhibitionary value of Egypt is well known in museum circles. In a report on the top ten ancient exhibits worldwide, Egypt came out as the clear frontrunner with the largest attendance figures for "Treasures of Ancient Egypt" at the National Gallery of Art in Washington: a staggering 430,772 people passed through the gates. It was second only to "A Century of Painting" at the Metropolitan Museum of Art in New York (449,935) for overall attendance throughout 2002. As the report went on to state: "the pulling power of all things Egyptian is second only to the appeal of the Impressionists" (Report 2003: 9). Other highly successful shows were "Eternal Egypt" in San Francisco with 208,870 people and in Kansas City with 114,434. The Louvre exhibition, "The Artists of Pharaoh," recorded 45,000 and "Christian Frescoes from Nubia" in Vienna recorded 160,000. Also impressive was the 156,509 visitors to "Burton, Tutankhamun and the

Table 7.1 Numbers of Visitors at Recent Exhibitions at the British Museum

Exhibition	Date	No. of visitors
Mysteries of Ancient China: New Discoveries from the Early Dynastiess	September 13, 1996 to January 5,1997	162,000
Ancient Faces: Mummy Portraits from Roman Egypt	March 14 to July 20, 1997	75,303
Maori	June 17 to November 1, 1998	39,638
Cracking Codes: The Rosetta Stone and Decipherment	July 10, 1999 to January 16, 2000	144, 851
Gilded Dragons: Buried Treasure from China's Golden Ages	October 23 to February 2000	42,994

Met's Egyptian Expedition" at the Metropolitan in New York. In the top ten list for 2002 half of the exhibits focused upon Egypt, four of those specifically on Pharaonic material. The numbers of visitors at recent exhibitions at the British Museum (Table 7.1) similarly testify to the popularity of Egyptian things. Some 145,000 people visited the exhibition centered around the Rosetta Stone entitled "Cracking Codes," only one (albeit famous) object in the collection, and focused upon the relatively dry topic of writing, as opposed to 162,000 who came to see a very much larger presentation of "Mysteries of Ancient China" as a civilization, and later only around 43,000 who saw China's buried treasure in 2000. Consider the small number of visitors who attended the Maori exhibition in 1998, not quite 40,000 people. "Cracking Codes" was an enormous success, supplemented with a superb catalogue (Parkinson 1999) and designer presentation, itself selling around 26,500 copies. And consumption of Egypt is signified in other related sales. For example, in the 1979 Tutankhamun exhibition in Toronto some $4,000 worth of chocolate in the shape of the famous death mask was sold on a daily basis over sixty days of the exhibition (Wall and Knapper 1981).

The Mummification of Desire: The British Museum

The British Museum forms one focus of this chapter because of the sophistication of their merchandising, stores and publications, and their open access policy; also, unlike museums such as the Metropolitan, the British

Museum officials are exceedingly helpful in providing figures for their sales and exhibitions. The British Museum is known for its vast storehouse of treasures, famous stores and merchandise, publishing house and books, lectures, tours, educational website and special exhibitions. In this manner the institution accords well with the idea that museums embrace social, sacred, cognitive and educational spheres (Kelly 1987: 16). Examining figures from the British Museum's chain of stores in London (Bloomsbury Street and Heathrow airport), their own British Museum Press and impressive on-line sites, it is clear that Egypt is their most successful draw card. Obviously no antiquities are marketed through the museum, so that stores capitalize on the consumer desire to own the object double in an endless series of reproductions manufactured at a smaller scale and with reduced expenditure. And they are good – I have bought many things myself and even when doing this research was drawn into the sticky webs of desire for Egyptian *things*: mouse mats, stationery, housewares, and books, all beautifully reproduced. As Howard Carter famously said when gazing upon the treasures of Tutankhamun, "wonderful things!"

> Like the Museum itself, our online shops contain a rich variety of books and gifts. Some have an educational or practical use; others are simply beautiful objects to give a distinctive touch to any home. Taking the exhibits as their inspiration, each tells a fascinating story and offers a permanent reminder of the wonders to be found in the Museum. Whether you are planning on indulging yourself or are looking for a unique gift, you can now browse our ranges by entering our Egyptian Shop, Exhibition Shop or Children's Shop and those who wish to peruse our complete range of books and gifts can do so by entering either the Gift or Book Shop. We hope you enjoy your visit, your order is greatly appreciated and the proceeds directly support the work of the Museum (http://www.britishmuseum.co.uk/).

Consumerism is thus seen as providing a benefit to culture and its on-going public presentation. The Trustees of The British Museum founded the British Museum Company Ltd in 1973 so as "to advance the educational aims of the Museum" (http://www.britishmuseum.co.uk/). Egypt's popularity is further reflected in the British Museum Company merchandising and its advertising on its official website. Unlike the other cultures represented in the collection, ancient Egypt is the only one to have its own store. The image of a mummy also visibly emblazons the Children's Store, where they focus upon selling mummy jigsaw puzzles, games, pencil sets, sweets, T-shirts and books. One that caught my eye was emblazoned with "I love my mummy." British Museum company practice is not dissimilar to that of other major institutions such as the Chicago Field Museum, encapsulating the appeal by simply exhorting, *Mummies. Mummies. And more mummies. Real ones. Need we say more?* Art enchants the mundane object, whereas its transmutation into design disenchants it. Turning design into a thing returns it to the shelf, the museum, art gallery, collection, and to the world of goods (Attfield 2000: 4). Some may argue, however, that different inspirations are at work here or that copies retain another level of enchantment, albeit replete with a different intensity from the original. On offer are "Magnetic Tut" fridge magnets replete with coffin, clothes, bandages, jewelry, crown, death mask, canopic jars, and so on. And while this may seem macabre in principle, children swarm around these objects in the store and around the real mummies upstairs. Egypt is effectively domesticated and within reach of all, irrespective of education or economics. Statues of the Gayer-Anderson cat; Bastet, ankh and lapis jewelry; lotus and hieroglyph scarves; *shabtis*; calendars; Predynastic blue hippos; miniatures of the gods; playing cards; Royal heads; and Rosetta Stone ties, T-shirts, socks, cups, journals, books, cups, candles, plaques, paper weights, puzzles, etc. As Geof Thompson, merchandising manager for the British Museum Company told me, the British Museum stands for authority and integrity, therefore its replicas must be both distinctive and authentic. The museum's role as an educator is also paramount: here the visitor is buying an education, so one does not have to be guilty about spending. He was adamant that Egypt was at the forefront of this connection and believed that this was largely because the museum had such a long-standing interest in Egypt and that this had guaranteed them their magnificent collection. In the museum the Egyptian galleries occupy great swathes of the ground floor and are typically packed with school groups doing projects and tour groups. An upper floor also houses the Roxie Walker Galleries that specialize in mummies and mortuary archaeology. As one long-time employee remarked, this is the most popular part of the museum, people love the mummies, and the Predynastic mummy named "Ginger" is perhaps the most popular exhibit in the entire museum.

Ancient Egypt reigns supreme for the British Museum Company. Three consumer spheres inform their sales agenda: souvenirs, gifts and cultural products. The largest-selling products are images of Anubis, Egyptian cats (specifically the Gayer-Anderson cat: see Figure 7.1), mummies, and the Rosetta Stone. There is a marked stress upon material connections with the collection. For example, Tutankhamun's image is not employed excessively since this is not part of the museum's collection, reiterating the importance of the local reproductions. Replicas are the most profitable category of object, followed by clothes and accessories, then perhaps food. Replicas take an enormous amount of effort and collaboration between the staff in the Egyptian Antiquities section of the museum and with the merchandising department. The company asserts that their replicas and gifts are based on objects in their collections and often directly molded from the originals: "our replicas are the closest that you can get to owning actual historical pieces." Here we see the salience of popular desire for the real and, since that is not possible for most, the replica forms the perfect substitute tinged with aura and magic. In addition, they produce a wide range of stationery, jewelry and accessories, decorative ornaments and other gifts inspired by objects and motifs within the collections. Appropriately the signage at the main store signals "Silks and Replicas." As one young schoolboy gasped, "Oh cool, you can buy a Rosetta stone!" Not surprisingly the Great Court shops and rest-aurants open at 9 a.m. whereas the collections are open to the public at 10 a.m.; and it is busy from 9 onwards daily. People enter the main store in the foyer in a steady stream before venturing toward the galleries. Many head straight for the bookstall to buy their books and guides before entering; invariably they *buy* before they *see*.

Egypt's disproportionate popularity is spatially marked. At the Children's Store in the newly constructed Great Court half the store is devoted to Egypt, while the rest serves Africa, Europe, Asia, the Americas, and so on. Greek and Roman culture probably ranks second in sales for children. At the main store and bookstore the majority of floor space and banner advertisements are devoted to Egypt. Marketing some time ago planned four distinct spheres: Egypt, British Museum, Greece and Rome, and Britain. More recently, the administration has had more explicit concerns for a universalizing strategy aimed at presenting global culture, and it will be interesting to observe the role of Egypt in that future scheme. But already the push is on for more and more Egyptian things, more games and toys, more popular books and new replicas. When I ask Geof Thompson why he thought Egypt was so popular, he seemed unsure, as if it were simply the given state of affairs. On reflection he cited the popularity of Art deco, as well as a sort of general public consciousness. He then offered that one can actually *see* Egypt at the British Museum, and it was both old and colorful. It is all these things and much more I believe, as I have argued above.

Well-known and respected, the British Museum Press markets a large number of Egyptian titles on-line and through its various stores and is part of their explicit policy of education. According to their on-line publicity:

The British Museum has a long history of publishing, dating back to the mid 18th century, with the first recorded publication of catalogues to the early collections in 1749. The British Museum Press was founded in 1973 and is the world's leading museum publisher. Around 60 books are published each year in the broad subjects of history, archaeology, ethnography, fine and decorative arts and numismatics for scholars, children and the layman.

Their *Dictionary of Ancient Egypt* is a bestseller, along with *How to Read Egyptian Hieroglyphs*. They draw upon history and their long involvement with things Egypt as validation: "5000 years of Ancient Egypt. One publisher" was the slogan that graced their bestseller, *The British Museum Dictionary of Ancient Egypt*. Brochures advertising their books feature Egypt heavily and place them purposively up front. Ancient Egypt also features heavily within children's books. And within the main museum bookstore there exists one of the most impressive collections of books on Egypt one can find, covering a vast range of topics: Egyptian art, mummies, gods, magic, women, queens, death, Pharaohs, myths, hieroglyphs, temples, social history, historiography, Nubia, the Copts, historic travelers, and more unusual topics such as Egypt in modern photography, modern art, and nineteenth-century postcards. Their books now appear in various languages, including Japanese. The British Museum Press also uses the iconic symbol of the mummy on the cover of its *A–Z Companion* for the museum, sold for a mere £6 and another bestseller.

Finally, the British Museum also specializes in expert-led tours overseas to archaeological and historical sites. As their publicity makes clear, in only a few years their outfit has grown to become not only the largest provider of museum tours in the UK but also one of the biggest in the world. The tours provide a way of sharing the museum's renowned specialist knowledge with interested groups of travelers, with tours organized to many of the cultural highlights of the world. Unsurprisingly, as cultural brokers for ancient Egypt, more tours are offered there than for any other country, and this is a salient sphere where education and entertainment/tourism coalesce. The British Museum employs experts, trained Egyptologists, who guide specialized tours around museums and archaeological sites. Their tours include "Essential Egypt," "Egypt Family Tour," "The Splendour that was Egypt," "Egypt: Story of the Nile," "Discover Egypt," etc. As they rightly assert: Who better to be your guide to understanding the diversity of Ancient Egypt than The British Museum? In sum, the British Museum and its company provide a total package – a very successful mix of education, entertainment, shopping, and travel with quality and integrity being their hallmarks. And it is salient that ancient Egypt is central to their public profile at every level. They are part of a new hybrid project that has its roots in past centuries yet is thoroughly future-oriented about its presentation of ancient culture to contemporary audiences.

Shopertainment, Infotainment, Edutainment

Given this success, why is there supposedly a crisis in the sphere of the museum, a crisis of identity? The collapsing of spheres and encompassing of diverse aims and offerings is key in this crisis. Museums are the cultural theme parks of high modernity since they now attempt to provide a total service, including everything from restaurants, entertainments, lectures, films, music, books, gifts, replicas, activities for children and, finally, the exhibits themselves. Despite this new reality, various publics hold rigid and circumscribed notions of the museum as a strictly cultural domain. Consider the outrage in London when the "Bond, James Bond" exhibit opened at the Science Museum. Public indignation focused upon the commercial Hollywood-style entertainment that targeted the masses (the niche market was avowedly 11-year-old boys) and attempted to pass as education. Yet this is an old dilemma. In 1913 the president of the Metropolitan published a monograph entitled *Art in Merchandise: Notes on the Relationship of Stores and Museums* (Belk 2001: 112), and described their collaboration with Macy's. Today of course fashion is tightly enmeshed within the fabric of the Metropolitan, whether in their stores or in their exhibitionary spaces (e.g. The Costume Institute: Bennet 1999). Given the long and fruitful collaboration in Euro-American culture one can only challenge the notion that "in the last century a separation of art and science and of festivity and commerce has taken place in these societies, with the objects and activities in each category fairly sharply distinguished in terms of audience, curatorial experience, and visual ideology" (Appadurai and Breckenridge 1999: 408).

The blurring of museum and theme park is no better evidenced than in the Las Vegas strip. Casinos, including the Bellagio and the Venetian, have significant art holdings (the Venetian showcases the Guggenheim Hermitage Museum), and the Luxor installed a to-scale simulacrum of Tutankhamun's tomb. This accords with the postmodern conflation of popular forms of entertainment or *low culture*, with its opposite *high culture*, in the guise of the museum and its related cultural spaces. Museums, casinos, theme parks and heritage sites are all heterotopic spaces. They are blurred and porous taxa; the museum is a consumer space while the casino is a cultural place, and so on. Both offer additional entertainment, media events and collections. There has been a progressive morphing of domains between education, entertainment and consumption. Collateral institutions of museums, heritage parks, theme parks, shopping malls, and casinos each capitalize upon the wonder, aura, uniqueness, singularity, and spectacle of their materials. "Capitalize" is the operative word here, given that these are all spheres of massive consumption. Throughout the twentieth century museums enlivened their exhibits with dioramas, natural habitats, period rooms and live demonstrations. The remarkable success of Disney theme parks was an additional influence, but it cannot suffice as a solitary explanation. Art indeed imitated life, evidenced by AMNH's exhibitions such as "The Science of Jurassic Park" and "The Lost World: The Life and Death of Dinosaurs" that exactly mirror the popular movie and sequels. Dinosaur replicas were provided by Spielberg's company and the taped tour featured the movies' scientist, Hollywood star Jeff Goldblum (Hannigan 1998: 99). During 1993 the Chicago Museum of Science, Buffalo Museum of Science, Denver Museum of Natural History and three other science museums hosted an exhibition around the TV series and films of *Star Trek*, replete with movie highlights and a "Starfleet Store" (Belk 2001: 120). Organizers proposed that *Star Trek* reinstated a sense of wonder about science and technology and offered a positive vision of the future. McDonaldization and Disneyfication are significant and overt economic and cultural processes only to be matched by the more subtle strategy of disguised market places that are the particular domain of the museum. But whereas Disney is all about illusion and hyperreality, museums retain their cachet because they possess *the real*.

Real and replica converge within the larger museum's edifice, containing the exhibition hall, the store, restaurant, cinema, and so on. Sculpture gardens are used for weddings; gift stores sell designer jewelry, home furnishings and world music; restaurants have become increasingly swanky. Indeed the most successful flagship museums in the US are supported by various revenues: gate receipts, individual memberships, foundation funding, private gifts and public funding from governments or universities, earned income and corporate sponsorships (Clark-Madison 2002: 54). The museum shop, the blockbuster show and the Disneyfication of the museum are the hallmarks of new configurations of cultural and exhibitionary spaces. The Metropolitan, having the most successful museum shop, grossed $65 million in 1988, $6.2 million of which was tax-free profit (Levine 1989: 94). It has outlets in Macy's, the New York Public Library, Soho and in upscale shopping centers in New

Jersey, Connecticut and Ohio, as well as five stores in Japan (Kelly 1993: 234). Their unofficial mascot is the popular blue faience Egyptian hippopotamus replica, nicknamed William (Levine 1989: 96). To achieve financial targets Chicago's Field Museum of Natural History hired a manager from Lord and Taylor, while the Art Institute of Chicago similarly hired from Nieman-Marcus (Belk 2001: 122). Museum stores like those at the Metropolitan or British Museum specialize in authentic reproductions from their own storerooms. At the Metropolitan head curators in specific departments approve these replications with exacting descriptions, with apparent customer consternation if the accompanying authentications are not forthcoming. On their website *Behind the Scenes of the Met Store*, they claim that "Every product created by the Museum is the result of careful research and expert execution by the Metropolitan's staff of art historians, designers, and master craftspeople, who ensure that each reproduction bears the closest possible fidelity to the original." And further, "when works of art are still under excavation, too large to move, or otherwise difficult to access" their mold-maker "goes off-site to make molds for the Metropolitan. These molds are used to create reproductions for sale . . ." Patrons attribute authenticity to those objects sold in museum shops, or at a minimum authentic museum-quality. Shop staff at the Metropolitan claim that their replicas are of higher quality than their rivals, the British Museum and the Louvre. This, of course, is debatable and one receives different answers depending upon who is interviewed. People would generally rather buy the same product/s at a museum shop than at any other retail outlet.

The Metropolitan also rents out its galleries for functions: cocktail parties, dinners, and corporate functions at costs upwards of $30,000 (Kelly 1993: 233). I have attended Egyptological events hosted at the Temple of Dendur, a perfect space reminiscent of a Pharaonic sacred lake. A similar cocktail party at the temple recently featured in a romantic Hollywood blockbuster *Maid in Manhattan*. Jennifer Lopez walked toward the temple wearing a densely pleated evening dress that was remarkably reminiscent of the famous curvaceous statue of Queen Nefertiti wearing pleated linen: perhaps a little too striking to be coincidence. One of the most popular destinations in the entire museum, *the real* (an ancient temple constructed in 15 BC by the Roman emperor Augustus) is housed within a supremely modernist architectural space where natural light gives the impression of exteriority coupled with the addition of papyrus and water within a conventional gallery. As a nodal point of the ground floor galleries, people can move around the space, apprehend its solid physicality, enter the temple, or sit and reflect, so that numerous tour groups and school parties come here to escape the glass-case atmosphere, given that the expansive inside/outside effect lends the feeling of a living museum. Dismantled to save it from the rising waters of Lake Nasser after the building of the Aswan High Dam, the temple was a gift to the United States from the Egyptian government in recognition of the American contribution to the international campaign to save the ancient Nubian monuments. The Dendur Temple has a unique biography of its own that remains to be fully narrated. This requires moving our scholarship beyond the instance of creation, the date and place of fabrication, toward the constitutive knowledge of the object and its accrued meanings through time, and the object's participation in forms of ongoing social life.

Based on observational studies of visitation at the Metropolitan, the British Museum, the Louvre, and various other international institutions, Kelly (1993: 232) consistently found that a staggering 30 percent of museum visitors never actually *visit* the galleries, even if they had traveled from overseas, it was a first-time visit, or they had paid a substantial sum to be taken on tour. Rather, they head directly for the store to buy a souvenir, replica or other things that signify and materialize their pilgrimage. Since the museum is a sacred space, purchasing replicas of its contents extends that process of sacralization and the concomitant acquisition of knowledge, virtuosity and cultural capital. Materialism can be repackaged as both noble and valuable. Even if one cannot afford the real, the copy retains the transcendent qualities of magic, aesthetics, wisdom or love. One might see this as an objectification of objects (Belk 2001: 147), accumulating new registers of meaning and experience. If one cannot view or possess the ancient original, there is always the replica or the postcard. If one cannot visit Egypt and experience archaeology in the real, there are other alternatives such as The Luxor Hotel and Casino. They are two evocative examples of the very same processes of desire for, and consumption of, things Egyptian.

False Coin of its Dream: The Luxor, Las Vegas

The story of Las Vegas as the ultimate postmodern city assumes legendary status amongst cultural theorists (Gottdiener, Collins, and Dickens 1999; Littlejohn 1999; Rothman 2002; Rothman and Davis 2002; Taylor 1997), particularly the aggressive hyperreal theming of its casinos and the collapsing of experiential spheres. Postmodern positioning views Vegas as the classic heterotopic space; a placeless place, both mirror and mirage, absolutely unreal, and only surface and shadow. It is considered a space of heterochrony, of timelessness that breaks with traditional temporal schemes. Foucault also saw museums as similarly constituted: "a place of all times that is itself outside of times, all epochs, all forms, all tastes" (Foucault 1986: 242). What is striking at The Luxor is the explicit amalgamation of consumption, entertainment, education and exhibition that work to full effect when situated around the icons of Egypt. Yet beyond the postmodern narratives of fluidity and play, Las Vegas presents us with a tightly controlled and disciplined geography. The Luxor is the perfect exhibitionary space (Bennet 1999), combining the *spectacle* of Egypt with the *surveillance* aspect of the casino's rigid monitoring systems, and with the *disciplining* nature of architecture specifically designed to control patrons. Our saturation within the culture of spectacle belies the modernist assumption that real and imaginary are valid distinctions (Rojek 1993). Luxor designers have exhibited a consummate dedication to Egyptian art, architecture and cultural custom at every level from the cutlery and carpeting to the enormous statuary, wall paintings and architecture itself. People pose for photographs with Egyptian statues just as they do in the real Luxor, imploding time/space specificities that

Figure 7.2 The Sphinx and pyramid of The Luxor Hotel and Casino. Photo by the author.

is typical of heterotopic spaces. Designers claim The Luxor is "a place to have an adventure," "it's a living thing" and "it will never close" (Morris 1994). Egyptian ritual objects of veneration, in their original ancient settings, have been transposed to the modern sphere, the pyramid, the obelisk, statues of gods and Pharaohs – only the understandings and inherent religiosity have changed. It is the perfect site for the flipside analysis of the reification of Egyptian objects and their potent materialities.

The Luxor is a hotel-casino; a thirty-storey pyramid of black glass sits in its geometrical splendor in the desert, not unlike the original great pyramid (Schull 2001). When it was built the 4,455-room casino cost $700 million; it is the second largest hotel in the world, employing 4,000 people. It receives between 15,000 and 20,000 visitors each day, according to Luxor marketing. The 47–acre domain mixes ancient Middle Eastern themes, featuring incongruous themed simulations resulting from a type of geographical dyslexia. Despite the rigorous theming and dedication to authentic reproduction by designers who copied from Egyptology books, two huge Mayan pyramids have surreptitiously crept into the construction: one in the pool area another on the entertainment level. Inside the casino is the largest atrium in the world, some 29 million cubic feet; one is able to encase not merely a dead Pharaoh but the gigantic mass of nine 747 airplanes (Gottdiener, Collins, and Dickens 1999: 39). Themed casinos like The Luxor are indicative of the new architainment: designers impute that you no longer need neon signage when you can employ dynamic architectures to sign casinos – the Excalibur, Caesar's Palace, and the Venetian are other examples of ancient theming. As one employee proudly stated: "Unlike some of the other casinos, The Luxor keeps its theme throughout the hotel. Others only go so far." As the promotional materials state:

> The Luxor is easily the most spectacular setting in all of Las Vegas. Luxor now has everything to make your trip a historic event. Settle into one of our lush Egyptian styled rooms, and then float the day away in our spectacular pool and private cabana area. As our guest at the Luxor rediscover a world of upscale shopping, wonder at the treasures of ancient Egypt and enjoy luxurious accommodations fit for royalty. Luxor stands as a shimmering monument to comfort, luxury and impeccable service.

Reproductions and simulations at this staggering scale reinforce the fantasy environment, and the close proximity of this tightly knit urban texture proffers a phantasmagoric landscape. Robust theming of exteriors (and in The Luxor's case, interiors) results in a hyperreal spectacle that in turn belies the real logic of commodity production. Some 30 million visitors come each year for the sex, glitter, fantasy, entertainment and risk. Vegas underscores Debord's notion of spectacle that is the defining attribute of industrial society (Gottdiener, Collins, and Dickens 1999: 93). In that sense Las Vegas is not atypical, it is simply an extreme signifier of symbolic capital, of fantasy and leisure, and amusing ourselves to death.

Figure 7.3 Sphinx and inscribed obelisk on the attractions floor, Luxor Hotel and Casino. Photo by the author.

Luxor Casino's pyramid is a vehicle that transforms and transports visitors to another time and place, past and future (Schull 2001: 395). This plays on the trope of the pyramid as time machine, popular in many films and other media. As Tschumi encapsulates it (cited in Taylor 1997), the pyramid is a figure of longing for transcendence and permanence. The pyramid, as a shape, supposedly exudes its own force, offering visitors weird and wonderful experiences of alterity, and perhaps luck. Guests claim to experience odd sensations from sleeping in the pyramid. As one masseuse at the Oasis Spa told me, "Lots of people come in needing a massage because they think the pyramid has negative energy." When I suggested that pyramid power was once thought to exert positive energy, she replied that "Some people say the pyramid makes them feel worse, others better." Originally The Luxor also featured a Nile boat ride that took patrons from the registration desk to the elevators that was also part of a larger "archaeological tour" replete with guides that took visitors back in time 4,000 years (Morris 1994). Sadly this attraction was subsequently closed and cemented over because the water became putrid, people frequently jumped into The Luxor's Nile, and the whole venture was deemed unhealthy. Vacation and death, the freedom to traverse worlds and ordinary experiences are also foregrounded in The Luxor's promotional materials. As Schull documents, some visitors literalize the connection by jumping to their deaths from the central atrium of the pyramid. Lore has it that many more suicides occur at The Luxor than its rival casinos. The Luxor is also dangerous ground outside the walls of the pyramid. Pilots claim to see the penetrating Xenon light, a 315,000-watt beam from the obelisk, visible ten miles into space. Drivers complain that the sun's blinding reflection off the glass has caused numerous car accidents, and nightly projected images from the eyes of the sphinx, ten storeys high and taller than the original, are likened to shooting lasers (Schull 2001: 396).

Like modern museums, The Luxor collapses entertainment and education, culture and economics, and forms part of the new experiential economy (see also Hall in press). While the museum was indelibly influenced by the rise of the department store and its taxonomic structures, the casino is deeply shaped by the contours of both museum and store, resulting in a modern cultural space that offers exhibits, restaurants, shops, activities, and so on. Described as "an oasis of entertainment," The Luxor casino boasts an "authentic reproduction" of the burial chamber of Tutankhamun, constructed in collaboration with Egyptologists. The president of the casino traveled to Egypt himself to conduct his own research (Schull 2001: 396), here again blurring the

Figure 7.4 Casino foyer inside pyramidal atrium, Luxor Hotel and Casino. Photo by the author.

boundaries between education and entertainment. During the opening week some fifty Egyptian officials were flown into Las Vegas to view the spectacle and to undoubtedly lend their own aura of authenticity. Visitors are greeted by an introductory video made by the BBC, hosted by the historian Christopher Frayling – and a piece of the Great Pyramid in a glass case sent as a gift by the Egyptian Tourism Department. While the museum has copies of many of the most spectacular objects, they are not accurately arranged because, as the soundtrack explains, "this affords you a better view." Looking through hacked glassed-in holes in fake walls, the whole effect is literally that of a robbed tomb, which is inevitably rather apt. The disembodied voice of Howard Carter escorts the visitor through the exhibit, much like the video guides at traditional museums; he explains the Egyptian processes of mummification and describes the functions of certain objects. In another form of object personification, a ventriloquist for Carter comments that these are objects awakened from 3,000 years of slumber. There is an aura of simulacrum, just as there was an aura with the original (Baudrillard 1997: 10–11). Nothing but the semblance of the king's body was ever present. The secret of The Luxor pyramid is that there is no pyramid (Taylor 1997: 248), and certainly no entombed Pharaoh and his accompanying treasure, although the specter of treasure pervades the casino. Since the opening of Tutankhamun's tomb, people have not been able to get enough of Egypt, to consume its luxuries and bask in its iconography. In fact, from the nineteenth century it has been a recurrent motif in art, film, clothing, décor and design. Tutankhamun is a constant presence throughout much of the casino from restaurant props, to decorative statues, to replicas, to children's toys. The voice of Carter tells us that "we are bringing him greater fame through showing him at The Luxor," and makes the obvious comparisons to other great cultures: Egypt is of course greater. And Tutankhamun has survived it all. Ancient objects shift representational contexts from antiquity to modernity, and the successive phases of the image move from the reflection of a profound reality to that which masks and denatures a profound reality; finally, the image has no relation to reality whatsoever: it is its own pure simulacrum (Baudrillard 1994a: 6). And it is a further simulacrum that greets the visitor after the museum: yet another store selling copies, and Luxor – and Egyptian-themed products primarily made in China. Two videos play simultaneously side by side: one shows the archaeology and architecture of Egypt discussed by renowned Egypt-ologists, the other shows the architecture and construction of the Luxor casino.

Aggressively themed and synergistic, The Luxor is the site of the mutual convergence of four active consumer systems: shopping, dining, entertainment and education. The Luxor also offers edutainment such as the *Mysteries of Egypt*, a National Geographic tour featuring Egypt's greatest star, Omar Sharif, recounting his homeland's legends. As he shares the myths and magic of the chambers of the sacred tomb of King

Figure 7.5 Tomb goods from the replica tomb of Tutankhamun, Luxor Hotel and Casino. Photo by the author.

Tutankhamun spectators are invited to look over his shoulder through magnificent Egypt and its treasures. Other imagineering efforts include *Secrets of the Luxor Pyramid*, written and directed by Douglas Trumbell, who also worked on *2001: A Space Odyssey, Close Encounters of the Third Kind, Star Trek,* and *Blade Runner.* As Trumbell quips, "you're not just looking at a movie, you're in the movie; you become a character" (quoted in Taylor 1997: 242–3). The theater itself operates as a time machine in full hyperreal spectacle. Blending the visualization of IMAX with an animated Disney ride, *In Search of the Obelisk* is one feature that, unlike the rest of the casino, makes no attempts at authenticity. Trumbell explains this obvious fact by exhorting that the production is based on a pre-Egyptian civilization, and that "everything you've ever seen in Egypt is a poor facsimile of what this high-tech civilization developed" (quoted in Morris 1994) as if this was somehow factual! Designers were at pains to present "a good future" where everything was nice and harmonious, recapping the idea of the pyramid as time-machine. Visitors are taken on an elevator ride that simulates a drop of some 1,000 feet, arriving in a dark, cavernous room populated with a two–storey faux sphinx with eyes that flash blue laser beams: Trumbell calls this styling "crypto-Egypto." Jaded attendants herd visitors into the theater where they experience a bone-crunching ride while watching a dramatic *Star Wars* genre film. The experience is devoid of anything archaeological or Egyptological; rather, this is science fiction at its worst. Fabricated and stagy, this is where Disneyfication reigns supreme and edutainment is abandoned. While this may seem unsurprising, it is significant given the relentless dedication to Egyptian theming in a casino where even the renovations are couched in antiquity: "Pardon the inconvenience, the Pharaoh is re-carpeting his home" was emblazoned on glossy signs placed near construction work.

The Luxor sells both the *real* and the *hyperreal*. In the aptly named "Treasure Chest" real antiquities from New York dealer Jerome Eisenburg are for sale: *shabti* $400, faience necklace $75, wooden coffin face $3,000, Ptah-Sokar Osiris figure $3,000 and, quite appropriately, many faience gaming pieces for around $400. One employee told me that teachers are their best clients, "they like that they are authentic," while other customers explain straight out that they cannot afford to buy "but they

Figure 7.6 Replicas and real antiquities at the "Treasure Chest," Luxor Hotel and Casino. Photo by the author.

just want to hold the antiquities." Customers have asked whether the salespeople are "frightened of the curse, I tell them I'm not because these antiquities have passed through many hands." In another store, "Secrets of Luxor," one salesperson claimed: "I've always been interested in Egypt and read a lot. I've learnt a lot since I worked here too." The store sells many academic books and videos, such as British Museum publications. As one assistant said: "People buy lots of books. They come here and they get hooked on Egypt." While some products in the store come directly from Egypt (leather goods, glass, papyrus) the vast majority are made in China and, as one assistant quipped, "People like things to come from Egypt, but when they see those copies from China, they don't care so much." In "The Cairo Bazaar" another assistant reiterated that "a lot of our stuff comes from Egypt" and explained that this was of interest to her customers. She also ventured "people like history" and relatedly that "people like to collect . . . some like the Luxor logo, some don't. They go from casino to casino collecting stuff." In fact there are more shops in The Luxor than in the British Museum or Metropolitan Museum of Art put together. Their stock in trade is pyramids, obelisks, statues of gods and Pharaohs, Tutankhamun replicas, mummies, and so on,

Figure 7.7 Excavating Egypt at the Pharaoh's Pheast Buffet, Luxor Hotel and Casino. Photo by the author.

iterating a clear focus on ritual and religion, specifically around the domain of death. Educational books and videos jostle for space alongside T-shirts, clothing, bags, replicas, prints, jewelry, glasses, home wares, toys, magnets, key-rings, pens, and stationery.

Guests at The Luxor can also consume Egypt, albeit in name only. Venues include the Nefertiti Lounge, Isis, Papyrus, Pharaoh's Pheast Buffet, Luxor Steakhouse and Nile Deli. In the Pyramid Café, for example, they boast "Traditional breakfast specialties to honor Pharaoh's cere-monial morning ritual" that include Nectars of the Nile, Eggs Benedict à la Cheops, Valley of the Kings Breakfast, and so on. Side dishes are framed as Sides of the Pyramid, whereas breads fall under the banner of The Royal Grainery. For lunch one can dine on the DeLuxor Burger, followed by a Temple of Luxor Banana Split. It is not only Egyptian statuary and architecture that is staggering in its magnitude. Rather, at the level of minutiae, it is the devotional detail shown to the mundane: wallpaper, crockery, bathroom tiles, fake papyrus plants, carpet motifs, lotus columns, faux sandstone walls, Egyptian moldings, gilt decorations, and hieroglyphs everywhere from floor to ceiling. Even the slot machines have salubrious names including Mummy Mayhem, Egyptian Treasures, Queen of the Nile, Cleopatra, and so on. The Baccarat room looks remark-ably like the White Chapel of Senwosret I in Luxor (Egypt). The main gaming floor is a giddying display of massive hieroglyph-clad ceilings, gaudy statues, decorative columns and slot machines flashing treasure! Ironically this recalls Harris's (1990: 57) charge that late nineteenth-century America had been "suborned by the machine or deluded by national conceit into an affection for meretricious ornament and senti-mental, crudely wrought art." That being said, I do not wish this chapter to stand as a critique of Egypt's place in replicatory regimes or as an assault on practices of popular consumption and representation. That, I believe, would be both an easy and superficial reading of the edutainment domain. The processes at work here are sophisticated and complex, aiming at both authenticity and experience, and are clearly not com-pletely divorced from our academic enterprises. It would be a mistake to dismiss them as belonging outside our remit; rather they are testament to the popularity of our own scholarly productions and perhaps the nar-rowing chasm between public and academic discourses.

Egypt Rising: Materialities Past and Future

Ancient Egypt possessed perhaps the earliest and best-known culture to fetishize material objects in ways moderns can apprehend: to adorn the body, replicate the self, immortalize and memorialize the individual, magically intervene into otherworldly spheres, to improve upon nature and to accumulate a wide array of things during life and subsequently take them to the grave. Egypt's legacy of embodied materiality and its specific cultural inheritance clearly demand our attention. Its particularities should be studied contextually, yet these object lessons have the interpretative power to contrast with our own culture and make us reflect on our philosophies of materiality. The highly charged nature of visualizing and materializing in ancient Egyptian society can be explored in relation to human agency, power, the desire to control fate and technologies of enchantment. From life to death the material world instantiated, reflected and shaped social life and, concomitantly, potential existence in the afterworld. Those same evocative Egyptian materials are still potent signifiers in Western culture and one can readily trace their appreciation in the modern world. The Luxor Casino may be an extreme example of Egypt and the saturation of its signifiers, but is in itself a monumental testament to the desire and longing that coalesces around the materiality of Egypt today. Thousands of years after the demise of Pharaonic Egypt as a coherent cultural sphere, so many lay people as well as scholars are fascinated with Egypt's tangible and spiritual achievements, although it is the overpowering physicality that serves as the bedrock for our fantasies and fascinations.

To evince this connection one need only consider the place of Egypt in museums and their connected spheres of consumption and replication. The modern museum, and its combined role as showcase and shopping center, offers reproductions and replications of the real Egypt. The conflation between museum and store is reiterated by the spatial logic of their entwined placement. The auratic quality of the ancient can then be desired and owned in the present in a very different sphere of value than in the original context. Although, as outlined with the example of the Gayer-Anderson cat, perhaps for some individuals these connections are not altogether unrelated. As suggested above, moderns revere the same things as ancients, a process of replication and reverence that has been reinvented and historically produced through the millennia. Ritual and religious objects are devotional materials that cultures both hold in awe and have venerated within their own discursive practices. At the heart of these processes lies the relationship of ancient material culture and its representation to the public. In the main, archaeology can only be presented through its artefactual nature – that is, its very thingness. As archaeologists, we cannot easily replicate the processes of archaeology; our technics and praxis, therefore the results of our labor, the objects themselves, become our disciplinary mode of production: objects are the immediate and tangible signs of the past as past and as memory.

Taking the contemporary consumption of ancient Egyptian materials, I have attempted to document the very peculiar discursive nature of modern relationships to Egypt's past through the processes of replication. Ancient objects store up an investment of human observation and emotion, they become physical receptacles of feeling and focus. Through things Egyptian we suffer the melancholia of loss and its confronting paradoxes: "the past is irrecoverable and that past is not past; the past is the resource for the future and the future is the redemption of the past; loss must be marked and it cannot be represented; loss fractures representation itself and loss precipitates its own modes of expression" (Butler 2003: 467). Egyptian art and archaeology hold a specific place in the Western imaginary and are perhaps the most salient signs of deep time and cultural difference, now lost. Loss creates longing. From Las Vegas casinos to British Museum gift stores, the popularity of copied Egyptian material culture far outstrips that of other ancient groups. Egyptian things occupy an iconic status that is so seductive for those who have come after, and their particular aesthetic is seemingly timeless. Our engagement with Egypt and with the materiality of the past more generally cannot be adequately encompassed by superficial notions of exoticism or Disneyfication, despite burgeoning trends in a globalized economy. Owning things Egyptian or their copies transfers part of the special resonant magic of their ancient culture to us as modern consumers. It is the spiritual resonance, esoteric and secret knowledge, notions of permanence and timelessness, aesthetics and bodily beauty, scientific achievement, and finally the possibility of life eternal, that are all tacitly embraced in both real and reproduced materials, and in the act of possessing them. Their efficacious and auratic qualities, that unique manifestation of distance, are then transmuted into the sphere of consumer possibility. Our vision of Egypt today is that of a mysterious world populated by pyramids, sphinxes, temples, tombs, statues, mummies and the accoutrements of death. In vain we attempt to grasp the myriad meanings and cultural cadences of their object world, but the link is eternally severed. What we simply have left are their things, the physical reminders and instantiations of the greatness that was Egypt.

Bibliography

Andreu, G. (2002). "Meretseger," in G. Andreu (ed.), *Les artistes de Pharaon: Deir el-Médineh et la Vallée des Rois*, pp. 275–81. Paris: Reunion des Musées Nationaux.

Appadurai, A. (1986a). "Introduction: commodities and the politics of value," in A. Appadurai (ed.), *The Social Life of Things: Commodities in Cultural Perspective*, pp. 3–63. Cambridge: Cambridge University Press.

—— Editor. (1986b). *The Social Life of Things: Commodities in Cultural Perspective*, Cambridge: Cambridge University Press.

Appadurai, A. and C. A. Breckenridge (1999). "Museums are good to think: heritage on view in India," in D. Boswell and J. Evans (eds), *Representing the Nation*, pp. 404–20. London: Routledge.

Apter, E. (1993). "Introduction," in E. Apter and W. Pietz (eds), *Fetishism and Cultural Discourse*, pp. 1–9. Ithaca, N.Y.: Cornell University Press.

Arendt, H. (1958). *The Human Condition*, Chicago, Ill.: University of Chicago Press.

—— (1968). "Introduction," in W. Benjamin (ed.), *Illuminations*, pp. 1–55. New York: Schocken Books.

Armstrong, R. P. (1981). *The Powers of Presence: Consciousness, Myth and Affecting Presence*, Philadelphia, Pa.: University of Pennsylvania Press.

Assmann, J. (1993). "Literatur und Karneval im Alten Ägypten," in S. Döpp (ed.), *Karnevaleske Phanomene in antiken und nachantiken Kulturen und Literaturen*, pp. 31–57. Trier: Verlag Trier.

—— (2001). *The Search for God in Ancient Egypt*, Ithaca, N.Y.: Cornell University Press.

Attfield, J. (2000). *Wild Things: Material Culture of Everyday Life*, Oxford: Berg.

Bachelard, G. (1994). *The Poetics of Space: The Classic Look at How We Experience Intimate Places*, Boston, Mass.: Beacon Press.

Baines, J. (1984). "Interpretations of religion: logic, discourse, rationality," *Göttinger Miszellen* 76: 25–54.

—— (1990). "Restricted knowledge, hierachy, and decorum: modern perceptions and ancient institutions," *Journal of the American Research Center in Egypt* 27: 1–23.

—— (1994). "On the status and purposes of ancient Egyptian art," *Cambridge Archaeological Journal* 4: 67–94.

—— (2002). "Egyptian letters of the New Kingdom as evidence for religious practice", *Journal of Ancient Near Eastern Religions* 1: 1–31.

Baines, J. and P. Lacovara (2002). "Burial and the dead in ancient Egyptian society: respect, formalism, neglect," *Journal of Social Archaeology* 2: 5–36.

Bakhtin, M. (1984). *Rabelais and His World*, Bloomington, Ind.: Indiana University Press.

Bal, M. (1994). "Telling objects: a narrative perspective on collecting," in J. Elsner and R. Cardinal (eds), *The Cultures of Collecting*, pp. 97–115. Cambridge, Mass.: Harvard University Press.

Balzac, H. de. (1844–46). *Cousin Pons*, New York: A. L. Burt Company.

Barthes, R. (1957). *Mythologies*, London: Paladin.

Bataille, G. (1988). *The Accursed Share: Volume I*, New York: Zone Books.

Baudrillard, J. (1990). *Seduction*, New York: St. Martin's Press.

—— (1993). *Symbolic Exchange and Death*, London: Sage.

—— (1994a). *Simulacra and Simulation*, Ann Arbor, Mich.: University of Michigan Press.

—— (1994b). "The system of collecting," in J. Elsner and R. Cardinal (eds), *The Cultures of Collecting*, pp. 7–24. Cambridge, Mass.: Harvard University Press.

—— (1996). *The System of Objects*, London: Verso.

—— (1997). *Art and Artefact*, London: Sage.

—— (1998). *The Consumer Society*, London: Sage.

—— (2001). *Impossible Exchange*, London: Verso.

Bauer, A. A. (2002). "Is what you see all you get? Recognizing meaning in archaeology," *Journal of Social Archaeology* 2: 37–52.

Belk, R. (1985). "Materialism: trait aspects of living in the material world," *Journal of Consumer Research* 12: 265–80.

—— (1991). "Possessions and the sense of past," in R. Belk (ed.), *Highways and Buyways: Naturalistic Research from the Consumer Behavior Odyssey*, pp. 287–92. Provo, Ut.: Association for Consumer Research.

—— (2000). "Are we what we own?," in A. L. Benson (ed.), *I Shop, Therefore I Am: Compulsive Buying and the Search for Self*, pp. 76–104. Northvale, N.J.: Jason Aronson.

—— (2001). *Collecting in a Consumer Society*, London: Routledge.

Bell, L. (1997). "The New Kingdom 'Divine' Temple: The example of Luxor," in B. E. Shafer (ed.), *Temples of Ancient Egypt*, pp. 127–84. Ithaca, N.Y.: Cornell University Press.

Belting, H. (1994). *Likeness and Presence: A History of the Image Before the Era of Art*, Chicago, Ill.: University of Chicago Press.

Bender, B. (1998). *Stonehenge: Making Space*, Oxford: Berg.

—— (2001). "Landscapes on the move," *Journal of Social Archaeology* 1: 75–89.

Benjamin, W. (1968). *Illuminations*, New York: Schocken Books.

—— (1979). "Doctrine of the similar (1933)," *New German Critique* 17: 65–9.

—— (1999). "Doctrine of the similar," in M. Jennings, H. Eiland, and G. Smit (eds), *Walter Benjamin: Selected Writings, Volume 2 (1927–1934)*, pp. 694–8. Cambridge, Mass.: Harvard University Press.

Bennet, T. (1995). *The Birth of the Museum: History, Theory, Politics*, London: Routledge.

—— (1999). "The exhibitionary complex," in D. Boswell and J. Evans (eds), *Representing the Nation*, pp. 323–61. London: Routledge.

Blake, E. C. (1999). "Identity mapping in the Sardinian Bronze Age," *European Journal of Archaeology* 2: 55–75.

Bleeker, C. J. (1967). *Egyptian Festivals: Enactments of Religious Renewal*, Leiden: E. J. Brill.

Bochi, P. A. (1994). "Images of time in ancient Egyptian art," *Journal of the American Research Centre in Egypt* 31: 55–62.

Bolton, L. (2001). "What makes Singo different: North Vanuatu textiles and the theory of captivation," in C. Pinney and N. Thomas (eds), *Beyond Aesthetics: Art and the Technologies of Enchantment*, pp. 97–115. Oxford: Berg.

Bomann, A. H. (1991). *The Private Chapel in Ancient Egypt*, London and New York: Kegan Paul International.

Boniface, P. and P. J. Fowler (1993). *Heritage and Tourism in "the Global Village"*, London: Routledge.

Bourdieu, P. (1977). *Outline of a Theory of Practice*, Cambridge: Cambridge University Press.

—— (1998). *Distinction: A Social Critique of the Judgement of Taste*, London: Routledge.

Bowdler, S. (1996). "Freud and archaeology," *Anthropological Forum* 7: 419–38.

Boyer, P. (1996). "What makes anthropomorphism natural: intuitive ontology and cultural representations," *Journal of the Royal Anthropological Institute* 2: 83–97.

Boym, S. (2001). *The Future of Nostalgia*, New York: Basic Books.

Bradley, R. (2000). *An Archaeology of Natural Places*, London: Routledge.

Brunner-Traut, E. (1979). *Egyptian Artists' Sketches: Figured Ostraka from the Gayer-Anderson Collection in the Fitzwilliam Museum, Cambridge*, Leiden: Nederlands Historisch-Archaeologisch Instituut te Istanbul.

Bruyère, B. (1930). *Rapport sur les Fouilles de Deir el Médineh (1929), Deuxième Partie*, Cairo: Imprimerie de l'Institut Français d'Archéologie Orientale.

—— (1939). *Rapport sur les Fouilles de Deir el Médineh (1934–1935), Troisème Partie FIFAO 16*, Cairo: Imprimerie de l'Institut Français d'Archéologie Orientale.

Buchli, V. (2002a). "Immateriality", Presented at an American Anthropological Association Meeting, New Orleans, November 22.

—— (2002b). "Introduction," in V. Buchli (ed.), *The Material Culture Reader*, pp. 1–22. Oxford: Berg.

Buchli, V. and G. Lucas. Editors. (2001). *Archaeologies of the Contemporary Past*, London: Routledge.

Butler, J. (2003). "Afterword: after loss, then what?," in D. L. Eng and D. Kazanjian (eds), *Loss: The Politics of Mourning*, pp. 467–77. Berkeley, Calif.: University of California.

Byrne, D. (2003). "Messages to Manila," in Many Exchanges: archaeology, history, community and the work of Isabel McBryde, *Aboriginal History* 11.

Campbell, C. (1987). *The Romantic Ethic and the Spirit of Modern Consumerism*, Oxford: Basil Blackwell.

Campbell, S. (2001). "The captivating agency of art: many ways of seeing," in C. Pinney and N. Thomas (eds), *Beyond Aesthetics: Art and the Technologies of Enchantment*, pp. 117–35. Oxford: Berg.

Chapman, J. (2000). *Fragmentation in Archaeology: People, Places, and Broken Objects in the Prehistory of South-Eastern Europe*, London: Routledge.

Chesson, M. Editor. (2001). *Social Memory, Identity and Death: Ethnographic and Archaeological Perspectives on Mortuary Rituals*, Washington: American Anthropological Association.

Chilton, E. Editor. (1999). *Material Meanings: Critical Approaches to the Interpretation of Material Culture*, Salt Lake City, Ut.: University of Utah Press.

Chippindale, C. and D. W. J. Gill. (2001). "On-line auctions: a new venue for the antiquities market," *Culture without Context* 9: 4–12.

Clark-Madison, M. (2002). "Museums for the masses," in *Hemispheres*, September, pp. 50–8.

Connerton, P. (1989). *How Societies Remember*, Cambridge: Cambridge University Press.

Coombe, R. J. (1998). *The Cultural Life of Intellectual Properties*, Durham, N.C.: Duke University Press.

Critchley, S. (2002). *On Humour*, London: Routledge.

D'Alleva, A. (2001). "Captivation, representation, and the limits of cognition: interpreting metaphor and metonymy in Tahitian *Tamu*," in C. Pinney and N. Thomas (eds), *Beyond Aesthetics: Art and the Technologies of Enchantment*, pp. 79–96. Oxford: Berg.

Danet, B. and T. Katriel (1994). "Glorious obsessions, passionate lovers and hidden treasures: collecting, metaphor, and the Romantic ethic," in S. H. Riggins (ed.), *The Socialness of Things*, pp. 23–61. Berlin and New York: Mouton de Gruyter.

Dant, T. (1999). *Material Culture in the Social World: Values, Activities, Lifestyles*, Philadelphia, Pa.: Open University Press.

Davis, N. Z. (1978). "Women on top: symbolic sexual inversion and political disorder in early modern Europe," in B. A. Babcock (ed.), *Reversible World: Symbolic Inversion in Art and Society*, pp. 147–90. Ithaca, N.Y.: Cornell University Press.

Davis, R. H. (1997). *Lives of Indian Images*, Princeton, N.J.: Princeton University Press.

Davis, W. (1996). *Replications: Archaeology, Art History, Psychoanalysis*, University Park, Pa.: The Pennsylvania State University Press.

de Certeau, M. (1984). *The Practice of Everyday Life*, Berkeley, Calif.: University of California Press.

Demarée, R. J. (1983). *The 3h Ikr n Rᶜ-Stelae: On Ancestor Worship in Ancient Egypt*, Leiden: Nederlands Instituut voor het Nabije Oosten te Leiden.

DeMarrais, E., L. J. Castillo, and T. Earle (1996). "Ideology, materialization, and power strategies," *Current Anthropology* 37: 15–86.

Der Manuelian, P. (1999). "Semi-literacy in Egypt: some erasures from the Amarna period," in E. Teeter and J. A. Larson (eds), *Gold of Praise: Studies on Ancient Egypt in Honor of Edward Wente*, pp. 285–98. Chicago, Ill.: Oriental Institute of the University of Chicago.

Derchain, P. (1975). "La perruque et le cristal," *Studien zur Altägyptischen Kultur* 2: 55–74.

Derrida, J. (1987). *Cinders*, Lincoln, Nebr.: University of Nebraska Press.

—— (1992). *Given Time: I. Counterfeit Money*, Chicago, Ill.: University of Chicago Press.

Desmond, J. (1999). *Staging Tourism*, Chicago, Ill.: University of Chicago Press.

Dobres, M. (2000). *Technology and Social Agency*, Oxford: Blackwell.

Dobres, M. and J. Robb. Editors. (2000). *Agency in Archaeology*, London: Routledge.

Douglas, M. (1992). "Rightness of categories," in M. Douglas and D. Hull (eds), *How Classification Works*, pp. 239–71. Edinburgh: Edinburgh University Press.

—— (1994). "The genuine article," in S. H. Riggins (ed.), *The Socialness of Things*, pp. 9–22. Berlin and New York: Mouton de Gruyter.

Douglas, M. and D. Hull (1992). "Introduction," in M. Douglas and D. Hull (eds), *How Classification Works*, pp. 1–12. Edinburgh: Edinburgh University Press.

Douglas, M. and B. Isherwood. (1996). *The World of Goods: Towards an Anthropology of Consumption*, London: Routledge.

Dreyer, G. (1986). *Der Tempel der Satet: die Funde der Frühzeit und des Alten Reiches*, Mainz am Rhein: Philip von Zabern.

Duncan, C. (1999). "From princely gallery to public art museum," in D. Boswell and J. Evans (eds), *Representing the Nation*, pp. 304–31. London: Routledge.

Dupré, J. (1993). *The Disorder of Things: Metaphysical Foundations of the Disunity of Science*, Cambridge, Mass.: Harvard University Press.

Eaton-Krauss, M. (1984). "Statuendarstellung," in W. Helck and E. Otto (eds), *Lexikon der Ägyptologie*, vol. V, pp. 1263–6. Wiesbaden: Otto Harrassowitz.

Eck, D. L. (1996). *Darsan: Seeing the Divine Image in India*, New York: Columbia University Press.

Eckardt, H. and H. Williams (2003). "Objects without a past? The use of Roman objects in Anglo-Saxon graves," in H. Williams (ed.), *Archaeologies of Remembrance: Death and Memory in Past Societies*, pp. 141–70. New York: Kluwer/Plenum.

Edmonds, M. (1999). *Ancestral Geographies of the Neolithic: Landscapes, Monuments and Memory*, New York: Routledge.

Egan, M. (1991). *Milagros: Votive Offerings from the Americas*, Santa Fe, N.M.: Museum of New Mexico.

Elia, R. J. (1995). "Conservators and unprovenanced objects: preserving the cultural heritage or servicing the antiquities trade?," in K. W. Tubb (ed.), *Antiquities Trade or Betrayed: Legal, Ethical and Conservational Issues*, pp. 244–55. London: Archetype.

—— (1997). "Looting, collecting, and the destruction of archaeological resources," *Nonrenewable Resources* 6: 85–98.

—— (2002). "Digging up dirt: antiquities case unearths corruption," *Wall Street Journal*, June 19 p. D7.

Ellen, R. F. (1988). "Fetishism," *Man* 23: 213–35.

Elsner, J. and R. Cardinal (1994). "Introduction," in J. Elsner and R. Cardinal (eds), *The Cultures of Collecting*, pp. 1–6. Cambridge, Mass.: Harvard University Press.

Eng, D. L. and D. Kazanjian (2003). "Introduction: mourning remains," in D. L. Eng and D. Kazanjian (eds), *Loss: The Politics of Mourning*, pp. 1–25. Berkeley, Calif.: University of California.

Errington, S. (1998). *The Death of Primitive Art and Other Tales of Progress*, Berkeley, Calif.: University of California Press.

Fane, D., I. Jacknis, and L. Breen. Editors. (1991). *Objects of Myth and Memory: American Indian Art at The Brooklyn Museum*, New York: The Brooklyn Museum.

Faulkner, R. O. (1985). *The Ancient Egyptian Book of the Dead*, London: British Museum Press.

Fernandez, J. and M. T. Huber (2001). "The anthropology of irony," in J. Fernandez and M. T. Huber (eds), *Irony in Action*, pp. 1–37. Chicago, Ill.: The University of Chicago Press.

Fischer-Elfert, H.-W. (1998). *Die Vision von der Statue im Stein*, Heidelberg: Universitätsverlag C. Winter.

Foertmeyer, V. A. (1989). Tourism in Graeco-Roman Egypt. Ph.D. Thesis, Princeton University.

Forman, W. and S. Quirke (1996). *Hieroplyphs and the Afterlife in Ancient Egypt*, London: British Museum Press.

Forrester, J. (1994). "'Mille e tre': Freud and collecting," in J. Elsner and R. Cardinal (eds), *The Cultures of Collecting*, pp. 224–51. Cambridge, Mass.: Harvard University Press.

Forty, A. (1999). "Introduction," in A. Forty and S. Küchler (eds), *The Art of Forgetting*. pp. 1–18. Oxford: Berg.

Foucault, M. (1970). "Theatrum philosophicum," *Critique* 282: 885–908.

—— (1972). *The Archaeology of Knowledge*, London: Routledge.

—— (1973). *The Order of Things*, New York: Pantheon.

—— (1986). "Of other spaces," in N. Mirzoeff (ed.), *The Visual Culture Reader*, pp. 237–44. London: Routledge.

Friedman, F. (1985). "On the meaning of some anthropoid busts from Deir el Medina", *Journal of Egyptian Archaeology* 71: 82–97.

—— (1994). "Aspects of domestic life and religion," in L. H. Lesko (ed.), *Pharaoh's Workers. The Villagers of Deir el Medina*, pp. 95–117. Ithaca, N.Y.: Cornell University Press.

Frood, E. (2003). "Ritual function and priestly narrative: the stelae of the High Priest of Osiris, Nebwawy," *Journal of Egyptian Archaeology* 90.

Gamman, L. and M. Makinen (1994). *Female Fetishism*, New York: New York University Press.

Gardiner, A. H. (1947). *Ancient Egyptian Onomastica, Volumes I & II*, Oxford: Oxford University Press.

Geary, P. (1986). "Sacred commodities: the circulation of medieval relics," in A. Appadurai (ed.), *The Social Life of Things: Commodities in Cultural Perspective*, pp. 169–91. Cambridge: Cambridge University Press.

Gell, A. (1992). "The enchantment of technology and the technology of enchantment," in J. Coote and A. Shelton (eds), *Anthropology, Art and Aesthetics*, pp. 40–63. Oxford: Oxford University Press.

—— (1998). *Art and Agency: An Anthropological Theory*, Oxford: Oxford University Press.

Georgoulake, E. (1997). "Votives in the shape of human body parts: shaping a framework," *Platon* 49: 188–206.

Gerstenblith, P. (2002). "United States v. Schultz," *Culture without Context* 10: 27–31.

Giddy, L. (1999). *The Survey of Memphis II. Kom Rabi'a: The New Kingdom and Post-New Kingdom Objects*, London: Egypt Exploration Society.

Gillings, M. and J. Pollard (1999). "Non-portable stone artefacts and contexts of meaning: the tale of Grey Wether (www.museums.ncl.ac.uk/Avebury/stone4.htm)", *World Archaeology: The Cultural Biography of Objects* 31: 179–93.

Glassie, H. (1999). *Material Culture*, Bloomington, Ind.: Indiana University Press.

Godelier, M. (1999). *The Enigma of the Gift*, Cambridge: Polity Press.

Goldwasser, O. (1995). *From Icon to Metaphor: Studies in the Semiotics of the Hieroglyphs*, Fribourg: University of Fribourg.

Goodman, N. (1992). "The new riddle of induction," in M. Douglas and D. Hull (eds), *How Classification Works*, pp. 24–41. Edinburgh: Edinburgh University Press.

Gosden, C. (2001). "Making sense: archaeology and aesthetics," *World Archaeology: Archaeology and Aesthetics* 33: 163–7.

Gosden, C. and Y. Marshall (1999). "The cultural biography of objects," *World Archaeology: The Cultural Biography of Objects* 31: 169–78.

Gottdiener, M., C. C. Collins, and D. R. Dickens (1999). *Las Vegas: The Social Production of an All-American City*, Oxford: Blackwell.

Graeber, D. (2001). *Toward an Anthropological Theory of Value*, New York: Palgrave.

Graves-Brown, P. Editor. (2000). *Matter, Materiality, and Modern Culture*, London and New York: Routledge.

Greenfield, J. (1989). *The Return of Cultural Treasures*, Cambridge: Cambridge University Press.

Habermas, J. (1987). *The Theory of Communicative Action: Volume 2*, Boston, Mass.: Beacon Press.

Halbwachs, M. (1992). *On Collective Memory*, London and Chicago, Ill.: University of Chicago Press.

Hall, M. (in press). "The reappearance of the authentic," in I. Karp *et al.* (eds), *Museum Frictions: Public Cultures/Global Transformations*, London: Routledge.

Hallam, E. and J. Hockey (2001). *Death, Memory and Material Culture*, Oxford: Berg.

Hamilakis, Y. (1999). "Stories from exile: fragments from the cultural biography of the Parthenon (or 'Elgin') marbles," *World Archaeology: The Cultural Biography of Objects* 31: 303–20.

Handler, R. (1986). "Authenticity," *Anthropology Today* 2: 2–4.

Hannigan, J. (1998). *Fantasy City: Pleasure and Profit in the Postmodern Metropolis*, London: Routledge.

Haraway, D. (1991). *Simians, Cyborgs and Women: The Reinvention of Nature*, London: Free Association Press.

Haraway, D. J. (1997). *Modest_Witness@Second_Millennium.FemaleMan©_ Meets_OncoMouse™*, New York: Routledge.

Hare, T. (1999). *ReMembering Osiris: Number, Gender, and the Word in Ancient Egyptian Representational Systems*, Stanford, Calif.: Stanford University Press.

Haring, B. (2003). "From oral practice to written record in Ramesside Deir el-Medina," *Journal of the Economic and Social History of the Orient* 46 (3): 249–72.

Harris, N. (1990). *Cultural Excursions: Marketing Appetites and Cultural Tastes in Modern America*, Chicago, Ill.: University of Chicago Press.

Havel, V. (1969). *The Garden Party*, London: Jonathan Cape.

Hegarty, P. (2000). *Georges Bataille: Core Cultural Theorist*, London: Sage.

Hegel, G. W. F. (1977). *Phenomenology of Spirit*, Oxford: Oxford University Press.

Helck, W. (1967). "Einige Bemerkungen zum Mundöffnungsritual", *Mitteilungen des Deutschen Archäologischen Instituts Abteilung Kairo* 22: 27–41.

Hodder, I. Editor. (1989). *The Meanings of Things: Material Culture and Symbolic Expression*, London: HarperCollins.

—— (1991). *Reading the Past*, Cambridge: Cambridge University Press.

—— Editor. (2000). *Towards Reflexive Method in Archaeology: The Example at Çatalhöyük*, Cambridge: McDonald Institute for Archaeological Research.

Hodel-Hoenes, S. (2000). *Life and Death in Ancient Egypt: Scenes from Private Tombs in New Kingdom Thebes*, Ithaca, NY: Cornell University Press.

Hoffmeier, J. K. (1985). *Sacred in the Vocabulary of Ancient Egypt*, Freiburg: Universitätsverlag Frieburg Schweiz.

Hornung, E. (1982). *Conceptions of God in Ancient Egypt: The One and the Many*, Ithaca, N.Y.: Cornell University Press.

—— (1992). *Idea into Image: Essays on Ancient Egyptian Thought*, New York: Timken.

Hoskins, J. (1998). *Biographical Objects: How Things Tell the Stories of People's Lives*, London and New York: Routledge.

Houlihan, P. F. (1996). *The Animal World of the Pharaohs*, Cairo: University of Cairo Press.

—— (2001). *Wit and Humour in Ancient Egypt*, London: The Rubicon Press.

Huyssen, A. (1995). *Twilight Memories: Marking Time in a Culture*, New York: Routledge.

Ingold, T. (2000). "Making culture and weaving the world," in P. Graves-Brown (ed.), *Matter, Materiality and Modern Culture*, pp. 50–71. London: Routledge.

—— (2003). "From the perception of archaeology to the anthropology of perception," *Journal of Social Archaeology* 3: 5–22.

Jackson, M. (1996). "Introduction: phenomenology, radical empiricism, and anthropological critique," in *Things as They Are: New Directions in Phenomenological Anthropology*, pp. 1–50. Bloomington, Ind.: University of Indiana Press.

James, H. (1987). *The Spoils of Poynton*, London: Penguin.

Janssen, J. J. (1975). *Commodity Prices from the Ramessid Period*, Leiden: E. J. Brill.

—— (1980). "Absence from work by the necropolis workmen of Thebes," *Studien zur Altägyptischen Kultur* 8: 127–52.

Johnson, M. H. (1989). "Conceptions of agency in archaeological interpretation", *Journal of Anthropological Archaeology* 8: 189–211.

Jones, A. (2001). "Drawn from memory: the archaeology of aesthetics and the aesthetics of archaeology in Earlier Bronze Age Britain and the present", *World Archaeology: Archaeology and Aesthetics* 33: 334–56.

Kan, S. (1989). *Symbolic Immortality: The Tlingit Potlatch of the Nineenth Century*, Washington, DC: Smithsonian Institution Press.

Keen, I. (2001). "Agency, history and tradition in the construction of 'Classical' music: the debate over 'authentic performance'," in C. Pinney and N. Thomas (eds), *Beyond Aesthetics: Art and the Technologies of Enchantment*, pp. 31–55. Oxford: Berg.

Keimer, L. (1940). "Jeux de la nature retouchés par la main de l'homme, provenant de Deir el-Médineh (Thèbes) et remontant au nouvel-empire", *Étude d'Égyptologie* 2: 1–21.

Keith-Bennett, J. L. (1988). "Anthropoid busts II: not from Deir el Medineh alone," *Bulletin of the Egyptological Seminar* 3: 43–72.

Kelly, R. (1987). "Museums as status symbols II: attaining a state of having been," in R. Belk (ed.), *Advances in Nonprofit Marketing*, pp. 1–38. Greenwich, Conn.: JAI Press.

—— (1993). "Discussion: vesting objects and experiences with symbolic meaning", *Advances in Consumer Research* 20: 232–4.

Kirkegaard, S. (1968). *The Concept of Irony*, Bloomington, Ind.: Indiana University Press.

Knappett, C. (2002). "Photographs, skeuomorphs and marionettes: some thoughs on mind, agency, and object," *Journal of Material Culture* 7: 97–117.

Kopytoff, I. (1986). "The cultural biography of things: commoditization as process," in A. Appadurai (ed.), *The Social Life of Things: Commodities in Cultural Perspective*, pp. 64–91. Cambridge: Cambridge University Press.

Kristeva, J. (1982). *Powers of Horror: an Essay on Abjection*, New York: Columbia University Press.

Krutchen, J.-M. (1992). "Un sculpteur des images divines ramesside," in M. Broze (ed.), *L'Atelier de l'Orfèvre: Mélanges offerts à Ph. Derchain*, pp. 107–18. Leuven: Peeters.

Küchler, S. (1993). "Landscape as memory: the mapping of process and its representation in a Melanesian society," in B. Bender (ed.), *Landscape: Politics and Perspectives*, pp. 85–106. London: Berg.

—— (1997). "Sacrificial economy and its objects: rethinking colonial collecting in Oceania," *Journal of Material Culture* 2: 39–60.

—— (1999). "The place of memory," in A. Forty and S. Küchler (eds), *The Art of Forgetting*, pp. 53–72. Oxford: Berg.

—— (2001). "Why knot? a theory of art and mathematics," in C. Pinney and N. Thomas (eds), *Beyond Aesthetics: Art and the Technologies of Enchantment*, pp. 57–77. Oxford: Berg.

—— (2002). *Malanggan: Art, Memory and Sacrifice*, Oxford: Berg.

Kunzle, D. (1978). "World upside down: the iconography of a European broadsheet type," in B. A. Babcock (ed.), *Reversible World: Symbolic Inversion in Art and Society*, pp. 39–94. Ithaca, N.Y.: Cornell University Press.

Lacan, J. (2001). *Ecrits: A Selection*, London and New York: Routledge.

Lakoff, G. (1987). *Women, Fire, and Dangerous Things: What Categories Reveal About the Mind*, Chicago, Ill: University of Chicago Press.

Latour, B. (1991). *We Have Never Been Modern*, Cambridge, Mass.: Harvard University Press.

—— (1996). *Petite Réflexion Sur le Culte Moderne des Dieux Faitiches*, Paris: Collection, Les Empecheurs de Penser en Rond.

—— (2000). "When things strike back: a possible contribution of 'science studies' to the social sciences," *British Journal of Sociology* 51: 107–23.

Layton, R. (1991). *The Anthropology of Art*, Cambridge: Cambridge University Press.

Le Goff, J. (1996). *History and Memory*, New York: Columbia University Press.

Leach, N. Editor. (1997). *Rethinking Architecture: A Reader in Cultural Theory*, London: Routledge.

Leach, W. (1993). *Land of Desire: Merchants, Power, and the Rise of a New American Culture*, New York: Vintage.

Lemonnier, P. (1992). *Elements for an Anthropology of Technology*, Ann Arbor, Mich.: University of Michigan Press.

—— Editor. (1993). *Technological Choices: Transformation in Material Cultures since the Neolithic*, London: Routledge.

Leroi-Gourhan, A. (1993). *Gesture and Speech*, Cambridge, Mass.: MIT.

Lévi-Strauss, C. (2001). *Myth and Meaning*, London: Routledge.

Levine, J. (1989). "Art chic," *Forbes* 148: 94, 96 (August 21).

Lévy-Bruhl, L. (1966). *How Natives Think*, New York: Washington Square Press.

Lichtheim, M. (1976). *Ancient Egyptian Literature: Volume II. The New Kingdom*, Berkeley, Calif.: University of California Press.

Littlejohn, D. Editor. (1999). *The Real Las Vegas*, Oxford: Oxford University Press.

Lowenthal, D. (1999). "Preface," in A. Forty and S. Küchler (eds), *The Art of Forgetting*. pp. xi–xiii. Oxford: Berg.

Lyotard, J.-F. (1993). *Libidinal Economy*, Bloomington, Ind.: Indiana University Press.

Malinowski, B. (1935). *Coral Gardens and Their Magic*, New York: American Book Company.

McDowell, A. G. (1992). "Awareness of the past in Deir el-Medina," in R. J. Demarée and A. Egberts (eds), *Village Voices*, pp. 95–109. Leiden: Centre of Non-Western Studies.

—— (1999). *Village Life in Ancient Egypt: Laundry Lists and Love Songs*, Oxford: Oxford University Press.

Mann, T. (1978). *Joseph and His Brothers*, Harmondsworth: Penguin.

Manniche, L. (1987). *Sexual Life in Ancient Egypt*, London and New York: Kegan Paul.

Mark, V. (1994). "Objects and their maker: bricolage of the self," in S. H. Riggins (ed.), *The Socialness of Things*, pp. 63–100. Berlin and New York: Mouton de Gruyter.

Marx, K. (1992). *Capital: A Critique of Political Economy*, New York: International Publishers.

Mauss, M. (1990). *The Gift: The Form and Reason for Exchange in Archaic Societies*, New York: W. W. Norton.

—— (2001). *A General Theory of Magic*, London: Routledge.

Merleau-Ponty, M. (1962). *The Phenomenology of Perception*, London: Routledge and Kegan Paul.

—— (1963). *The Structure of Behavior*, Boston, Mass.: Beacon Press.

Merriman, N. (1989). "Museum visiting as a cultural phenomenon," in P. Vergo (ed.), *The New Museology*, pp. 149–71. London: Reaktion Books.

Meskell, L. M. (1994). "Deir el Medina in hyperreality: seeking the people of Pharaonic Egypt," *Journal of Mediterranean Archaeology* 7: 193–216.

—— (1996). "The somatisation of archaeology: institutions, discourses, corporeality," *Norwegian Archaeological Review* 29: 1–16.

—— (1998). "An archaeology of social relations in an Egyptian village," *Journal of Archaeological Method and Theory* 5: 209–43.

—— (1999). *Archaeologies of Social Life: Age, Sex, Class etc. in Ancient Egypt*, Oxford: Blackwell.

—— (2000). "Re-embedding sex: domesticity, sexuality and ritual in New Kingdom Egypt," in R. Schmidt and B. Voss (eds), *Archaeologies of Sexuality*, pp. 253–62. London: Routledge.

—— (2002). *Private Life in New Kingdom Egypt*, Princeton, N.J.: Princeton University Press.

—— (2003). "Memory's materiality: ancestral presence, commemorative practice and disjunctive locales," in R. van Dyke and S. E. Alcock (eds), *Archaeologies of Memory*, pp. 34–55. Oxford: Blackwell.

—— (n.d.). "Sites of violence: terrorism, tourism and heritage in the archaeological present," in L. M. Meskell and P. Pels (eds), *Embedding Ethics: Shifting Boundaries of the Anthropological Profession*, Oxford: Berg.

Meskell, L. M. and R. A. Joyce (2003). *Embodied Lives: Figuring Ancient Maya and Egyptian Experience*, London: Routledge.

Miller, D. (1985). *Artefacts as Categories: A Study of Ceramic Variability in Central India*, Cambridge: Cambridge University Press.

—— (1987). *Material Culture and Mass Consumption*, Oxford: Blackwell.

—— (1995). "Consumption and commodities," *Annual Review of Anthropology* 24: 141–61.

—— (1997). "Consumption and its consequences," in H. Mackay (ed.), *Consumption and Everyday Life*, London: Sage.

—— Editor. (1998a). *Material Cultures: Why Some Things Matter*, Chicago, Ill.: University of Chicago Press.

—— (1998b). *A Theory of Shopping*, Ithaca, N.Y.: Cornell University Press.

—— (2001a). "Alienable gifts and inalienable commodities," in F. Myers (ed.), *The Empire of Things*, pp. 91–115. Santa Fe: School of American Research.

—— (2001b). *The Dialectics of Shopping*, Chicago, Ill.: University of Chicago.

—— (in press) "Introduction," in D. Miller (ed.), *Materiality*, Durham, N.C.: Duke University Press.

Miller, D. and C. Tilley (1996). "Editorial," *Journal of Material Culture* 1: 5–14.

Minault-Gout, A. (2002). *Carnets de pierre*, Paris: Hazan.

Montserrat, D. and L. M. Meskell (1997). "Mortuary archaeology and religious landscape at Graeco-Roman Deir el Medina", *Journal of Egyptian Archaeology* 84: 179–98.

Moreland, J. (1999). "The world(s) of the cross," *World Archaeology: The Cultural Biography of Objects* 31: 194–213.

Morenz, S. (1973). *Egyptian Religion*, Ithaca, N.Y.: Cornell University Press.

Morris, S. (1994). *The Making of the Luxor* (video), New York: Circus Circus Enterprises.

Munn, N. D. (1986). *The Fame of Gawa: A Symbolic Study of Value Transformation in a Massim (Papua New Guinea) Society*, Durham, N.C.: Duke University Press.

Myers, F. (2001). "Introduction: the empire of things," in F. Myers (ed.), *The Empire of Things*, pp. 3–61. Santa Fe: School of American Research.

O'Hanlon, M. and R. L. Welsch. Editors. (2000). *Hunting the Gatherers: Ethnographic Collectors, Agents and Agency in Melanesia, 1870s–1930s*. Oxford: Bergham Books.

Omlin, J. A. (1973). *Der Papyrus 55001 und seine satirisch-erotischen Zeichnungen und Inschrifen*, Turin: Museo Egizio di Torino.

Oring, E. (1992). *Jokes and Their Relations*, Lexington, Ky.: University of Kentucky Press.

Ortner, S. B. (1996). *Making Gender: The Politics and Erotics of Culture*, Boston, Mass.: Beacon Press.

Parkinson, R. B. (1997). *The Tale of Sinuhe and other Ancient Egyptian Poems*, Oxford: Clarendon Press.

—— (1999). *Cracking Codes: The Rosetta Stone and Decipherment*, London: British Museum Press.

—— (2002). *Poetry and Culture in Middle Kingdom Egypt: A Dark Side to Perfection*, London: Continuum.

—— (2003). "'No one is free from enemies': voicing opposition in literary discourse," in H. Felber (ed.), *Feinde und Aufrhrer. Konzepte von Gegnerschaft in der Literatur des Mittleren Reiches*. Leipzig: Abhandlungen der Sachsischen Akademie der Wissenschaften zu Leipzig.

Patterson, T. C. (2003). *Marx's Ghost: Conversations with Archaeologists*, Oxford: Berg.

Pearce, S. M. (1995). *On Collecting: An Investigation into Collecting*, London: Routledge.

—— (1998). *Collecting in Contemporary Practice*, London: Sage.

Pearson, M. and M. Shanks (2001). *Theatre/Archaeology*, London: Routledge.

Pels, P. (1998). "The spirit of matter: on fetish, rarity, fact, and fancy," in P. Spyer (ed.), *Border Fetishisms: Material Objects in Unstable Places*, pp. 91–121. New York: Routledge.

—— (2002). "'Materialism,' 'Spiritualism' and the modern fear of matter and materiality," Presented at an American Anthropological Association Meeting, New Orleans, November 22.

Pietz, W. (1993). "Fetishism and materialism: the limits of theory in Marx," in E. Apter and W. Pietz (eds), *Fetishism and Cultural Discourse*, pp. 119–51. Ithaca, N.Y.: Cornell University Press.

Pinch, G. (1993). *Votive Offerings to Hathor*, Oxford: Griffith Institute.

—— (1994). *Magic in Ancient Egypt*, London: British Museum Press.

Pinney, C. and N. Thomas. Editors. (2001). *Beyond Aesthetics: Art and the Technologies of Enchantment*, Oxford: Berg.

Pollard, J. (2001). "The aesthetics of depositional practice," *World Archaeology: Archaeology and Aesthetics* 33: 315–33.

Poovey, M. (1998). *A History of The Modern Fact*, Chicago, Ill.: University of Chicago Press.

Preucel, R. W. and A. A. Bauer (2001). "Archaeological pragmatics," *Norwegian Archaeological Review* 34: 85–96.

Price, S. (1989). *Primitive Art in Civilized Places*, Chicago, Ill.: University of Chicago Press.

Quirke, S. (1992). *Ancient Egyptian Religion*, London: British Museum Press.

Rainbird, P. (1999). "Entangled biographies: western Pacific ceramics and the tombs of Pohnpei," *World Archaeology: The Cultural Biography of Objects* 31: 214–24.

Ratzel, F. (1896). *The History of Mankind*, London: Macmillan and Co.

Report. (2003). "Antiquities top ten," *The Art Newspaper*, vol. 133 (February), p. 9.

Riggins, S. H. (1994). "Introduction," in S. H. Riggins (ed.), *The Socialness of Things*, pp. 1–6. Berlin and New York: Mouton de Gruyter.

Ritner, R. K. (1993). *The Mechanics of Ancient Egyptian Magical Practice*, Chicago, Ill.: Oriental Institute University of Chicago.

—— (1995). "The religious, social, and legal parameters of traditional Egyptian magic," in M. Meyer and P. Mirecki (eds), *Ancient Magic and Ritual Power*, pp. 43–60. Leiden: E. J. Brill.

Robins, G. (1996). "Dress, undress, and the representation of fertility and potency in New Kingdom Egyptian Art," in N. B. Kampen (ed.),

Sexuality in Ancient Art. pp. 27–40. Cambridge: Cambridge University Press.

—— (2001). *Egyptian Statues,* Princes Risborough: Shire Publications.

Rojek, C. (1993). *Ways of Escape: Modern Transformations in Leisure and Travel,* London: Macmillan Press.

Rorty, R. (1989). *Contingency, Irony, and Solidarity,* Cambridge: Cambridge University Press.

Rothman, H. K. (2002). *Neon Metropolis: How Las Vegas started the Twenty-First Century,* New York: Routledge.

Rothman, H. K. and M. Davis. Editors. (2002). *The Grit Beneath the Glitter: Tales from the Real Las Vegas.* Berkeley, Calif.: University of California Press.

Rowlands, M. (2002). "A materialist approach to materiality," Presented at an American Anthropological Association Meeting, New Orleans, November 22.

Russmann, E. R. (2001). *Eternal Egypt: Masterworks of Ancient Art from the British Museum,* Berkeley, Calif.: University of California Press.

Russmann, E. R. and D. Finn (1989). *Egyptian Sculpture: Cairo and Luxor,* Austin, Tex.: University of Texas Press.

Saitta, D. J. (1994). "Agency, class, and archaeological interpretation," *Journal of Anthropological Archaeology* 13: 201–27.

Saunders, N. J. (1999). "Biographies of brilliance: pearls, transformations or matter and being c. AD 1492," *World Archaeology: The Cultural Biography of Objects* 31: 243–57.

—— (2001). "A dark light: reflections on obsidian in Mesoamerica," *World Archaeology: Archaeology and Aesthetics* 33: 220–36.

Schiffer, M. B. (1999). *The Material Life of Human Beings,* London: Routledge.

Schull, N. D. (2001). "Oasis/Mirage: fantasies of nature in Las Vegas," in B. Herzogenrath (ed.), *From Virgin Land to Disney World: Nature and its Discontents in the USA of Yesterday and Today,* pp. 377–402. Amsterdam: Rodopi.

Scott, J. C. (1990). *Domination and the Arts of Resistance: Hidden Transcripts,* New Haven, Conn.: Yale University Press.

Seip, L. P. (1999). "Transformations of meaning: the life history of a Nuxalk mask," *World Archaeology: The Cultural Biography of Objects* 31: 272–87.

Serres, M. (1987). *Statues,* Paris: François Bourin.

Shafer, B. E. (1997). "Temples, priests, and rituals: an overview," in B. E. Shafer (ed.), *Temples in Ancient Egypt,* pp. 1–30. Ithaca, N.Y.: Cornell University Press.

Shelton, A. Editor. (1995). *Fetishism: Visualising Power and Desire*, London: Lund Humphries Publishers.

Simmel, G. (1979). *The Philosophy of Money*, Boston, Mass.: Routledge & Kegan Paul.

Simpson, W. K., E. F. Faulkner, and E. F. Wente Jr. (1972). *The Literature of Ancient Egypt*, New Haven, Conn.: Yale University Press.

Stallybrass, P. (1998). "Marx's coat," in P. Spyer (ed.), *Border Fetishisms: Material Objects in Unstable Places*, pp. 183–207. New York: Routledge.

Strathern, M. (1999). *Property, Substance and Effect: Anthropological Essays on Persons and Things*, London: Athlone.

—— (2001). "The patent and the Malanggan," in C. Pinney and N. Thomas (eds), *Beyond Aesthetics: Art and the Technologies of Enchantment*, pp. 259–86. Oxford: Berg.

Tambiah, S. J. (1984). *The Buddhist Saints of the Forest and the Cult of Amulets*, Cambridge: Cambridge University Press.

Taube, K. (1989). "Ritual humor in Classic Maya religion," in W. F. Hanks and D. R. Rice (eds), *Word and Image in Maya Culture: Explorations in Language, Writing, and Representation*, pp. 351–81. Salt Lake City, Ut.: University of Utah Press.

Taussig, M. (1980). *The Devil and Commodity Fetishism in South Africa*, Chapel Hill, N.C.: University of North Carolina Press.

—— (1993a). "Maleficium: state fetishism," in E. Apter and W. Pietz (eds), *Fetishism and Cultural Discourse*, pp. 217–47. Ithaca, N.Y.: Cornell University Press.

—— (1993b). *Mimesis and Alterity: A Particular History of the Senses*, New York: Routledge.

Taylor, J. H. (2001). *Death and the Afterlife in Ancient Egypt*, London: British Museum Press.

Taylor, M. C. (1997). *Hiding*, Chicago, Ill.: University of Chicago Press.

Te Velde, H. (1967). *Seth, God of Confusion: A Study of his Role in Egyptian Mythology and Religion*, Leiden: E. J. Brill.

Themelis, P. G. (1994). "Ancient Greek cult practice from the epigraphical evidence," in R. Hagg (ed.) *Proceedings of the Second International Seminar on Ancient Greek Cult*, pp. 101–22. Stockholm: Swedish Institute at Athens.

Thomas, N. (1991). *Entangled Objects: Exchange, Material Culture and Colonialism in the Pacific*, Cambridge, Mass.: Harvard University Press.

—— (1994). *Colonialism's Culture: Anthropology, Travel and Government*, Princeton, N.J.: Princeton University Press.

—— (1999). *Possessions: Indigenous Art/Colonial Culture*, London: Thames and Hudson.

—— (2001). "Introduction," in C. Pinney and N. Thomas (eds), *Beyond Aesthetics: Art and the Technologies of Enchantment*, pp. 1–12. Oxford: Berg.

Tilley, C. Editor. (1990). *Reading Material Culture*, Oxford: Blackwell.

—— (1994). *A Phenomenology of Landscape: Places, Paths and Monuments*, Oxford: Berg.

Torres, G. (1997). *The Force of Irony: Power in the Everyday Life of Mexican Tomato Workers*, Oxford and New York: Berg.

Traunecker, C. (1989). "Le Château de l'Or de Thoutmosis III et les magasins nord du temple d'Amon," *Cahiers de Recherches de l'Institut de Papyrologie et d'Egyptologie de Lille: Sociétés Urbaines en Égypte et au Soudan* 11: 89–111.

Turfa, J. M. (1994). "Anatomical votives and Italian medical traditions," in R. D. de Puma and J. Small (eds), *Murlo and the Etruscans: Art and Society in Ancient Etruria*, pp. 224–40. Madison, Wis.: Wisconsin Studies in Classics.

Turner, V. (1969). *The Ritual Process*, Chicago, Ill.: Aldine.

—— (1982). *From Ritual to Theatre: The Human Seriousness of Play*, New York: PAJ Publications.

Tyler, E. B. (1977) *Primitive Culture*, New York: Gordon Press.

Valbelle, D. (1985). *"Les Ouvriers de la Tombe". Deir el Médineh à l'époque ramesside, BdE 96*, Cairo: Institut Français d'Archéologie Orientale.

Van Dijk, J. (1995). "Maya's chief sculptor Userhet-Hatiay," *Göttinger Miszellen* 148: 29–34.

Van Dyke, R. and S. E. Alcock. Editors. (2003). *Archaeologies of Memory*, Oxford: Blackwell.

Vandier d'Abbadie, J. (1946). *Ostraca figurés de Deir el Médineh. Troisème Fascicule*, Cairo: l"Institute Français d'Archéologie Orientale.

Vico, G. (1984). *The New Science of Giambattista Vico*, Ithaca, N.Y.: Cornell University Press.

Wall, G. and C. Knapper (1981). *Tutankhamun in Toronto*, Department of Geography Publication, University of Waterloo.

Watson, P. (2002). "The investigation of Frederick Schultz," *Culture without Context* 10: 21–6.

Weiner, A. (1985). "Inalienable wealth," *American Ethnologist* 12: 210–27.

—— (1992). *Inalienable Possessions: The Paradox of Keeping-While-Giving*, Berkeley, Calif.: University of California Press.

Wente, E. (1990). *Letters from Ancient Egypt*, Atlanta, Ga.: Scholars Press.

Wilkinson, R. H. (1992). *Reading Egyptian Art*, New York: Thames and Hudson.

Williams, H. Editor. (2003). *Archaeologies of Remembrance: Death and Memory in Past Societies*, New York: Kluwer/Plenum.

Wood, M. (1998). "The use of the Pharaonic past in modern Egyptian nationalism," *Journal of the American Research Center in Egypt* 35: 179–96.

Wylie, A. (2002). *Thinking from Things: Essays in the Philosophy of Archaeology*, Berkeley, Calif.: University of California Press.

Zandee, J. (1960). *Death as an Enemy According to Ancient Egyptian Conceptions*, Leiden: E. J. Brill.

Index

'ning Source UK Ltd.
Keynes UK
'f1830060616

'UK00016B/231/P